Interpreting

The New National Planning Policy Framework

Alistair Mills

Barrister, Landmark Chambers

External College Lecturer in Law,
Magdalene College, Cambridge

BATH PUBLISHING

Published October 2018

ISBN 978-1-9164315-2-2

Bath Publishing Limited

27 Charmouth Road

Bath

BA1 3LJ

Tel: 01225 577810

email: info@bathpublishing.co.uk

www.bathpublishing.com

Bath Publishing is a company registered in England: 5209173

Registered Office: As above

to Josephine,

with sparkling eyes

Acknowledgments

In writing this book, professionally, and in my wider life, I have had the good fortune to be supported by a number of extraordinary people. I am grateful to all my family, friends, and colleagues from whom I have taken more than I could ever give in return.

It is standard practice for an author to thank his or her publishers. In this case, however, this is much more than a ritual incantation. David Chaplin and Helen Lacey at Bath Publishing have been ideal publishers. They have provided gentle guidance whilst not being constraining. Their ability to turn around this project so rapidly has been thoroughly impressive.

I am grateful to my friends and family who put up with me and have been encouraging during the course of the production of this book. Charles Ogilvie and Dr Stuart Murray are better friends than I deserve. The Vicar and congregation of St Mark's Kennington keep my feet on the ground and lift my mind and soul up from planning policy and court cases. My grandmother, Mrs Valerie Douglass, is a constant support as well as a close friend. My sister and brother in law, Dr Susanna Mills and Dr Diarmuid Coughlan, have provided encouragement and good cheer. My parents, the Rev Roger and Mrs Sarah Mills, shouldered the incalculable burden of having me to stay for part of the time when I was writing this book, and have been a blessing to me in so many other ways.

I am extremely lucky in my colleagues at Landmark Chambers and at Magdalene College, Cambridge. At Landmark, I am grateful to all those who have provided encouragement, advice, and helpful discussions, including Charlie Banner, David Elvin QC, Christopher Katkowski QC, Graeme Keen QC, Hannah Gibbs, Heather Sargent, James Maurici QC, Richard Clarke, Richard Moules, Rupert Warren QC, Stephen Morgan and Zack Simons. They have greatly improved this book. My roommates Richard Clarke and Hannah Gibbs are patient with me beyond explanation, as well as being fantastic company. My excellent clerks, Richard Bolton and Matthew Dowdall, have arranged matters with their customary skill so I have had time to dedicate to writing. At Magdalene, I am grateful in particular to Dr Neil Jones, for initially inviting me and continuing to let me teach for the college.

John Rhodes OBE of Quod was kind enough to take time to discuss the NPPF with me. Dr Joanna Bell of St John's College, Cambridge generously read chapters of this book in draft at very short notice. Dr Stuart Murray likewise read part of the book and provided helpful comments. I am very grateful to them all; any errors, of course, remain my own.

There are two people without whom I would not survive a career in the law. David Blundell of Landmark Chambers, who has been a friend and mentor to me for many years, has given me countless hours of his time. His astonishing kindness is matched only by his legal ability and wisdom. My wife, Josephine, brings me endless joy. I love her more than I could ever say, and she loves me more than I could ever understand. It is to her that this book is dedicated.

Alistair Mills

Landmark Chambers, London

9 October 2018

v

Contents

Chapter 5: Principles of Plan-making and Decision-taking

Chapter 6: Residential Development

Chapter 7: Business, Economy, Retail and Town Centres

Chapter 8: Communities, Transport, Effective Use of Land and Design

Chapter 9: Supporting High Quality Communications

Chapter 10: The Green Belt

Chapter 11: Climate Change, Flooding and Coastal Change

Chapter 12: Conserving and Enhancing the Natural Environment

Chapter 13: Conserving and Enhancing the Historic Environment

Chapter 14: Minerals

Chapter 15: Challenging Decisions Interpreting the NPPF

Index

Table of Cases

Table of NPPF References

Abbreviations and References

The following abbreviations are used in this book:

AONB	Area of Outstanding Natural Beauty
BC	Borough Council
CC	County Council or City Council
CPR	Civil Procedure Rules
DC	District Council
DMPO	Town and Country Planning (Development Management Procedure) (England) Order 2015
GPDO	Town and Country Planning (General Permitted Development) (England) Order 2015
LBC	London Borough Council
MBC	Metropolitan Borough Council
MDC	Metropolitan District Council
NPPF	National Planning Policy Framework, Published by Ministry of Housing, Communities and Local Government
PCPA	Planning and Compulsory Purchase Act 2004
PPG	Planning Practice Guidance, Published by Ministry of Housing, Communities and Local Government
PPG2	Planning Policy Guidance 2 (pre-NPPF national policy on the Green Belt)
SSCLG	Secretary of State for Communities and Local Government
SSSI	Site of Special Scientific Interest
TCPA	Town and Country Planning Act 1990

Chapter 1

Introduction

1.01 The NPPF is the primary expression of national planning policy for England. The status of national planning policy is explained in greater detail in Chapter 2, but it is of significance both in plan-making, and the making of individual decisions.

1.02 This book is intended to be a guide to the meaning of the new NPPF, with particular focus on the lessons learned from judicial interpretation of the original version of the NPPF. Judicial decisions are significant in this context, as the correct interpretation of planning policy (both in development plans and in the NPPF) is a matter of law. Put another way, it is not a matter of planning judgment for a decision-maker. It is not enough for the decision-maker to reach an interpretation of policy which is reasonable, or plausible. The interpretation which is reached has to be right, and it is the courts who decide which interpretation is right.

1.03 Although the idea of the original NPPF was that planning policy could be clearly and shortly expressed, it gave rise to a considerable amount of litigation regarding how the wording should be interpreted. The amount of litigation may in some ways be a cause of regret (the delay to development; the cost; the risk of decision-makers taking a defensive approach). Some may suggest that the lawyers are to blame for this. On the other hand, a conclusive interpretation of terms or phrases in policy does promote the consistency of decision-making, and makes some aspects of the planning process more certain.

1.04 For some time, I have collected decisions interpreting the NPPF in an online resource on Landmark Chambers' website, entitled A Digest of Decisions. Some of this will now have fallen away; some of the policies which the courts were interpreting having been materially amended by the new NPPF. However, much of the judicial wisdom will apply to the new NPPF as much as to the old.

1.05 At the time of writing, it is very much "early days" of the second NPPF; the new wording is yet to be hammered out in the courts, and the PPG is yet to be comprehensively amended to reflect the new NPPF. Chapters will be able to go into more depth where there has been substantial judicial consideration of the original NPPF, and there has been little changing in the wording brought about by the new NPPF.

1.06 The NPPF Digest was largely made up of quotations from judicial decisions, with little commentary on the decisions or the NPPF itself. This book takes a different approach: cases are explained in more detail, and there is less use of quotation.

1.07 Chapter 2 seeks to explain the nature of planning policy, which is not necessarily self-evident. Chapter 3 considers some general principles which emerge from the case law as to how the courts have sought to interpret the NPPF. The subsequent chapters provide an explanation of specific policy to be found in the NPPF. The final chapter considers how the interpretation of the NPPF may feature in challenges to decisions.

1.08   Reading this book is not intended to be a substitute to reading the NPPF itself. Neither does it provide a commentary on every single paragraph of the NPPF. The publishers and I decided not to include the NPPF as an appendix to the book: this would substantially increase the printed length of this book with a document which is freely available online.

1.09   This book is heavily indebted to the judges who have carefully construed and interpreted the meaning of the NPPF. I hope that two elements of the style of my writing do not cause offence: where a judge has changed judicial rank (for instance, been promoted from the High Court to the Court of Appeal), I have not used the phrase "as s/he then was" when referring to a decision made prior to the promotion. Secondly, I do not generally refer to a judge as "his/her Lordship/Ladyship" in the text. No disrespect whatsoever is meant by these stylistic decisions.

1.10   Where there is a reference in the form "NPPF 100", this is referring to paragraph 100 of the new NPPF. A reference to a paragraph of the previous NPPF will not use this form, instead referring to "(para. x)". Where there is a judicial decision referring to a paragraph of the original NPPF, I have used the paragraph reference of the equivalent paragraph in the new NPPF. In quotations, the paragraph numbers have been replaced in square brackets. This is so even though the text of the old NPPF may not be identical to the new NPPF. Whilst this approach is not perfect, it is less cumbersome than referring to the paragraph numbers of the original NPPF which is no longer in force.

1.11   The contents of this book are for educational purposes only, and do not constitute legal advice. The bulk of the manuscript was delivered to the publishers on 3 September 2018; it has however been possible to make some amendments since that stage.

Chapter 2

The Nature and Status of National Planning Policy

Introduction

2.01   The NPPF is the primary expression of the government's planning policy for England. What, however, is national planning policy? What is its status? How does it relate to planning policy in local plans and neighbourhood plans?

2.02   The Ministerial announcement accompanying the publication of the NPPF described it as a "rule book".[1] This is something of a misnomer: the NPPF is not a book, and it does not contain rules. The status of the NPPF is a matter of some complexity, since it is at a lower legal status than local planning policy, but nevertheless informs the making of it. Understanding the system requires examination of the legislative regime regarding decision-making on planning applications.

Section 38(6)

2.03   Section 38(6) of the PCPA provides:

> "If regard is to be had to the development plan for the purpose of any determination to be made under the planning Acts the determination must be made in accordance with the plan unless material considerations indicate otherwise."

2.04   This means that the starting-point for the determination of a planning application is the provisions of the statutory development plan (including any neighbourhood plans), rather than the NPPF. However, the result indicated in a development plan is not binding; it can be outweighed by other material considerations.

2.05   Related to section 38(6) PCPA is section 70(2) of the Town and Country Planning Act 1990. Section 70(2) provides:

> "In dealing with an application for planning permission or permission in principle the authority shall have regard to —
>
> (a) the provisions of the development plan, so far as material to the application,
>
> (aza) a post-examination draft neighbourhood development plan, so far as material to the application,
>
> (aa) any considerations relating to the use of the Welsh language, so far as material to the application;
>
> (b) any local finance considerations, so far as material to the application, and
>
> (c) any other material considerations.

2.06   As the NPPF itself says, it is a material consideration in planning decisions (NPPF

---

[1]   https://www.gov.uk/government/news/governments-new-planning-rulebook-to-deliver-more-quality-well-designed-homes (accessed 8 October 2018).

2). The terms of the NPPF can therefore indicate a result different to that expressed in national planning policy. It is also the case that, as the House of Lords said in *City of Edinburgh Council v Secretary of State for Scotland*,[2] development plan policies can pull in different directions. The terms of national planning policy can provide an indication to a decision-maker which of those directions to take.

2.07   In *City of Edinburgh*, the local planning authority had refused planning permission for a food store and petrol filling station. Planning permission was, however, granted on appeal to the Secretary of State whose reporter[3] found that greater weight should attach to material considerations other than the development plan,[4] including planning guidance which post-dated the development plan. This decision was challenged by the local planning authority, ultimately unsuccessfully.

2.08   Lord Clyde gave the main judgment. He acknowledged that the legislative status of the development plan made is more than "simply one of the material considerations". However, he went on to say that "the priority given to the development plan is not a mere mechanical preference for it".

2.09   The weight to be given to the different material considerations is not a matter of law for the court. It is a matter of planning judgment, for the decision-maker (Lord Clyde in *City of Edinburgh*, quoting Glidewell LJ in *Loup v Secretary of State for the Environment*[5] and Lord Hoffmann in *Tesco Stores Ltd v Secretary of State for the Environment*; more recently Lindblom J in *Crane v Secretary of State for Communities and Local Government*[6] and the Supreme Court in *Hopkins Homes Ltd v SSCLG*[7] endorsed this approach).

2.10   Lord Clyde set out the correct approach in *City of Edinburgh*, p.1459:

> "it will obviously be necessary for the decision-maker to consider the development plan, identify any provisions in it which are relevant to the question before him and make a proper interpretation of them. His decision will be open to challenge if he fails to have regard to a policy in the development plan which is relevant to the application or fails properly to interpret it. He will also have to consider whether the development proposed in the application before him does or does not accord with the development plan. There may be some points in the plan which support the proposal but there may be some considerations pointing in the opposite direction. He will require to assess all of these and then decide whether in light of the whole plan the proposal does or does not accord with it. He will also have to identify all the other

---

[2]   [1997] 1 WLR 1447. This is well-established: see also *Tesco Stores Ltd v Secretary of State for the Environment* [1995] 1 WLR 759.

[3]   The Scottish equivalent of a Planning Inspector.

[4]   It is accepted that the Scottish legislation, section 18A of the Town and Country Planning (Scotland) Act 1972 is materially equivalent to the English legislation.

[5]   (1995) 71 P&CR 175.

[6]   [2015] EWHC 425 (Admin).

[7]   [2017] UKSC 37; [2017] 1 WLR 1865.

material considerations which are relevant to the application and to which he should have regard. He will then have to note which of them support the application and which of them do not, and he will have to assess the weight to be given to all of these considerations. He will have to decide whether there are considerations of such weight as to indicate that the development plan should not be accorded the priority which the statute has given to it. And having weighed these considerations and determined these matters he will require to form his opinion on the disposal of the application. If he fails to take account of some material consideration or takes account of some consideration which is irrelevant to the application his decision will be open to challenge. But the assessment of the considerations can only be challenged on the ground that it is irrational or perverse."

2.11   Lord Hope described the presumption in favour of the development plan as a "presumption of fact", and not a "governing or paramount one".

2.12   What *City of Edinburgh* tells us is that, whilst the statutory development plan has priority, and is more than just a material consideration for the purposes of section 38(6) PCPA, it is capable of being overridden by other material considerations (including subsequent planning guidance). Whether the provisions of the development plan are overridden on the facts of a particular application is a matter of planning judgment for the decision-maker. If the decision-maker has identified the material considerations, then the court will not interfere unless the decision is irrational or perverse. In *R (West Berks DC and Reading BC) v SSCLG*,[8] the Court of Appeal went so far as hold that the principles that (i) weight is a matter for the decision-maker and (ii) development plan policy may be superseded by more recent guidance means that "no systematic primacy is to be accorded to the development plan" (para. 20).

2.13   Section 38(6) was again considered by the Court of Appeal in *BDW Ltd v SSCLG*.[9] A Planning Inspector had dismissed a developer's appeal against the local planning authority's refusal of planning permission for residential development on a farmland site. Lindblom LJ helpfully identified at para. 21 five points regarding section 38(6):

(1)   The duty is to give the development plan priority, whilst weighing the other material considerations in the balance;

(2)   The decision-maker must understand the relevant provisions of the plan, which may sometimes pull in different directions;

(3)   The subsection does not dictate how the decision-maker is to carry out her function, and a two-stage exercise is not essential;

(4)   The duty can be carried out only if the decision-maker identifies whether the proposal complies with the development plan as a whole;

(5)   The NPPF does not displace or modify the duty in section 38(6).

---

[8]   [2016] EWCA Civ 441; [2016] 1 WLR 3923.

[9]   [2016] EWCA Civ 493; [2017] PTSR 1337.

2.14   On the facts of *BDW Ltd*, the outcome of the appeal before the Inspector turned on a single policy in the development plan, which was the policy of central relevance to the appeal. The Inspector found that the proposal was not in accordance with that policy. The proposal was therefore contrary to the development plan as a whole (para. 33).

2.15   Whether a proposal is in accordance with the development plan is a different question to whether the development plan is out of date by virtue of being inconsistent with the NPPF. In *R (Sienkiewicz) v South Somerset DC*,[10] Ouseley J held that a local authority had erred in taking into account the weight to be given to a development plan policy due to consistency with the NPPF when considering whether the proposal complied with the development plan. This was "muddying of the waters". As Ouseley J stated at para. 44, "[t]he NPPF is but another material consideration; it may mean that conflict with the development plan is to be given less weight, but it cannot bear upon whether the conflict exists in the first place". Conversely, the terms of a development plan document cannot bear on the interpretation of the NPPF: *R (Boot) v Elmbridge BC*,[11] para. 36.

The Power to Make National Planning Policy

2.16   The ability of the Secretary of State to make national planning policy is well established, but the source of this power is not obvious. In *R (Alconbury Developments Ltd) v Secretary of State for the Environment*,[12] Lord Hoffmann described it as "the business of the Secretary of State, aided by his civil servants, to develop national planning policies and co-ordinate local policies" (para. 123). Lord Clyde stated (para. 140) "[b]y means of a central authority some degree of coherence and consistency in the development of land can be secured. National planning guidance can be prepared and promulgated and that guidance will influence the local development plans and policies which the planning authorities will use in resolving their own local problems." If there is going to be national planning policy, Lord Clyde said, it is consistent with the principle of democracy that this such policy should be devised by a minister answerable to Parliament.

2.17   In the High Court decision in *R (Cala Homes (South) Ltd) v Secretary of State for Communities and Local Government*,[13] Lindblom J held at para. 50:

> "The power of a minister to issue a statement articulating or confirming a policy commitment on the part of the government does not derive from statute. As was noted by Cooke J. in *Stringer* (at p.1295), s.1 of the Town and Country Planning Act 1943 imposed on the minister a general duty to secure consistency and continuity in the framing and execution of a national policy for the use and development of land. Although that duty was repealed by the Secretary of State in the Environment Order 1970, [Leading Counsel

---

[10]   [2015] EWHC 3704 (Admin); [2016] PTSR 815.

[11]   [2017] EWHC 12 (Admin); [2017] 2 P&CR 6.

[12]   [2001] UKHL 23; [2003] 2 AC 295.

[13]   [2011] EWHC 97 (Admin); [2011] 1 P&CR 22.

for the Secretary of State] submitted, and I accept, that it still accurately describes the political responsibility of the Secretary of State for planning policy. The courts have traditionally upheld the materiality of such policy as a planning consideration."

2.18   The decisions in *R (West Berks DC and Reading BC) v SSCLG*[14] of the High Court and the Court of Appeal[15] concerned the lawfulness of national planning policy made in relation to the requirement of developers to provide affordable housing. Holgate J's decision, in finding the policy unlawful, was reversed by the Court of Appeal. Holgate J however did accept (para. 108) the Secretary of State's submission, following from the decision in *Alconbury*, that the Secretary of State "sits at the apex of the planning system in England and Wales and as such he is entitled to set *national* policy relevant to the determination of planning matters" (emphasis in original).

2.19   The Court of Appeal observed, in relation to the power to create national planning policy (para. 12):

> "the Secretary of State's power to formulate and adopt national planning policy is not given by statute. It is an exercise of the Crown's common law powers conferred by the royal prerogative."

2.20   The nature and scope of the Royal Prerogative is disputed by constitutional law scholars. However, the general essence is that there are certain powers which the monarch (in practice, Government Ministers) have which arise from the monarch's historical status. These include the power to make treaties, to pardon criminals, and to declare war.

2.21   The Court of Appeal's view was doubted by the Supreme Court in *Hopkins Homes Ltd v SSCLG*,[16] paras 19-20. Although the parties had agreed in their written documentation that the Secretary of State's power to make national planning policy emerged from the Royal Prerogative, the Supreme Court questioned this. Referring to the decision in *Alconbury*, Lord Carnwath JSC said that it was "clearly correct" that the Secretary of State's powers derived expressly or by implication from the Planning Acts, giving him "overall responsibility for oversight of the planning system". This fact is reflected in the Secretary of State's powers in terms of plan preparation, and more generally in his powers of intervention in the planning process.

2.22   Lord Carnwath JSC went on to state (para. 21):

> "It is important…in assessing the effect of the Framework, not to overstate the scope of this policy-making role. The Framework itself makes clear that as respects the determination of planning applications (by contrast with plan-making in which it has statutory recognition), it is no more than "guidance" and as such a "material consideration"… It cannot, and does not purport to, displace the primacy given by the statute and policy to the

---

[14]   [2015] EWHC 2222 (Admin); [2016] PTSR 215.

[15]   [2016] EWCA Civ 441; [2016] 1 WLR 3923.

[16]   [2017] UKSC 37; [2017] 1 WLR 1865.

statutory development plan. It must be exercised consistently with, and not so as to displace or distort, the statutory scheme."

Implication for Interpretation

2.23   The general approach to the interpretation of national planning policy is considered elsewhere [see Chapter 3: The Interpretation of Policy]. At present it is worth saying that it follows from the source of the power to create national planning policy being planning legislation, that policy must be consistent with that legislation. Relatedly, it can be assumed that (to the extent that there is doubt about the interpretation of national planning policy) it must be interpreted in a manner consistent with the statutory scheme.

2.24   The different status of the development plan on the one hand, and other material considerations such as the NPPF on the other, has an impact upon the interpretation of development plan policies. In *Colman v SSCLG*,[17] an early case on the interpretation of the NPPF concerning a proposal for the construction of wind turbines in Devon, local plan policies were inconsistent with the NPPF. The claimant argued that local plan policies should be interpreted in line with the (subsequent) policies in the NPPF. The High Court rejected this argument (para. 23). This was in part because a material consideration is "conceptually distinct" from considerations in the development plan. Objectives in the development plan, on the one hand, and in national planning policy, were therefore of a different kind. They should not be mixed together.

2.25   The fact that the source of the power to make planning policy is statutory does not make the NPPF itself a statute, and does not mean that the NPPF should be interpreted as if it were a statute. The courts have repeatedly stressed that it should not be interpreted in such a manner (see Chapter 3: The Interpretation of Policy).

2.26   *Cawrey v SSCLG*[18] concerned a challenge by a developer to the decision of a Planning Inspector, dismissing an appeal against the refusal of planning permission for residential development. Gilbart J expressed matters crisply, stating at para. 45 that the "NPPF is not to be used to obstruct sensible decision-making. It is there as policy guidance to be had regard to in that process, not to supplant it". The NPPF's status as a policy document means that it does not do away with the importance of a decision-maker "taking a properly nuanced decision in the round".

The Practical Significance of National Planning Policy

2.27   National planning policy has significance in both the making of development plans, and in decisions on planning applications.

Plan-making

2.28   In the formulation of local plans, an Inspector appointed by the Secretary of State must assess whether a draft plan submitted for examination is sound. Soundness is

---

[17]   [2013] EWHC 1138 (Admin).

[18]   [2016] EWHC 1198 (Admin).

not defined in legislation, but is explained in the NPPF. NPPF 35(d) makes clear that, to be sound, a plan must be "[c]onsistent with national policy - enabling the delivery of sustainable development in accordance with the policies in this Framework".

2.29   If asked to do so, the Inspector must recommend modifications of the document that would make it sound (section 20(7C) PCPA). The Secretary of State himself can intervene in the process, including by requiring the Inspector to consider specified matters (section 20(6A)(b) PCPA).

2.30   If the Secretary of State considers that a local development is unsatisfactory, he may, prior to adoption, direct the local planning authority to modify the document, and the authority must comply with the direction (section 21(1)-(2) PCPA). The Secretary of State may also direct that a draft development plan document is submitted to him for approval (section 21(4) PCPA).

2.31   The PCPA permits the Secretary of State to direct the revision of a local development document, in accordance with a timetable set by the Secretary of State (section 26). The Secretary of State also has a default power to prepare or revise a document, or to give directions as to the authority in relation to the preparation or revision of the document, if he thinks that a local planning authority are failing or omitting to do anything it is necessary for them to do in connection with the preparation, revision or adoption of a development plan document (section 27(1)-(2) PCPA).

2.32   The Secretary of State's planning policy as expressed in the NPPF will be significant for these decisions.

2.33   In relation to the examination of draft neighbourhood plans, the Examiner must consider whether the draft document meets the basic conditions, including whether "having regard to national policies and advice contained in guidance issued by the Secretary of State, it is appropriate to make the order" (Town and Country Planning Act 1990, Schedule 4B, para. 8(1)-(2)).

Decision-taking

2.34   The role of national planning policy in the context of decision-taking is more subtle. The case-law considered above indicates that the statutory development plan has priority: it is the starting-point. National planning policy is a material consideration which may indicate that a decision is taken otherwise than in accordance with the development plan. It must therefore be taken into account. The PPG states:[19]

> "The National Planning Policy Framework represents up-to-date government planning policy and must be taken into account where it is relevant to a planning application or appeal. If decision takers choose not to follow the National Planning Policy Framework, clear and convincing reasons for doing so are needed. A development that is consistent with the National Planning Policy Framework does not remove the requirement to determine the application in accordance with the development plan unless there are other material considerations that indicate otherwise."

---

[19]   PPG, Section on Determining a planning application, para. 010.

2.35   The weight to be given to national or local planning policy is a matter of planning judgment for the decision-maker.[20] On the facts of a particular proposal, if there is a conflict between national planning policy and the terms of the development plan, it is open to the decision-maker to follow the policy in the development plan. As Lindblom LJ stated in *East Staffordshire BC v SSCLG*,[21] at para. 14:

> "it is for the decision-maker to decide what weight should be given to NPPF policy in so far as it is relevant to the proposal. Because this is government policy it is likely to command significant weight, but the court will not intervene unless the weight given to it by the decision-maker can be said to be unreasonable in the *Wednesbury* sense".[22]

2.36   The significance of the Secretary of State's national planning policy is made all the greater by the fact that the Secretary of State can call in planning applications for his own consideration (or, if there is an appeal to the Planning Inspectorate against refusal or non-determination of an application, the appeal can be recovered for the Secretary of State's own determination). When making a decision for himself as to whether to grant planning permission, the Secretary of State may be expected to give considerable weight to the planning policy he has published. This would be permitted, as weight is a matter for the decision-maker.

2.37   In *West Berks*, the Secretary of State had made a Written Ministerial Statement expressing national planning policy (which was also expressed in the PPG) regarding requiring developers of small sites for residential development to provide planning contributions including to affordable housing. The policy was that such contributions should not be required on small sites. At the hearing before Holgate J, Leading Counsel for the Secretary of State made a statement seeking to explain the new policy. This included that it would "*normally* be inappropriate" to require contributions from the small sites.

2.38   The claimants argued that the Secretary of State was attempting to prioritise national planning policy over local planning policy, which was in breach of the statutory primacy of the development plan. Whilst this persuaded Holgate J in the High Court, the Court of Appeal rejected this argument. According to the Court of Appeal, the Secretary of State "may well prefer his own policy to that of the development plan in case of conflict", and it is obvious that a decision-maker who promulgates a policy wishes it to be followed (para. 25). Therefore, it is lawful for the Secretary of State to "express his view as to the weight to be given to his policy" (para. 23).

2.39   Despite all the complexity of case law set out in this book, national planning policy

---

[20]   The extract from the PPG pre-dates the decision of the Supreme Court in *Hopkins Homes Ltd v SSCLG* [2017] UKSC 37; [2017] 1 WLR 1865, and the new NPPF. There may be some doubt as to whether the requirement for a "convincing" reason to justify not following the NPPF is required: a decision-maker may be simply entitled to say that in an exercise of judgment he gives greater weight to other factors.

[21]   [2017] EWCA Civ 893; [2018] PTSR 88.

[22]   The reference to a '*Wednesbury* sense' is to the decision of the Court of Appeal in *Associated Provincial Picture Houses Ltd v Wednesbury Corporation* [1948] 1 KB 223; a decision which is "*Wednesbury* unreasonable" is a decision which is so unreasonable that no reasonable decision-maker could have made it.

must be seen in the context that it is a means to an end, not the end itself (*Mansell v Tonbridge and Malling BC*,[23] para. 41). As Gilbart J stated in *R (Irving) v Mid-Sussex DC*,[24] para. 48, "The NPPF is not to be used to obstruct sensible decision-making. It is there as policy guidance to be had regard to in that process, not to supplant it".

The Inability to Override Local Planning Policy

2.40   It is not unlawful for national planning policy to express aims or to seek results different to that in local planning policies. In *R (McCarthy and Stone Retirement Lifestyles Limited) v Mayor of London*[25], Ouseley J held at para. 42 that "the NPPF contains advice which conflicts with development plans up and down the country, and is not on that account unlawful".

2.41   Although it is lawful to have inconsistent national and local policy, there are restrictions on what national policy may seek to do. Prior to the entry into force of the Localism Act 2011, there was a tier of planning policy which provided direction for development at a regional level, through the medium of Regional Strategies. It was a policy of the Coalition Government which entered office in 2010 to abolish this tier of planning control as part of the policy of localism. The abolition of regional strategies took effect by the Localism Act. The lead-up to the legislative change gave rise to litigation.

2.42   In *R (Cala Homes (South) Limited) v Secretary of State for Communities and Local Government*,[26] the Court of Appeal considered the legality of a letter from the government's Chief Planner, telling decision-makers to take into account the Government's intention to revoke regional strategies as a material consideration. The Court of Appeal held that the letter was not unlawful, but held at para. 26:

> "If the Chief Planning Officer's letter had advised local planning authorities to ignore the policies in the regional strategies, or to treat them as no longer forming part of the development plan, or to determine planning applications otherwise than in accordance with them because the Government proposed to abolish them, or if it had told decision-makers what weight they should give to the Government's proposal, then such advice would have been unlawful."

2.43   In *West Berks*, the Court of Appeal considered that the Secretary of State was not entitled to seek by the policy as set out in the WMS to "countermand or frustrate the effective operation of sections 38(6) and 70(2)". Planning policy must be consistent with the statutory scheme within which it operates. The Court of Appeal explained the passage quoted above from *Cala Homes*, saying that the examples given would "all have urged or instructed local planning authorities to act outside the statute" (para. 23).

2.44   Therefore, whilst a national planning policy may express a policy which is different

---

[23] [2017] EWCA Civ 1314; [2018] JPL 176.

[24] [2016] EWHC 1529 (Admin); [2016] PTSR 1365.

[25] [2018] EWHC 1202 (Admin); [2018] JPL 1106.

[26] [2011] EWCA Civ 639; [2011] JPL 1458.

to that set out in the development plans of various local planning authorities, and whilst that national planning policy may express the weight which it would wish to be given to that national planning policy, it would be unlawful for the national planning policy to instruct decision-makers to act contrary to the statutory scheme, including telling them to ignore the provisions of the development plan. It would also, presumably, be unlawful to set up national planning policy as a direct rival to a development plan, by saying that decisions are to be taken in accordance with the national planning policy unless material considerations indicated otherwise. Whilst the weight to be given to various considerations is a matter for a decision-maker, the development plan remains the starting-point.

The Formulation of National Planning Policy

2.45   When creating national planning policy, are there any matters which the Secretary of State has to take into account?

2.46   This was a matter considered by the Court of Appeal in *West Berks*. The Secretary of State argued that there were no particular considerations which the Secretary of State was bound to take into account. The Court of Appeal held there was a limited restriction on what the Secretary of State had to take into account (or could not take into account):

   •   The Secretary of State could not make policy which was inconsistent with section 38(6) PCPA or section 70(2) TCPA;

   •   The Secretary of State could not introduce by virtue of his policy matters which were not proper planning considerations at all.

2.47   The categories given by the Court of Appeal are broad. So long as national planning policy does not require the decision-maker to ignore the development plan, or some similar clear requirement to breach the statutory duties,[27] then the first limb will be satisfied. The scheme of planning legislation does not necessarily tend to one policy goal or another. In *Tesco Stores Ltd v Secretary of State for the Environment*,[28] Lord Hoffmann held (complete with a quotation from Larkin) that the Secretary of State's basic policy of permitting development unless it would cause demonstrable harm to interests of acknowledged importance is not required by the TCPA: a policy that planning permission should be granted only for good reason would also be consistent with the legislation.

2.48   In relation to the second limb, the scope of proper planning considerations is wide. A consideration can be relevant to a planning consideration if it serves a planning purpose, and a consideration serves a planning purpose if it relates to the character of the use of land (*Newbury District Council v Secretary of State for the Environment*[29],

---

[27] For instance, a policy which downplayed the importance of protecting listed buildings as enshrined in section 66(1) of the Planning (Listed Buildings and Conservation Areas) Act 1990.

[28] [1995] 1 WLR 759.

[29] [1981] AC 578.

Westminster City Council v Great Portland Estates Plc[30]).

2.49   The Court's approach in *West Berks* was on the basis that the Secretary of State's power did not come from statute, but from the common law. On the basis of the decision of the Supreme Court in *Hopkins Homes*, this would now appear to be wrong. However, this seems not to affect the practical implication of the decision in terms of what considerations can be taken into account. Whether the Secretary of State had taken into account all the considerations required by law was a matter in dispute before Dove J in *R (Richborough Estates Ltd) v SSCLG*.[31] A collection of housebuilders brought a challenge to the lawfulness of new national planning policy concerning housing land supply and neighbourhood planning. They argued that the Secretary of State failed to have regard to material considerations including the need for further research about the effectiveness of neighbourhood planning, and the approach to the assessment of housing need within neighbourhood area. The Secretary of State argued, on the basis of the decision of the Court of Appeal in *West Berks*, that so long as the policy was not contrary to the planning legislation, and did not introduce considerations which were not properly planning considerations, the formulation of policy was a matter for the Secretary of State with which the court should not interfere. Dove J held at para. 33:

> "it is clear that the judgment in the *West Berkshire* case [2016] PTSR 982 is both in point in relation to the issues raised by the claimants in relation to a failure to have regard to obviously material considerations, and is binding upon this court. As the court in that case observed, the legislative framework does not lay down criteria for assessing the merits of planning policy which has been made, nor does it lay down those matters which the defendant should or should not have regard to when making national policy. Provided, therefore, that the policy produced does not frustrate the operation of planning legislation, or introduce matters which are not properly planning considerations at all, and is not irrational, the matters which the defendant regards as material or immaterial to the determination of the policy being issued is a matter entirely for the defendant."

2.50   As such, the Secretary of State did not have to take into account the matters which the claimants alleged had been ignored. However, in any event, Dove J considered that they had not been left out of account (para. 34). In Dove J's consideration of the principle from *West Berks*, no difficulty appears to have been caused by virtue of the fact that the Supreme Court in *Hopkins Homes* disagreed with the Court of Appeal's views regarding the source of the Secretary of State's powers to make national planning policy.

2.51   Dove J rejected the further argument that the Secretary of State's practice was such as to give rise to an expectation that a Written Ministerial Statement in relation to national planning policy concerning housing would not be made without there being a process of consultation. The argument failed on the facts: the Secretary of

---

[30]   [1985] 1 AC 661.
[31]   [2018] EWHC 33 (Admin); [2018] PTSR 1168.

State did not have a consistent practice of consultation prior to issuing a Written Ministerial Statement on the topic (para. 75).

'Out of Date' Local Plan Policies

2.52　In the *City of Edinburgh* case,[32] Lord Clyde gave as an example of where material considerations indicate that planning permission should be granted, notwithstanding an application not in accordance with the development plan, a situation where "a particular policy in the plan can be seen to be outdated and superseded by more recent guidance". As such, a major impact of national planning policy upon development control decisions can be to render policies in the development plan out of date.

2.53　This is relevant to weight: whilst a decision-maker is generally entitled to give whatever weight she wishes to factors in the planning balance, the fact that a development plan policy is out of date is potentially relevant to the weight to be given to the policy.[33] Furthermore, NPPF 11 indicates that, where the policies which are most important for determining the application are out of date, then a more favourable test for applicants for permission will apply.

---

[32]　[1997] 1 WLR 1447.

[33]　This is notwithstanding the indication in *Hopkins Homes* that the focus is whether the presumption in favour of sustainable development (now in NPPF 11) applies.

Chapter 3

The Interpretation of Policy

Introduction

3.01 This book as a whole is about the interpretation of the NPPF, which is an expression of national planning policy, drafted by the Secretary of State. Most chapters deal with the policies of the NPPF relating to different topics, and how they have been or might be interpreted. This chapter sets out some general principles of interpretation for the NPPF, which may provide some assistance where novel questions of interpretation arise.

3.02 This chapter will address the following questions:

(i) Who has the last word in the interpretation of planning policy?

(ii) What are the general principles of interpreting planning policy?

(iii) What is the relevance of the interpretation of pieces of legislation for the interpretation of the NPPF?

(iv) What is the relevance of previous planning policy for interpreting the NPPF?

(v) Is the PPG relevant to interpreting the NPPF?

(vi) Are other policy documents relevant to interpreting the NPPF?

(vii) What is the relevance of previous decisions interpreting the NPPF?

The Courts and the Interpretation of Planning Policy: An Objective Approach

3.03 The Supreme Court held in *Tesco Stores Ltd v Dundee CC*[1] that the courts have the final word on the correct interpretation of local plan policy. Whilst the creation of policy is a matter for the policy-maker, how that policy should be interpreted - what it really means - is a matter of law. This means that it is not enough for a decision-maker to argue that the interpretation which it reached of its own policy (or a policy produced by another body) was <u>reasonable</u>. It must have reached the legally <u>correct</u> interpretation.[2]

3.04 The local planning authority in *Tesco Stores* argued that the interpretation of planning policy was a matter of planning judgment, that a court could quash a decision on the basis of the interpretation of policy only if the decision-maker had attached to words a meaning which they were not capable of bearing. This argument was rejected by the Supreme Court. Development plan policy has statutory force, and it is necessary for a decision-maker to proceed on a proper understanding of the development plan. Planning policy may leave certain questions for the application

---

[1] [2012] UKSC 13; [2012] PTSR 983.

[2] That said, the courts will be likely to quash a decision for a misinterpretation of policy only where the misinterpretation was material to the decision [see Chapter 15: Challenging Decisions Interpreting the NPPF].

of the policy to particular facts. However, Lord Reed JSC stated at para. 19, "planning authorities do not live in the world of Humpty Dumpty: they cannot make the development plan mean whatever they would like it to mean".[3]

3.05   Whilst the decision of the Supreme Court was based on the context of the interpretation of development plan policies, and the reasoning referred to the statutory basis for such policies, Lord Reed did also rely upon the wider administrative law principle that the benefit of consistency and direction in the exercise of discretion indicates that "policy statements should be interpreted objectively in accordance with the language used, read as always in its proper context" (para. 18).

3.06   It is well established that the approach of the Supreme Court now applies not only to development plan policies but also to the interpretation of the NPPF. In *St Albans v Hunston Properties Ltd*,[4] Sir David Keene noted the context of *Tesco Stores Ltd* being the statutory development plan, but held at para. 4 that "it would seem difficult to distinguish between such a policy statement and one contained in non-statutory national policy guidance".

3.07   Whilst the court is the interpreter of policy, it must not forget that it is not the author of policy. The court has the power only to interpret the policy which is laid down by the appropriate body. "It is not the role of the court to add to or refine the policies of the NPPF, but only to interpret them when called upon to do so, to supervise their application within the constraints of lawfulness, and thus to ensure that unlawfully taken decisions do not survive challenge" (*Hallam Land Management Ltd v SSCLG*,[5] para. 50, Lindblom LJ).

3.08   The implication of the court being the interpreter of policy means that the views of the interpreter are not determinative. As Sullivan LJ stated in *Redhill Aerodrome Ltd v SSCLG*,[6] "[the NPPF] means what it says, and not what the Secretary of State would like it to mean". This objective approach is emphasised by the decision of Coulson J in *Forest of Dean DC v SSCLG*.[7] Coulson J took a dismissive approach to a submission on the part of the Secretary of State regarding his intention (para. 27):

> "Although [Counsel for SSCLG] submitted that it was always the SSCLG's intention to create [a] route by which the presumption in favour of development will not apply, I have had no regard to that submissions. It is irrelevant to the true meaning… The policy is a function of the NPPF itself; not what counsel tell me that the SSCLG intended it to say."

3.09   Likewise, the evidence as to what the parties' position was at an inquiry is unlikely to be of particular relevance to a court's determination of whether a Planning

---

[3]   This is presumably a nod to the famous dissenting speech of Lord Atkin in *Liversidge v Anderson* [1942] AC 206, regarding wartime detention, rejecting an argument that the Home Secretary had an unconditional authority to detain.

[4]   [2013] EWCA Civ 1610; [2014] JPL 599.

[5]   [2018] EWCA Civ 1808.

[6]   [2014] EWCA Civ 1386; [2015] PTSR 274.

[7]   [2016] EWHC 421 (Admin); [2016] PTSR 1031.

Inspector had erred in the interpretation of the policy. Ouseley considered in *Europa Oil and Gas Ltd*[8] that evidence of a party's position "does not go very far, since the error, if error it is, is one of interpretation of planning policy, an issue in the first place for the [I]nspector and then for the court. Evidence may be of little value in that context, however forensically appealing it may be to extract it…" (para. 35).

3.10 Although the Secretary of State's interpretation of his own policy is not determinative, that does not mean that it is not helpful to the court to know what it is. In *Watermead Parish Council*,[9] Lindblom LJ found that it was not necessary to reach a concluded view on the interpretation of the NPPF in relation to the presumption in favour of sustainable development. He declined to give a definitive view on the point. In reaching this view, Lindblom LJ considered that it was relevant that the Secretary of State was not represented before the court, in order to give his views on the correct interpretation of his policy. Lindblom LJ stated at para 45:

> "Because it arises from planning policy produced and published by the Government, and because it bears on decision-making not only by local planning authorities but also by the Secretary of State and his [I]nspectors, it is, I think, an issue on which this court would undoubtedly benefit from having submissions on behalf of the Secretary of State. This is not to suggest that the court might adopt an interpretation of planning policy urged upon it by the author of that policy if it is not the correct interpretation. It is simply to recognise the advantage the court would have in being told what the Secretary of State understands his own department's policy to mean, and how he intends it to operate, not least because he is the minister responsible for overseeing and managing the planning system in this country."

3.11 When the same point of interpretation of the NPPF arose more directly in the issues before the court in *East Staffordshire BC v SSCLG*,[10] the Court of Appeal (Lindblom LJ again giving the leading judgment) was willing to provide a definitive interpretation. Referring to para. 45 of *Watermead*, Lindblom LJ noted that the conclusion which he had reached on the interpretation of the NPPF was on which the "Secretary of State has expressly acknowledged and emphasised in this appeal" (para. 22(2)).

3.12 Although the personal views of the Secretary of State (or his officials) do not determine the meaning of a policy, the High Court has admitted witness evidence on behalf of the Secretary of State regarding the department's views on the meaning of policy. In *Good Energy Generation Ltd v SSCLG*,[11] Lang J was considering a challenge to the refusal of planning permission on appeal for wind farm development. One ground of challenge was that the Planning Inspector unlawfully disregarded benefits provided by the development. In the course of considering this ground, Lang J considered what is now NPPF 152, on the support to be given to community-led initiatives for renewable and low-carbon energy. An official from the Ministry

---

[8]   [2013] EWHC 2643 (Admin); [2014] 1 P&CR 3.

[9]   [2017] EWCA Civ 152; [2018] PTSR 43.

[10]   [2017] EWCA Civ 893; [2018] PTSR 88.

[11]   [2018] EWHC 1270 (Admin); [2018] JPL 1248.

of Housing, Communities and Local Government provided a witness statement, in which he acknowledged that the interpretation of policy is a question of law for the courts, but stated on behalf of the Government that the provision of the NPPF was not meant to include the proposals put forward by the claimant. Lang J stated this at para. 85:

> "The Claimant made no objection to the Secretary of State adducing Mr Watson's evidence. I found it helpful in identifying the intended scope of the [NPPF and PPG]. Nonetheless, I did not give it any weight in deciding whether these particular schemes came within the scope of the [NPPF or the PPG], because of the caution to be applied to *ex post facto* evidence filed by decision-makers."

3.13 Although Lang J disregarded the evidence as it related to the particular facts before her, she does appear to have considered it useful evidence in relation to the "intended scope" of national planning policy. Given the objective approach that the courts take to the interpretation of policy, this is a surprising approach, and is difficult to reconcile with the decision of Coulson J in *Forest of Dean* (it should not make a difference whether the Secretary of State's view on the meaning of policy is expressed in a witness statement, or in submissions from his barrister). It remains to be seen whether the courts will take such an approach in circumstances where the admission of such evidence is disputed by one of the parties.

3.14 The fact that the Secretary of State is the author of national planning policy means that, if he does not agree with the interpretation of it reached by the courts, he can amend the policy so as to more clearly reflect his intentions. However, unlike the PPG which has been amended frequently since its introduction, the original NPPF was left unchanged from its publication in March 2012 to its replacement with the new NPPF in July 2018. As long ago as the decision of the Court of Appeal in *Hunston Properties Ltd* in December 2013,[12] Sir David Keene called upon the Secretary of State "to review and to clarify what his policy is intended to mean", finding it difficult to construe. This call was not taken up with urgency (possibly because the Secretary of State was satisfied with the interpretation the Court of Appeal reached in *Hunston Properties Ltd*).

3.15 The objective approach to interpretation in the planning context does not just apply to development plan policy and national policy; in *Rainbird v LB Tower Hamlets*,[13] the High Court considered what approach to take to a guidance document regarding planning for daylight and sunlight, published by the Building Research Establishment. John Howell QC, sitting as a Deputy Judge of the High Court, considered at para. 81 that it was not open to the local planning authority merely to take any reasonable approach to the interpretation of the BRE Guide. The local planning authority had to take the legally correct approach (and the same would apply to a decision taken by the Secretary of State or a Planning Inspector on appeal). The meaning of the BRE Guide was a matter for the court, bearing in mind that it was "not an

---

[12] At para. 4.

[13] [2018] EWHC 657 (Admin).

enactment but rather…advice aimed primarily (but not exclusively) at designers".[14]

3.16   Care should be applied when considering previous judicial decisions interpreting the NPPF. In *Ceg Land Promotions II Ltd v SSCLG*,[15] Ouseley J considered his previous decision regarding valued landscapes in *Stroud DC v SSCLG* [see Chapter 12: Conserving and Enhancing the Natural Environment].[16] Ouseley J considered that *Stroud* was not authority for all it had been held up to be, specifically a requirement that in order to be a valued landscape, a site must have "demonstrable physical attributes". This was merely the phrase that the Planning Inspector had happened to have used in the decision under challenge in *Stroud DC*, and Ouseley J in *CEG Land Promotions* disavowed any such test in law (para. 58). There is thus a warning that the terms of a judgment will be strongly influenced by the facts of the decision it is considering, and the wording used by the judge may arise due to the way the decision-maker has phrased the decision. Wording from one particular judgment should not be lifted into a case concerning different facts, without carefully considering the implications of the change in context.

What are the General Principles of Interpretation?

3.17   Before turning to the detail of the cases, these can be summarised as follows:

(i)   Planning policy is not to be interpreted in an overly-legalistic way;

(ii)   Planning policy may pull in different directions;

(iii)   Interpretation of policy is a different matter to the application of policy to the facts;

(iv)   The views of specialist Planning Inspectors are entitled to respect;

(v)   Planning policies are to be practical, and are directed towards planning professionals and the public;

(vi)   Planning policy is to be interpreted in its context;

(vii)   Planning policy is to be interpreted as a whole.

3.18   Whilst planning policies are to be interpreted by courts, that does not mean that they are to be interpreted in an overly-legalistic way. As Lord Reed JSC stated in *Tesco Stores Ltd* at para. 19:[17]

> "[it is not right] that such statements should be construed as if they were statutory or contractual provisions. Although a development plan has a legal status and legal effects, it is not analogous in its nature or purpose to a statute or contract. As has often been observed, development plans are full of broad statements of policy, many of which may be mutually reconcilable, so that in a particular case one must give way to another."

---

[14]   Para. 82.
[15]   [2018] EWHC 1799 (Admin).
[16]   [2015] EWHC 488 (Admin).
[17]   [2012] UKSC 13; [2012] PTSR 983.

3.19   The same reasoning applies to the interpretation of the NPPF: *Redhill Aerodrome Ltd v SSCLG*.[18]

3.20   The courts have been critical of interpretation which is overly legalistic. The court's role "must not be overstated": *East Staffordshire BC v SSCLG*,[19] para. 9. Not only may an overly legalistic interpretation be a waste of time and mental effort, it may lead to the wrong interpretation. As the Court of Appeal held in *Braintree DC v SSCLG*,[20] at para. 27:

> "Our task, as [counsel] submitted, is to construe the words of the policy itself, reading them sensibly in their context. This is not a sophisticated exercise, and it need not be difficult. It is, in fact, quite straightforward. Planning policies, whether in the development plan or in the NPPF, ought never to be over-interpreted. As this case shows, over-interpretation of a policy can distort its true meaning–which is misinterpretation."

3.21   The Supreme Court commented on the "over-legalisation" of policy in *Hopkins Homes Ltd v SSCLG*.[21] Lord Carnwath JSC noted the comments of Lord Hoffmann in *Tesco Stores Ltd v Secretary of State for the Environment*[22] that the broad statements of policy in development plans may pull against each other: Lord Carnwath applied this to the NPPF. Over-legalisation is particularly problematic in a document which was intended to be read by a non-expert audience. In a very significant passage, Lord Carnwath stated at paras 25-26:

> "25. It must be remembered that, whether in a development plan or in a non-statutory statement such as the NPPF, these are statements of policy, not statutory texts, and must be read in that light. Even where there are disputes over interpretation, they may well not be determinative of the outcome... Furthermore, the courts should respect the expertise of the specialist planning inspectors, and start at least from the presumption that they will have understood the policy framework correctly. With the support and guidance of the planning inspectorate, they have primary responsibility for resolving disputes between planning authorities, developers and others, over the practical application of the policies, national or local...
>
> 26. Recourse to the courts may sometimes be needed to resolve distinct issues of law, or to ensure consistency of interpretation in relation to specific policies, as in the *Tesco* case. In that exercise the specialist judges of the Planning Court have an important role. However, the judges are entitled to look to applicants, seeking to rely on matters of planning policy in applications to

---

[18]   [2014] EWHC 2476 (Admin). The High Court's decision was overturned on appeal: [2014] EWCA Civ 1386; [2015] PTSR 274, but Sullivan LJ in the Court of Appeal expressly adopted Patterson J's approach on this point.

[19]   [2017] EWCA Civ 893; [2018] PTSR 88.

[20]   [2018] EWCA Civ 610; [2018] 2 P&CR 9.

[21]   [2017] UKSC 37; [2017] 1 WLR 1865.

[22]   [1995] 1 WLR 759, 780.

quash planning decisions (at local or appellate level), to distinguish clearly between issues of interpretation of policy, appropriate for judicial analysis, and issues of judgment in the application of that policy; and not to elide the two."

3.22 Does the same respect to be given to the expertise of Planning Inspectors apply to decisions taken by local planning authorities? There is some indication that it should be. In *Mansell v Tonbridge and Malling BC*,[23] Sir Terence Etherton C noted that the reports of planning officers for decisions to be made by a planning committee of a local planning authority "are not, and should not be, written for lawyers, but for councillors who are well-versed in local affairs and local factors. Planning committees approach such reports utilising that local knowledge and much common-sense" (para. 63). Lindblom LJ referred at para. 41 to Parliament assigning the decision-making function "not to judges, but–at local level–to elected councillors with the benefit of advice given to them by planning officers, most of whom are professional planners".

3.23 Lindblom LJ made some trenchant observations regarding "excessive legalism" in *East Staffordshire BC*. Faced with an appeal against a decision in which the High Court had referred to "residual scope for the exercise of discretion", and "an algorithm to describe the process laid down in [NPPF 11]", as well as posing the question "[h]ow exceptional is exceptional?",[24] Lindblom LJ stressed the need to adopt a simple approach. At para. 50, he stated:

"The court should always resist over complication of concepts that are basically simple. Planning decision-making is far from being a mechanical, or quasi-mathematical activity. It is essentially a flexible process, not rigid or formulaic. It involves, largely, an exercise of planning judgment, in which the decision-maker must understand relevant national and local policy correctly and apply it lawfully to the particular facts and circumstances of the case in hand, in accordance with the requirements of the statutory scheme."

3.24 Notwithstanding these comments, Lindblom LJ in the recent case of *Samuel Smith Old Brewery (Tadcaster) v North Yorkshire CC*[25] quashed the decision of a local planning authority to grant planning permission, where the officer report disclosed an error in the interpretation of Green Belt policy. Lindblom LJ noted previous warnings about excessive legalism at para. 33, but nevertheless found that the court must intervene where a planning decision "has been made by a local planning authority on the basis of a misunderstanding and misapplication of national planning policy".

3.25 Whilst the precise meaning of aspects of national planning policy may prove a matter of fascination for lawyers, litigants and courts, they are not to lose sight of the purpose of national planning policy: "the making of planning policy is not an end in

---

[23] [2017] EWCA Civ 1314; [2018] JPL 176.

[24] In *Trustees of the Barker Mill Estates v SSCLG* [2016] EWHC 3028 (Admin); [2017] PTSR 408, Holgate J considered that the decision of the High Court in *East Staffordshire BC* as an illustration of the risk of this field becoming too legalistic.

[25] [2018] EWCA Civ 489.

itself, but a means to achieving reasonably predictable decision-making, consistent with the aims of the policy-maker" (*Mansell v Tonbridge and Malling BC*, para. 41).

3.26   The fact that policy is not a statute does not necessarily mean that a hands-off approach needs to be taken to the interpretation of it. Indeed, in *Euro Garages Ltd v SSCLG*,[26] Jefford J used the fact that the NPPF is not a statute as a justification for reading words into one paragraph of the previous version of the NPPF, which she viewed as otherwise not entirely making sense. Her insertion of words was "a sensible reading" and accorded with other policy in the NPPF (para. 18).[27]

3.27   Planning policy does not exist in a vacuum and is supposed to be practical. Policies are "designed to shape practical decision-taking, and should be interpreted with that practical purpose clearly in mind" (*Canterbury CC v SSCLG*,[28] para. 23(ii)). In *Canterbury CC*, Dove J also noted the audience of planning policies: they are to be applied by planning professionals and the public. This perhaps reflects the criticism of a legalistic argument by Ouseley J in *R (Robb) v South Cambridgeshire DC*,[29] para. 33, stating that "[t]his is an argument that would have been well received in a tribunal dealing with a taxing statute or chancery litigation 100 years or so ago. It is not an argument sensibly to be addressed on the meaning of policy in the 21st century. It is perfectly obvious that a degree of common sense has to attend the understanding of these policies."

3.28   A key aspect of interpretation of the NPPF is that the NPPF must be interpreted as a whole. Hickinbottom J so held as long ago as the decision of the High Court in *Bayliss v SSCLG*,[30] at para. 18. In the High Court, Ouseley J took a holistic approach to the interpretation of the NPPF in *Europa Oil and Gas Ltd v SSCLG*.[31] In his approach to the meaning of the phrase "mineral extraction" in Green Belt policy, Ouseley J reinforced his conclusion by reference to the section of the original NPPF specifically about the use of minerals. In the Court of Appeal's decision in the same case,[32] Richards LJ held at para. 16 that it would be "very surprising" were a term to have a different meaning in later passages in the NPPF, without a clear indication.

3.29   The fact that the NPPF should be interpreted as a whole indicates that the three objectives of the planning system, set out in NPPF 8, are capable of playing a part in the interpretation of the rest of the NPPF. Although NPPF 9 states that the objectives are "not criteria against which every decision can or should be judged", they should be delivered through "the application of policies" in the NPPF [see Chapter 4: Sustainable Development]. This echoes the approach of Lindblom LJ

---

[26]   [2018] EWHC 1753 (Admin).

[27]   The wording of the NPPF has changed between the first and second versions, such that Jefford J's insertions are no longer necessary.

[28]   [2018] EWHC 1611 (Admin).

[29]   [2017] EWHC 594 (Admin).

[30]   [2013] EWHC 1612 (Admin).

[31]   [2013] EWHC 2643 (Admin); [2014] 1 P&CR 3.

[32]   [2014] EWCA Civ 825; [2014] PTSR 1471.

in *Braintree DC v SSLCG*.[33]

3.30 A creative approach to the interpretation of the NPPF as a whole persuaded the High Court, but not the Court of Appeal, in *Redhill Aerodrome Ltd*. The claimant argued that the changes to national planning policy as a whole meant that the meaning of "any other harm", in the context of Green Belt policy, had changed as between national planning policy pre-dating the NPPF, and the version to be found in the NPPF. Earlier national guidance, set out in Planning Policy Guidance 2, was considered in the High Court in *River Club v SSCLG*.[34] The High Court had held in *River Club* that "any other harm" meant any harm whatsoever, not limited to harm to the Green Belt. The claimant in *Redhill Aerodrome Ltd* argued that the fact that the NPPF introduced distinct policy tests for certain contexts (particularly the test for residual harm to the highways network) meant that the meaning of "any other harm" meant "any other harm to the Green Belt", being a different interpretation to that given to PPG2 in *River Club*. Whilst Patterson J agreed in the High Court, her decision was reversed by the Court of Appeal. The Court of Appeal considered that the changes to national planning policy had not been so major as to result in a change in the established meaning of words in significant national policy. This case is considered further below in terms of the guidance it gives on the relevance of previous national planning policy to the interpretation of the NPPF.

3.31 The fact that the NPPF should be interpreted as a whole is in fact one aspect of a wider principle, which is that policy must be read in its proper context. In Canterbury CC, Dove J noted at para. 23(iii) that the context of a policy "will include its subject matter and also the planning objectives which it seeks to achieve and serve. The context will also be comprised by the wider policy framework within which the policy sits and to which it relates. This framework will include, for instance, the overarching strategy within which the policy sits". Patten LJ put the matter nicely in *Lloyd v SSCLG*,[35] at para 74, when he said "[o]ne is reminded of Lord Hoffmann's dictum that no one has ever made an acontextual statement,[36] and that applies as much to the construction of the national and local policies at issue in this case as it does to everything else."

3.32 The overall approach to the interpretation of policy was expressed in memorable fashion by Gilbert J in *Dartford BC v SSCLG*,[37] para. 42:

> "For those of us who have swum for several years in the waters of Town and Country Planning, it has been striking that NPPF, a policy document, could sometimes have been approached as if it were a statute, and as importantly, as if it did away with the importance of a decision maker taking a properly nuanced decision in the round, having regard to the development plan (and

---

[33] [2018] EWCA Civ 610; [2018] 2 P&CR 9.

[34] [2009] EWHC 2674 (Admin); [2010] JPL 584.

[35] [2014] EWCA Civ 839; [2014] JPL 1247.

[36] Lord Hoffmann used the phrase in *Kirin-Amgen Inc v Transkaryotic Therapies Inc (No. 2)* [2004] UKHL 46; [2005] 1 All ER 667 (a case about patents) at para. 64.

[37] [2016] EWHC 649 (Admin).

its statutory significance) and to all material considerations".

What is the Relevance of Legal Provisions?

3.33   The early decision of the Court of Appeal in *Europa Oil and Gas Ltd v SSCLG*[38] would tend to suggest that the scope for interpreting the NPPF by reference to other documents or policies is limited. Richards LJ held at para. 15: "[o]n the face of it, the NPPF is a stand-alone document which should be interpreted within its own terms. It even contains a glossary (Annex 2) which explains familiar planning terms such as "local plan" and "planning condition", cross-referring as appropriate to legislation." However, whilst the starting-point for the interpretation of the NPPF is going to be the wording of the document itself, read as a whole, the NPPF needs also to be read in its context.

3.34   If a term is used in the NPPF, and it is also found in legislation, is the interpretation of the term in that legislation also taken to be the correct interpretation of the term found in policy? The answer to this question is not straightforward: the courts have found that the legislative definition does not apply to the interpretation of policy in one context, but have at other times referred to legislative meaning when construing the NPPF. The basic position appears to be that the meaning of a word in legislation will be relevant only if the NPPF is correctly interpreted as incorporating that definition.

3.35   The relevance of the legislative meaning of a term arose in the context of policy on the AONB, National Parks and the Broads.[39] "Major development" is heavily restricted by policy in those areas. However, the meaning of the phrase was left undefined in the original version of the NPPF. In *Aston v SSCLG*,[40] the High Court rejected an argument that the prescriptive meaning of the phrase as found in the Town and Country Planning (Development Management Procedure) Order 2010 should apply where the phrase is used in the NPPF. The claimant's argument that "major development" should have a homogenous meaning across planning law and policy was rejected; Wyn Williams J held that there was no need for the phrase to have a uniform meaning wherever used in the planning context. The correct approach to construction is to consider the phrase "in the context of the document in which it appears" (para. 93). Whilst a precise definition was suitable for the procedural rules in the Development Management Procedure Order, the question of whether development in the AONB was major was much more suitable for the exercise of planning judgment by the decision-maker. This decision was followed by Lindblom J in *R (The Forge Field Society) v Sevenoaks DC*,[41] and also by

---

[38]   [2014] EWCA Civ 825; [2014] PTSR 1471.

[39]   This precise example has now been covered by Footnote 55 of the amended NPPF, which makes it clear that the meaning of the phrase is a matter for the decision maker, and the issue is dealt with in detail elsewhere [see Chapter 12: Conserving and Enhancing the Natural Environment]. However, what is relevant for the purposes of this chapter is the approach which the courts took to interpretation of policy, rather than the precise content of policy.

[40]   [2013] EWHC 1936 (Admin); [2014] 2 P&CR 10.

[41]   [2014] EWHC 1895 (Admin); [2015] JPL 22.

Stuart-Smith J in *R (JH and FW Green Ltd) v South Downs National Park Authority*.[42]

3.36   There have, however, been contexts in which the courts have viewed it as relevant to have regard to the terms of legislation to determine the meaning of policy in the NPPF. In *Fordent Holdings Ltd v SSCLG*,[43] HHJ Pelling QC, sitting as a Judge of the High Court, considered the meaning of Green Belt policy. At paras 17-18 he held that the meaning of the word "development" in the phrase "inappropriate development" was the same as that in section 55 TCPA. It could therefore include material changes of use. The Judge stated of the meaning of the word development: "[t]his is the meaning adopted generally in a planning law context. No other meaning is suggested". Presumably, what counts is not only that this is the meaning of the word in the planning law context, but in the context of the planning system generally, including planning policy. Ouseley J had taken the same approach as HHJ Pelling QC in *Europa Oil and Gas Ltd v SSCLG*,[44] at para. 53. Although not spelling out his reasoning in great detail, Ouseley J stated that the language of policy documents using the phrase "engineering operation" is clearly drawing on the concept of engineering operation as included in section 55 TCPA (which includes engineering operations in the definition of development).

3.37   On appeal against Ouseley J's decision,[45] the Court of Appeal considered an argument that the meaning of the phrase "mineral extraction" in the NPPF should be informed by the meaning of "extraction" in legislation. The appellant was seeking to argue that a different approach should be taken to the exploration for minerals, and the extraction of minerals which are known to be present. The appellant referred to various legislative provisions, which were said to be reflected in PPG2, the predecessor to the Green Belt policies in the NPPF. Richards LJ did not view this as a useful exercise, stating that although he saw the force of the argument that expressions in PPG2 echoed the definitions and distinctions in the legislation, it was unnecessary to reach a conclusion on the point, as what was being interpreted was the NPPF, which had replaced PPG2.

3.38   In another case concerning the Green Belt, the Court of Appeal considered in *Lloyd v SSCLG*[46] the question of whether the word "building" in the NPPF included a mobile home. In finding that it did not, Sullivan LJ found that NPPF 145 did not "operate in a vacuum". It operated in a "detailed statutory context", which distinguished between operational development and change of use, extends the definition of caravan to include a mobile home, and treats the stationing of a caravan as a use of land rather than as a building operation (paras 39-42).

3.39   The High Court considered NPPF policy regarding the construction of new buildings in the Green Belt in *Bromley LBC v SSCLG*.[47] The claimant council argued that

---

[42]   [2018] EWHC 604 (Admin).

[43]   [2013] EWHC 2844 (Admin); [2013] 2 P&CR 12.

[44]   [2013] EWHC 2643 (Admin); [2014] 1 P&CR 3.

[45]   [2014] EWCA Civ 825; [2014] PTSR 1471.

[46]   [2014] EWCA Civ 839; [2014] JPL 1247.

[47]   [2016] EWHC 595 (Admin); [2016] PTSR 1186.

an aspect of NPPF policy supported the operational development comprised in the construction of the building, but not the change of use of the site to residential use [see Chapter 10: The Green Belt]. In rejecting this argument, David Elvin QC, sitting as a Deputy High Court Judge, noted section 75 TCPA, the effect of which is that, where planning permission is granted for the erection of a building, then if no use is specified for the building, the permission is to be construed as including permission to use the building for the purpose for which it is designed. The Judge held at para. 41:

> "As new buildings, it appears clear to me that the Government must have had in mind the use of the buildings (set in the context of [section 75 TCPA]) given the clear language of the paragraph and its frequent reference, where intended, to the use of the new buildings."

3.40   The fact that the courts take the approach that a decision-maker does not necessarily have to trawl every use of a particular phrase in planning law and policy likely reflects the courts' wider principle that the interpretation of policy is not to be an overly-legalistic exercise. However, where a planning professional would understand a term as being used in a legal sense, then the courts are likely to take such an approach to the interpretation of the NPPF.

What is the Relevance of Previous National Planning Policy, Replaced by the NPPF?

3.41   The original NPPF brought about a number of changes to national planning policy guidance previously in force. However, in many respects, the new policy in the NPPF appeared to maintain the previous policy, albeit in fewer words. This gives rise to potentially difficult questions: to what extent should the interpretation of the NPPF be guided by the interpretation of now-revoked planning policy?

3.42   The Court of Appeal considered this question in *Europa Oil and Gas Ltd v SSCLG*.[48] The Court of Appeal had been presented with sophisticated argument regarding the relevance of meanings of terms in legislation, terms which were then found in PPG2, the predecessor to national Green Belt policy in the NPPF. The appellant argued that the meaning of the terms in the legislation therefore applied to the NPPF. The Court of Appeal did not find this approach persuasive (para. 32), Richards LJ stating that "[t]he NPPF replaced the earlier guidance (though not of course the legislation) and, so far as material, was more than a simple carry-across of the language used in the guidance it replaced."

3.43   In *Redhill Aerodrome Ltd v SSCLG*[49], a challenge was brought to the decision of a Planning Inspector on the basis that the interpretation of PPG2 could not apply to the NPPF. The change alleged related to the meaning of the phrase "any other harm" in NPPF 144 - did this mean any other harm to the Green Belt, or any other harm whatsoever? The High Court in *River Club v SSCLG*[50] had held that the

---

[48]   [2014] EWCA Civ 825; [2014] PTSR 1471.

[49]   [2014] EWCA Civ 1386; [2015] PTSR 274.

[50]   [2009] EWHC 2674 (Admin); [2010] JPL 584.

phrase as it appeared in PPG2 referred to any harm whatsoever. The High Court agreed with the claimant's argument that the meaning of the phrase had been changed with the advent of the NPPF. The Court of Appeal disagreed, overturning the High Court's decision. Part of the Court of Appeal's reasoning was based on the fact that the Secretary of State had shown no intention to change Green Belt policy in the way suggested by the claimant. The Court of Appeal held that the "fundamental aim of Green Belt policy" remained unchanged. The impact assessment carried out in relation to the NPPF indicated no change to Green Belt policy in this respect. Decisions of the Secretary of State made since the publication of the NPPF on individual planning applications did not indicate any approach different to that in *River Club*.

3.44   Sullivan LJ did not consider that these factors were conclusive (para. 17), the interpretation of the NPPF being a matter of law, not a matter of what the Secretary of State would like it to mean. However, he was influenced by the fact that "if the [NPPF] has effected this change in Green Belt policy it is clear that it has done so unintentionally".

3.45   In *R (Timmins) v Gedling BC*,[51] Richards LJ considered his earlier comments in *Europa Oil and Gas*, but, referring to *Redhill Aerodrome*, held that that "previous guidance… remains relevant" (para. 24). He reached his conclusion on the meaning of the NPPF, noting also the position under PPG2 ("[t]o the extent that it is relevant to look back at the position under PPG2… I do not accept that reference to PPG2 justifies a different interpretation…"). He agreed with counsel for the claimants that the fact that a matter is not referred to in the impact assessment into the NPPF is not determinative as to whether there is a change in policy.

3.46   The fact that the claimant's argument constituted a change from previous Green Belt policy was also relevant in *R (Lee Valley Regional Park Authority) v Epping Forest DC*.[52] The claimants were arguing that, notwithstanding the terms of NPPF 145(a), there could be harm to the openness of the Green Belt caused by buildings for agriculture and forestry. The Court of Appeal was not persuaded. PPG2 was explicit on the point in issue. Whilst the NPPF was not so explicit, "[i]f the Government had meant to abandon [the] distinction between "inappropriate" and appropriate development, one would have expected so significant a change in national policy for the Green Belt to have been announced".[53]

3.47   In *Tandridge DC v SSCLG*,[54] it was common ground between the parties that the replacement building exception for new buildings in the Green Belt should be approached in the same way as the decision in *R (Heath and Hampstead Society) v Camden LBC* interpreted that exception, as it had previously existed in PPG2.[55]

---

[51]   [2015] EWCA Civ 10; [2015] PTSR 837.

[52]   [2016] EWCA Civ 404; [2016] Env LR 30.

[53]   Para. 22.

[54]   [2015] EWHC 2503 (Admin).

[55]   [2008] EWCA Civ 193; [2008] 2 P&CR 13.

3.48   However, care must be taken to ensure that decision-makers (and courts) do not place too much reliance on previous versions of policy. In *Turner v SSCLG*,[56] Sales LJ noted that the policy to be interpreted was that in the NPPF, rather than PPG2, which (as was relevant to the matter in question) was "expressed in materially different terms" from the NPPF. Sales LJ considered that Green J in the High Court in *Timmins v Gedling BC*[57] had placed too much emphasis on the interpretation of PPG2 in previous case law.[58]

3.49   The Court of Appeal considered an unpromising argument regarding the interpretation of the phrase "previously developed land" in the context of the Green Belt in *Dartford BC v SSCLG*.[59] The Court of Appeal found the interpretation of the NPPF to be clearly contrary to the claimant council's interpretation [see Chapter 10: The Green Belt]. The claimant relied upon statements made by a minister when introducing changes to previous versions of planning policy, prior to the NPPF. Lewison LJ referred to *Timmins* and *Turner*, finding that "at least in the case of the Green Belt, previous policy guidance remained relevant". However, in a passage which poses a warning to potential challengers seeking to make such arguments, he held that he did not "consider that previous policy guidance should be invoked in order to create ambiguities in the NPPF where the language of that document is clear" (para. 20).

3.50   In a case <u>not</u> relating to the Green Belt, Lindblom LJ warned about the dangers of relying too heavily on the interpretation of non-NPPF policy in *Warners Retail (Moreton) Ltd v Cotswold DC*.[60] Whilst the policies were "similar in broad intent", they were "not in identical terms" (para. 45). Even a judgment of the Supreme Court interpreting the different policy should not be read across as if it were a decision about the NPPF, which it was not.

3.51   The Secretary of State can be assumed to be aware of judicial decisions interpreting the NPPF. Therefore, if a court judgment states that the Government policy leads to a surprising conclusion, but the Secretary of State elected not to make a change to the policy when amending the NPPF, it can be assumed that he wished the surprising interpretation to remain. In *R (East Meon Forge and Cricket Ground Protection Association (acting by its Chairman George Bartlett)) v East Hampshire DC*,[61] Lang J held that a certain aspect of national planning policy referred only to loss of a heritage asset, rather than harm to it. She stated that she was unaware why this would be, but as the NPPF did consistently draw a distinction between harm and loss, she was driven to that conclusion. The Secretary of State did not change this

---

[56]   [2016] EWCA Civ 466; [2017] 2 P&CR 1.

[57]   [2014] EWHC 654 (Admin).

[58]   As it happens, the High Court decision in *R (Heath and Hampstead Society) v Camden LBC* [2007] EWHC 977 (Admin); [2007] 2 P&CR 19.

[59]   [2017] EWCA Civ 141; [2017] PTSR 737.

[60]   [2016] EWCA Civ 606. The policies in question were Scottish development plan policies considered by the Supreme Court in *Tesco Stores Ltd v Dundee CC* [2012] UKSC 13; [2012] PTSR 983.

[61]   [2014] EWHC 3543 (Admin).

aspect of the NPPF when publishing the amended version of the NPPF, and so it can be assumed that he wished to maintain this distinction between loss and harm.[62]

3.52 What is the guiding principle to be drawn from all these various decisions? Notwithstanding the brief comment of Lewison LJ in *Dartford BC*, it is unlikely that there is any distinct approach relating to the Green Belt. Perhaps all that can be said is that the meaning of previous policy will be unlikely to be determinative of the interpretation of the NPPF; the degree to which it will be of assistance in interpreting the NPPF will depend upon the level of similarity between the previous policy and the paragraph of the NPPF in question, viewed in its context.

What is the Relevance of Other Policy to the Interpretation of the NPPF?

3.53 The early decision of the Court of Appeal in *Europa Oil and Gas* would tend to suggest that other policy is not relevant to the interpretation of the NPPF: the NPPF is a standalone document. However, there seem to be some exceptions to this proposition. Indeed, the amended version of the NPPF cannot be said to be an entirely standalone document: it refers to numerous other documents, including the Planning Policy for Traveller Sites, the PPG, United Nations General Assembly Resolution 42/187, legislation, Government strategies and circulars, and Building for Life 12: The sign of a good place to live (Birkbeck D and Kruczkowski S (2015)).

The PPG

3.54 There is considerable overlap between the PPG and the NPPF. Can the PPG be taken into account in the interpretation of the NPPF? In *Braintree DC v SSCLG*,[63] counsel for the Secretary of State argued that it would be inappropriate in principle to use the PPG when interpreting policies of the NPPF. Lindblom LJ stated at para. 36:

> "This is not something we have to decide, because the meaning of the policy we are dealing with here is plain on its face and requires no illumination from the PPG or any other statement of national policy or guidance. But I doubt that it would be right to exclude the guidance in the PPG as a possible aid to understanding the policy or policies to which it corresponds in the NPPF. There may be occasions when that is necessary. But this, in my view, is not such a case."

3.55 Lindblom LJ also considered that the interpretation of the policy which he had reached seemed "entirely consistent" with guidance in the PPG (para. 37). Lindblom LJ referred extensively to the PPG in *Catesby Estates Ltd v Steer*[64] regarding the concept of the setting of a listed heritage asset, finding that the PPG explains the concept of setting in the Glossary of the NPPF. Lindblom LJ said this of the PPG

---

[62] By contrast, the Secretary of State reinstated the general category of change of use as a class of development capable in certain circumstances of being appropriate development in the Green Belt in NPPF 146, on the back of judicial decisions noting that this class had been omitted from the original NPPF despite existing in previous national policy.

[63] [2018] EWCA Civ 610; [2018] 2 P&CR 9.

[64] [2018] EWCA Civ 1697.

in *R (Save Britain's Heritage) v Liverpool CC*,[65] para. 26:

> "We are concerned here not with planning policy of the kind contained in the NPPF but with practice guidance whose role, largely, is to amplify published policy. … the Government's planning policy for England is in the NPPF. The [PPG] supplements and explains policies in the NPPF, and assists in their application. And it should be construed, if it can be, consistently with them."

3.56 This paragraph states that the PPG should (if possible) be construed consistently with the NPPF, rather than the other way around; but this does tend to suggest that these publications by the Secretary of State should be read as a piece, if possible. In the High Court in *St Modwen Developments Ltd v SSCLG*,[66] Ouseley J held that the PPG was an aid to the interpretation of the NPPF, which is not to be interpreted as a statute or a contract: "when the policy-maker produces a subordinate document to expand on what he has previously said, which does not and is not expressly intended to contradict it, that document may assist the Court in understanding what was intended in the first place and why…". Lindblom LJ in the Court of Appeal[67] referred to the PPG as amplifying a footnote to the NPPF. He did not embrace the PPG as a tool for interpreting the NPPF in terms as broad as those expressed by Ouseley J, but neither did he distance himself from them. Lindblom LJ also referred to the amplifying role of the PPG in *R (DLA Delivery Ltd) v Lewes DC*,[68] when he found that a major theme of the NPPF (that the planning system should boost significantly the supply of housing) was "amplified in the PPG". In *Trustees of the Barker Mill Estates v SSCLG*[69] Holgate J referred to the PPG at para. 31 as providing "[m]ore detailed guidance" on the assessment of objectively assessed need for housing than the NPPF.

3.57 Ouseley J considered a challenge to a grant, on appeal, of prior approval for permitted development rights for change the use of premises from retail to residential use in *Patel v SSCLG*.[70] He considered an argument that compliance with the development plan had to be considered. One limb of this argument proceeded by reference to the NPPF. Ouseley J rejected this argument: the prior approval mechanism did not require compliance with the development plan. In the course of considering this argument, Ouseley J considered the PPG "for what it is worth", describing it as "a Government document of lower status then [sic] the NPPF". The PPG was not however material to the matter which Ouseley J had to decide.

3.58 The original NPPF was published in 2012; the PPG was first released in 2014. Ouseley J's reasoning in *St Modwen Developments* was based in part on the PPG being subsequent to the NPPF. Assuming that Ouseley J was correct in relation to the original NPPF, can the existing PPG be a guide to the interpretation of the

---

[65] [2016] EWCA Civ 806; [2017] JPL 39.

[66] [2016] EWHC 968 (Admin).

[67] [2017] EWCA Civ 1643; [2018] PTSR 746.

[68] [2017] EWCA Civ 58; [2017] PTSR 949.

[69] [2016] EWHC 3028 (Admin); [2017] PTSR 408.

[70] [2016] EWHC 3354 (Admin).

new version of NPPF? Other than in the few cases where the PPG was amended on the publication of the new NPPF, the various sections of the PPG have a preliminary warning:[71]

> "Planning practice guidance will, where necessary, be updated in due course to reflect changes to the National Planning Policy Framework (the new version of which was published in July 2018). Where any hyperlinks direct users to the previous National Planning Policy Framework (2012), please disregard these. If you'd like an email alert when changes are made to planning guidance please subscribe."

3.59   Once the process of reviewing the PPG to reflect changes to the NPPF has been completed, it seems likely that the PPG is capable of being a guide to the interpretation of the NPPF as before. Until such a point, it is more risky to rely on the PPG as a guide to interpretation, particularly if the wording of the NPPF has changed between the first and second versions of it. References to the PPG elsewhere in this book should be read subject to this warning.

Other Policy Documents

3.60   The High Court considered an alleged misinterpretation of Green Belt policy in the NPPF in *R (Boot) v Elmbridge BC*.[72] In defending the challenge, the local planning authority relied upon the existence of development plan policy which had different wording to that in the NPPF. Supperstone J agreed with the claimant that the wording of this policy "has no bearing on the proper interpretation of the NPPF" (para. 36).

3.61   In *LB Bromley*, the developer sought to rely upon a Governmental consultation paper on proposed changes to the NPPF, in relation to the correct interpretation of the NPPF. The Judge rejected this argument (para. 46): the consultation paper did not constitute Government policy, and "it is plainly untenable to construe the NPPF by reference to a document which was published over three and a half years later". There is a potential question as to the extent to which this decision is consistent with the approach the courts have taken to the relevance of the PPG in interpreting the NPPF. However, it may be that the PPG is a special case: as it is published on behalf of the Secretary of State, and is (in part) to inform the application of the NPPF, there are strong grounds for it being used as a guide to the interpretation of the NPPF.

What is the Relevance of Decisions Interpreting the First NPPF?

3.62   As the NPPF has been changed by the amendments made to it in 2018, what the courts have said about the original version does not necessarily follow to the amended version. To what extent will changes to the NPPF mean that established case law is up for grabs? Are we likely to see a fresh round of extensive litigation?

3.63   The answer to these questions is, as ever, contextual. Absent the ingenuity of an

---

[71]   https://www.gov.uk/government/collections/planning-practice-guidance, accessed 30 August 2018.

[72]   [2017] EWHC 12 (Admin); [2017] 2 P&CR 6.

argument such as in *Redhill Aerodrome Ltd* (remembering that such an argument failed), it is highly likely that where paragraphs of the new NPPF replicate the previous version, then interpretations of those paragraphs should remain the same. Where the changes to the NPPF are only to clarify the wording and make no substantive change to policy, then likewise the interpretations will remain the same.

3.64 Unless there is a clear change in policy (the clarity likely to depend in part upon whether any intention to make the change was shown in the Government's Consultation, or response to Consultation), then it seems likely that the courts will not radically change the judicial interpretations of national policy. This in part reflects the frustrations which the courts have about the number of legal challenges brought on the grounds of policy interpretation, and dislike of legalistic approaches. In *Mansell v Tonbridge and Malling BC*,[73] Lindblom LJ held that the meaning of the presumption in favour of sustainable development had been settled by the Court of Appeal's decision in *East Staffordshire BC v SSCLG*,[74] and it was therefore no longer justified to quote earlier High Court decisions on the topic.

3.65 Some precise guidance given by the courts will be changed by the new NPPF. For instance, in *Calverton Parish Council v Nottingham CC*,[75] Jay J set out how he considered how to approach the release of land from the Green Belt. He described his advice as a "counsel of perfection" (para. 52). However, it would no longer be a counsel of perfection, given the requirement added in the new NPPF to consider alternatives (NPPF 137). Likewise, in *IM Properties Development Ltd v Lichfield DC*,[76] Patterson J considered that there was no requirement when considering Green Belt release that the release be a last resort. This now needs to be reconsidered in the light of NPPF 137. However, in the absence of such clear changes, it will take some considerable persuasion to seek the courts to reach a different interpretation to that of the first NPPF.

3.66 Judicial decisions are not the only public decisions which interpret the NPPF: the decisions of Planning Inspectors and the Secretary of State may make express findings regarding the interpretation of the NPPF (and, indeed, officer reports to local planning authorities). Holgate J gave a warning about relying too heavily on decisions which relate truly to the specific facts of the development proposed, in *Parkhurst Road Ltd v SSCLG*,[77] para. 27:

> "There is a risk of attaching too much importance to the decisions of individual Inspectors, particularly where their conclusions were heavily dependent upon the circumstances of the cases before them and the nature of the evidence and submissions they received, with all their attendant strengths and weaknesses specific to that appeal. Reliance upon such decisions may take up a disproportionate amount of time and may distract parties from preparing

---

[73] [2017] EWCA Civ 1314; [2018] JPL 176.

[74] [2017] EWCA Civ 893; [2018] PTSR 88.

[75] [2015] EWHC 1078 (Admin).

[76] [2014] EWHC 2440 (Admin); [2014] PTSR 1484.

[77] [2018] EWHC 991 (Admin).

suitable and sufficient information to deal with the circumstances and issues which arise in their own case."

Chapter 4

Sustainable Development

Introduction

4.01　The presumption in favour of sustainable development, found in para. 14 of the old NPPF, gave rise to difficulty and litigation. How did the presumption operate: was it necessary to find that development was sustainable before deciding that the presumption applied? Was it the function of para. 14 to determine when development was sustainable? Or did para. 14 in fact determine when the presumption in favour applied?

4.02　Case law has given clarity to a number of difficult issues. The new NPPF, in the form of NPPF 11, does not replicate the old para. 14 exactly. Given the wide scope of application of this policy, it will be interesting to see how decision-makers (and courts) approach the new wording.

4.03　Issues concerning sustainable development are not restricted to NPPF 11. There have been major changes in the approach of the NPPF to this topic.

The Structure of Chapter 2 of the NPPF

4.04　NPPF 7-10 introduce the concepts of sustainable development. NPPF 11 sets out the presumption in favour of sustainable development, which is at the heart of national planning policy. NPPF 12 explains how the presumption in favour of sustainable development fits with the statutory status of the development plan (which arises from section 38(6) PCPA and section 70(2) TCPA). NPPF 13 apportions responsibility to neighbourhood plans for shaping and directing development which is outside strategic policies in local plans or spatial development strategies. NPPF 14 modifies the presumption in favour of sustainable development where the application concerns a site which is covered by a recent neighbourhood plan.

The Approach to Sustainable Development

4.05　NPPF 7 summarises the objective (rather than provides a definition) of sustainable development as "meeting the needs of the present without compromising the ability of future generations to meet their own needs", with a footnote referring to Resolution 42/187 of the United Nations General Assembly. To an extent, this downgrades the profile of the Resolution in the NPPF from previous policy. In the original NPPF, a green box[1] considered in eight lines the Resolution.

4.06　In the amended NPPF, the approach of the Resolution to sustainable development is said to be "[a]t a very high level" (and the green box has gone). This is perhaps unsurprising. The General Assembly definition is at a high level of generality, and

---

[1]　The only other green box contained the presumption in favour of sustainable development, in the old para. 14.

has not featured heavily in judicial decisions interpreting the NPPF.[2]

4.07   The approach of the NPPF to sustainable development follows two steps:

(1)   Achieving sustainable development means pursuing three over-arching objectives set out in NPPF 8;

(2)   The objectives themselves delivered through preparation and application of plans and application of policies in the NPPF (NPPF 9).

4.08   The three over-arching dimensions in NPPF 8 (the economic role, the social role and the environmental role) replicate those from para. 7 of the old NPPF, with some slight differences. The three dimensions have been re-labelled: no longer "roles", they are now "objectives". The economic objective has a reference to improved productivity which did not feature in the previous NPPF. The social objective refers to the safe built environment, and refers to both current and future needs.

4.09   The role of the three objectives has changed as between the old and new versions of the NPPF. In the original NPPF, the three roles were criteria for decision-makers to take into account. In *Fordent Holdings Ltd v SSCLG,*[3] HHJ Pelling QC noted at para. 6 that the it is necessary to focus on all three requirements, rather than one at the expense of the other. Lewis J in *Cheshire East Council v SSCLG*[4] stated that sustainable development "has three aspects which need to be considered". An example of a correct approach by a decision-maker under the old NPPF can be seen in *Amstel Group Corporation v SSCLG.*[5] At paras 22ff, Lang J explains that the Planning Inspector gave proper consideration to the three dimensions of sustainability, and identifies the paragraphs of the decision letter in which the dimensions were considered. However, even in para. 7 of the old NPPF, the bullet points did not constitute an exhaustive description or definition of the roles which made up sustainable development: *Keith Langmead Ltd v SSCLG.*[6]

4.10   NPPF 9 tells us that the three objectives are to be delivered through the plan-making stage, and through the application of the policies in the NPPF: "they are not criteria against which every decision can or should be judged". This has the potential for making a considerable change to the nature of decision-making.

4.11   This does not mean that the objectives in NPPF 8 are irrelevant, and can be ignored. They are factors to be taken into account in plan-making. But they are also tools for the interpretation of the rest of the NPPF: this would appear to be the case from the reference to the delivery of the objectives through the application of policies in the NPPF, in NPPF 9. In *Braintree DC v SSCLG,*[7] the Court of Appeal

---

[2]   It featured in a challenge regarding good design and the nature of sustainability in *Scrivens v SSCLG* [2013] EWHC 3549 (Admin); [2014] JPL 521, Collins J [see Paragraph 4.22]. The challenge was unsuccessful. Collins J again mentioned it in *R (Morris) v Wealden DC* [2014] EWHC 4081 (Admin).

[3]   [2013] EWHC 2844 (Admin); [2013] 2 P&CR 12.

[4]   [2014] EWHC 3536 (Admin); [2015] Env LR 10.

[5]   [2018] EWHC 633 (Admin); [2018] JPL 1013.

[6]   [2017] EWHC 788 (Admin); [2017] JPL 1031.

[7]   [2018] EWCA Civ 610; [2018] 2 P&CR 9.

was considering the meaning of "new isolated homes in the countryside" in NPPF 79. Lindblom LJ set out his own view on the meaning of the phrase, before checking this interpretation against the "broader context of the policies for sustainable development in the NPPF and guidance in the PPG" (para. 33). This included the considerations now found in NPPF 8. Lindblom LJ found that his interpretation was consistent with these policies (para. 35).

4.12   NPPF 9 stresses that planning policies should take local circumstances into account, and reflect the "character, needs and opportunities" of areas. This may have the result of making less strict what might otherwise seem to be absolute requirements set out in the NPPF. For instance, NPPF 63 states local planning authorities should not seek affordable housing for residential developments on development of a scale beneath a certain threshold [see Paragraph 6.63]. This has some similarities with the national policy originally expressed in a Written Ministerial Statement to Parliament on 28 November 2014. In the course of the litigation in *R (West Berks DC and Reading BC) v SSCLG*,[8] it became clear that it would be lawful for local authorities to depart from this position, if they considered there to be local circumstances justifying their doing so. NPPF 9 provides a short-cut towards such a position: the NPPF itself says generally that local circumstances need to be taken into account.

The Presumption in Favour of Sustainable Development

4.13   The presumption in favour of sustainable development is said to be at the heart of the NPPF (NPPF 10), and this is "[s]o that sustainable development is pursued in a positive way".

4.14   Whilst the presumption is "at the heart" of the NPPF, it is no longer described as being a "golden thread running through both plan-making and decision-taking". This phrase featured in the equivalent of NPPF 11 in the old NPPF. However, it caused a degree of confusion. In *Trustees of the Barker Mill Estates v SSCLG*,[9] Holgate J rejected an argument that the "golden thread" suggested the existence of a presumption in favour of sustainable development outside NPPF 11.

4.15   NPPF 11(d)(ii) is generally known as the "tilted balance". In *Hopkins Homes*, the Supreme Court stated that the effect of the application of the tilted balance means that the decision-maker "should… be disposed to grant the application unless the presumption can be displaced". NPPF 11, combined with national policy regarding housing land supply, "give no comfort to local planning authorities who allow their plans to become stale" (*Grand Union Investments Ltd v Dacorum BC*,[10] Lindblom J, para. 78). However, Sir David Keene in *City and District Council of St Albans v Hunston Properties Ltd* held (para. 31)[11] that it was not the right approach to treat a local planning authority has having "only itself to blame" if it were behind in producing a local plan, and therefore the application of objectively assessed need

---

[8]   [2016] EWCA Civ 441; [2016] 1 WLR 3923.

[9]   [2016] EWHC 3028 (Admin); [2017] PTSR 408.

[10]   [2014] EWHC 1894 (Admin).

[11]   [2013] EWCA Civ 1610; [2014] JPL 599.

figures for housing "produced a shortfall and led to permission being granted on protected land, such as Green Belt, when that would not have happened if there had been a new-style local plan in existence". Such an approach did not reflect that planning decisions are to reflect the public interest, and are "not to be used as some form of sanction on local councils".[12]

4.16   The sole case in which the NPPF has been interpreted by the Supreme Court, *Hopkins Homes Ltd v SSCLG*,[13] Lord Carnwath JSC explained the 'tilted balance' in these words (para. 54):

> "In the absence of relevant or up-to-date development plan policies, the balance is tilted in favour of the grant of permission, except where the benefits are 'significantly and demonstrably' outweighed by the adverse effects, or where 'specific policies' indicate otherwise."

4.17   Whilst many of the cases relating to the tilted balance have concerned whether or not a local planning authority can demonstrate a five-year supply of housing land, and the consequences of a failure to be able to do so, Lord Carnwath JSC noted at para. 55 that NPPF 11 does not concern housing policy alone. In relation to the new version of the NPPF, this remains true, although it is notable that Footnote 7 (regarding out of date policies) does relate solely to housing development.

4.18   The presumption in favour of sustainable development was considered in detail by the Court of Appeal in *East Staffordshire BC v SSCLG*.[14] A developer had been refused planning permission for residential development. The developer's appeal against this refusal was successful before a Planning Inspector. The local planning authority persuaded the High Court to quash the Inspector's decision.[15] The developer appealed against this decision.

4.19   The Court of Appeal considered conflicting High Court decisions on the question of whether a presumption in favour of sustainable development existed outside of NPPF 11: *Wychavon DC v SSCLG* indicating that there was,[16] *Cheshire East BC v SSCLG*[17] and *Barker Mill* indicating that there was not. Lindblom LJ agreed with the analysis of Holgate J in *Barker Mill*. The following propositions emerge following the decision of the Court of Appeal:

- The definition of sustainable development is different from the concept of a presumption in favour of sustainable development.

- The presumption in favour of sustainable development is conclusively found

---

[12]   The decision of Holgate J in *R (West Berkshire DC and Reading BC) v SSCLG* [2015] EWHC 2222 (Admin); [2016] PTSR 215, who referred at paras 18-19 to the NPPF containing policy "sanctions", seems to run counter to this. Holgate J's decision was reversed by the Court of Appeal: [2016] EWCA Civ 441; [2016] 1 WLR 3923.

[13]   [2017] UKSC 37; [2017] 1 WLR 1865.

[14]   [2017] EWCA Civ 893; [2018] PTSR 88.

[15]   The decision of Green J in [2016] EWHC 2973 (Admin); [2017] PTSR 386.

[16]   [2016] EWHC 592 (Admin); [2016] PTSR 675.

[17]   [2016] EWHC 571 (Admin); [2016] PTSR 1052.

in NPPF 11. There is no other presumption in the NPPF, whether express or implied.

- NPPF 11 not only explains the effect of the presumption in favour of sustainable development, but the circumstances in which it applies, in terms of plan-making and decision-taking.

- Even if the presumption applies, this does not displace the requirement to apply section 38(6) PCPA.

- The presumption in favour of sustainable development is a presumption of policy only. It is not a statutory presumption.

- Merely because proposed development does not benefit from the presumption in favour of sustainable development does not mean that permission should necessarily be refused.

- Conversely, merely because a proposal has the benefit of the 'tilted balance' does not mean that it will necessarily be granted planning permission.

- The presumption in favour of sustainable development is not a substitute for the exercise of planning judgment, which remains a matter for the decision-maker (not the court).

4.20   The Inspector, having been influenced by the decision in *Wychavon DC*, applied a presumption in favour of sustainable development outside of NPPF 11. The Inspector had therefore erred in law, and the decision was quashed. The Court of Appeal did not agree that the result would have been the same were it not for the Inspector's error.

4.21   At least in terms of the wording in the original NPPF, the Court of Appeal considered the meaning of the presumption to be settled. In *Mansell v Tonbridge and Malling BC*,[18] Lindblom LJ stated at para. 40:

> "In [earlier] cases, judges in the Planning Court have offered various interpretations of NPPF policy for the "presumption in favour of sustainable development", and have explained how, in their view, the presumption should work. There is no need for that to continue. After the decision of the Court of Appeal in *Barwood v East Staffordshire BC*, it is no longer necessary, or appropriate, to cite to this court or to judges in the Planning Court any of the first instance judgments in which the meaning of the presumption has been considered."

4.22   In *Scrivens v SSCLG*,[19] the claimant had sought to introduce a comprehensive view of sustainable development. He said that the NPPF, and Directive 2010/31/EU, contained five elements, to which he referred as "the Pentalogy". These requirements included that "sustainable" means that "nature's resources must not be used faster than they can be replenished naturally". By contrast, Collins J considered

---

[18]   [2017] EWCA Civ 1314; [2018] JPL 176.
[19]   [2013] EWHC 3549 (Admin); [2014] JPL 521.

that what is sustainable in particular circumstances will depend on a number of factors. Sustainability is not limited to the Pentalogy, given that the former includes the economic impact of development, and whether development is unsightly. The claimant argued that compliance with the Pentalogy was conclusive: if development complied with the Pentalogy, then permission should be granted. This argument was rejected. It was open to decision-makers to take into account other matters. The better view, on the basis of NPPF 11 and the decisions of the Court of Appeal in *East Staffordshire BC* and the Supreme Court in *Hopkins Homes*, is that decision-makers should not focus on deciding in the abstract whether the proposed development would constitute sustainable development; the focus is upon the application of the presumption in favour of sustainable development.

4.23   There is a single presumption in favour of sustainable development, which has consequences for both plan-making and decision-taking. Plans must positively seek opportunities to meet development needs. They must be sufficiently flexible to adapt to even rapid change (NPPF 11(a)). The starting point for strategic policies is that they should, as a minimum, meet objectively assessed needs for housing and other uses, not only for their own area but those which cannot be met in neighbouring areas (NPPF 11(b)). This starting point is departed from in either of two circumstances:

(1)   The application of particular policies in Footnote 6 provides a "strong reason for restricting the overall scale, type or distribution of development in the plan area" (NPPF 11(b)(i)) or

(2)   The adverse impacts of staying with the starting point would "significantly and demonstrably outweigh the benefits, when assessed against the policies in [the NPPF] taken as a whole" (NPPF 11(b)(ii)).

4.24   In terms of decision-making, the presumption in favour of sustainable development means granting planning permission without delay for proposals which comply with the development plan (NPPF 11(c)). A change from the previous version of the NPPF is that, to benefit from the presumption, the development plan must be up-to-date.[20] NPPF 11(d) may cause the most controversy:

"where there are no relevant development plan policies, or the policies which are most important for determining the application are out-of-date, granting permission unless:

(i)   the application of policies in [the NPPF] that protect areas or assets of particular importance provides a clear reason for refusing the development proposed; or

(ii)   any adverse impacts of doing so would significantly and demonstrably outweigh the benefits, when assessed against the policies in this Framework taken as a whole."

4.25   It has been said that NPPF 11(d) applies in circumstances where there is a policy

---

[20]   With thanks to Kate Olley for pointing this out.

lacuna: *R (Midcounties Co-operative Ltd) v Forest of Dean DC*,[21] para. 12.

4.26   It is well established that, even if policies are found to be out-of-date, and the tilted balance applies, the weight to be given to those policies remains a matter for the decision-maker. This is clear from the decision of Lord Carnwath JSC in *Hopkins Homes Ltd*, and has recently been restated by the Court of Appeal in *Hallam Land Management Ltd v SSCLG*.[22] In *Hallam Land*, the Court of Appeal held that it was not sufficient for a Planning Inspector to merely find that a local planning authority lacks a five-year supply of housing land; an Inspector must identify the broad extent of the shortfall. Whilst the tilted balance acts in favour of the grant of permission, it still requires the various matters on either side of the balance to be identified. As Lindblom LJ held at para. 47:

> "The policy in [NPPF 11] requires the appropriate balance to be struck and a balance can only be struck if the considerations on either side of it are given due weight. But in a case where the local planning authority is unable to demonstrate five years' supply of housing land, the policy leaves to the decision-maker's planning judgment the weight he gives to relevant restrictive policies. Logically, however, one would expect the weight given to such policies to be less if the shortfall in the housing land supply is large, and more if it is small. Other considerations will be relevant too: the nature of the restrictive policies themselves, the interest they are intended to protect whether they find support in policies of the NPPF, the implications of their being breached, and so forth."

4.27   Nevertheless, it is not necessary for the Inspector to assess the <u>exact</u> extent of the housing land shortfall (para. 48).

4.28   In an early decision on the NPPF, *Langton Homes Ltd v SSCLG*,[23] Foskett J held that a demonstrable shortfall in five-year supply "might well demand a more forceful application of the presumption", but a mere alleged shortfall "will not necessarily neutralise the application of NPPF 11, but "will demand less of an emphasis upon it depending on other material considerations". In *Hopkins Homes*, the Supreme Court identifies the main significance of a housing shortfall as to trigger the effect of the tilted balance in NPPF 11. It seems likely that, after the decision of the Supreme Court, a principle that the tilted balance can be applied to a greater or lesser extent depending on how clear it is that there is a housing shortfall is no longer good law. Given *Hallam Land* suggests that a Planning Inspector should give at least a broad extent of housing land supply shortfall, it seems unlikely that it would be acceptable for the Inspector to decline to give a definitive answer to whether there is such a shortfall at all (or to rely upon an alleged, but not demonstrated, shortfall). The existence of a shortfall is a binary question (there is either a shortfall or there is not). This is a different kind of question to considering the extent of a shortfall (which can be greater or lesser). This approach would be consistent with the finding of

---

[21] [2014] EWHC 3059 (Admin); [2015] JPL 288, decision of Hickinbottom J.

[22] [2018] EWCA Civ 1808.

[23] [2014] EWHC 487 (Admin).

Lindblom J in *Phides Estates (Overseas) Limited v SSCLG*,[24] in finding (at para. 40) that "the decision-maker must establish… whether there is a shortfall".

4.29   Lord Carnwath JSC contrasted his approach to weight with an earlier understanding of the NPPF, whereby it was assumed that, if a policy were deemed to be out-of-date by virtue of the local planning authority lacking a five-year supply of housing, then the policy would in practice be given minimal weight; Lord Carnwath referred to *Cotswold DC v SSCLG*.[25] Similarly, in *Tewkesbury BC v SSCLG*,[26] Males J had stated that a plan "which is based on outdated information, or which has expired without being replaced, is likely to command relatively little weight" (para. 13). Whilst this is expressed in terms of likelihood, decisions after *Hopkins Homes* would generally recognise that weight is a matter for the decision-maker alone.

4.30   In *Crane v SSCLG*,[27] Lindblom J referred to findings that "out of date policies… are likely to command little weight" (para. 58). However, at para. 74 he went on to state:

> "[NPPF 11] does not say that where "relevant policies" in the development plan are out of date, the plan must therefore be ignored. It does not prevent a decision-maker from giving as much weight as he judges to be right to a proposal's conflict with the strategy in the plan, or, in the case of a neighbourhood plan, the "vision"…."

4.31   The reluctance on the part of the courts to lay down any guidance regarding weight to be given to decisions may be reflected in the decision of the Court of Appeal in *East Staffordshire DC*. At first instance,[28] Green J had suggested that NPPF 11 provides a "strong gravitational pull", and that it "should yield only as an exception to the norm where there exists objective and substantial reasons which can be readily demonstrated to a high degree of probative value and which takes into account the particular reasons why a development has been found to collide with the Local Plan" (para. 22). Green J did not express a concluded view as to "exactly how exceptional "exceptional" actually is", but he viewed this as capable of being explored in an appropriate case. The Court of Appeal found it unnecessary to give any further guidance on this question, it not being necessary to the determination of the appeal, but stressed that weight is a matter for the decision-maker. At para. 50, Lindblom LJ held:

> "I would, however, stress the need for the court to adopt, if it can, a simple approach in cases such as this. Excessive legalism has no place in the planning system, or in proceedings before the Planning Court, or in subsequent appeals to this court. The court should always resist over complication of concepts that are basically simple. Planning decision-making is far from being a mechanical, or quasi-mathematical activity. It is essentially a flexible

---

[24]   [2015] EWHC 827 (Admin).

[25]   [2013] EWHC 3719 (Admin).

[26]   [2013] EWHC 296 (Admin); [2013] LGR 399.

[27]   [2015] EWHC 425 (Admin).

[28]   [2016] EWHC 2973 (Admin); [2017] PTSR 386.

process, not rigid or formulaic. It involves, largely, an exercise of planning judgment, in which the decision-maker must understand relevant national and local policy correctly and apply it lawfully to the particular facts and circumstances of the case in hand, in accordance with the requirements of the statutory scheme. The duties imposed by section 70(2) [TCPA] and section 38(6) [PCPA] leave with the decision-maker a wide discretion. The making of a planning decision is, therefore, quite different from the adjudication by a court on an issue of law…"

4.32   Lord Carnwath JSC said of the predecessor to NPPF 11 at para. 55 of *Hopkins Homes*:

"It has to be borne in mind… that [NPPF 11] is not concerned solely with housing policy. It needs to work for other forms of development covered by the development plan, for example employment or transport. Thus, for example, there may be a relevant policy for the supply of employment land, but it may become out-of-date, perhaps because of the arrival of a major new source of employment in the area. Whether that is so, and with what consequence, is a matter of planning judgment… This may in turn have an effect on other related policies, for example for transport. The pressure for new land may mean in turn that other competing policies will need to be given less weight in accordance with the tilted balance. But again that is a matter of pure planning judgment, not dependent on issues of legal interpretation."

4.33   There are two footnotes to NPPF 11(d). Footnote 7 qualifies policies which are out-of-date, and states:

"This includes, for applications involving the provision of housing, situations where the local planning authority cannot demonstrate a five-year supply of deliverable housing sites (with the appropriate buffer, as set out in paragraph 73); or where the Housing Delivery Test indicates that the delivery of housing was substantially below (less than 75% of) the housing requirement over the previous three years. Transitional arrangements for the Housing Delivery Test are set out in Annex 1."

4.34   This will be considered in Chapter 6 regarding residential development.

4.35   In the previous version of the NPPF, it was made clear by a footnote that the policy regarding decision-taking was subject to material considerations indicating otherwise. This is not expressed within NPPF 11 itself, but this omission is unlikely to make a difference to decision-making: as a matter of law, it would be necessary for decision-makers to take into account material considerations other than the NPPF in any event.

4.36   An important change between the original and the revised versions of the NPPF is the amendment of NPPF 11(d) to refer to situations "where there are no relevant development plan policies". This replaces the reference in the original NPPF to policies which were "absent" or "silent". The distinction between these two meanings was considered by Lindblom J in *Bloor Homes East Midlands Ltd v SSCLG*.[29] Lindblom J expressly found the concepts to be distinct (para. 45). Fortunately, this fine distinction is one which no longer exists in national policy. In *Bloor Homes*, Lindblom J held that whether policies were absent was a question of fact; whether they were silent was a question of fact and/or construction of the relevant document, or both. Whether the courts take a similar approach to the question of whether there are any relevant development plan policies remains to be seen. Silence, Lindblom J held, was a matter which it may be for the court to decide (para. 49). It may be the most consistent approach with previous case law to say that the existence of relevant development plan policies is a question of fact, but it is possible that the courts will decide that whether a policy is relevant is a matter of law.[30]

4.37   In *Trustees of the Barker Mill Estates v SSCLG*,[31] Holgate J held that the previous version of the NPPF indicated that, in order not to be silent, the development plan would need to have a policy which was "sufficient to enable the acceptability of the proposal to be judged in principle". It may be that the sufficiency limb of the test does not appear in the new NPPF.

4.38   As was held in *R (Wynn-Williams) v SSCLG*,[32] references to out-of-date policy in the NPPF must be considered in the light of NPPF 213, which includes:

> "…existing policies should not be considered out-of-date simply because they were adopted or made prior to the publication of this Framework. Due weight should be given to them, according to their degree of consistency with this Framework (the closer the policies in the plan to the policies in the Framework, the greater the weight that may be given)."

4.39   It is important that a decision-maker actually follows this approach, rather than making a different assessment of whether a policy is out-of-date. In *Daventry DC v SSCLG*,[33] Lang J considered that the ambit of NPPF 213 is broad. It requires assessment of the extent to which policies are consistent with all NPPF policies. Lang J found that the approach in NPPF 213 is not mechanistic, but rather evaluative ("nuanced"). The Court of Appeal upheld Lang J's decision.[34]

4.40   The application in *Daventry DC* was considered against a development plan, which included a Local Plan adopted in 1997 (some policies having been saved in September 2007). The evidence base for the policies was long out of date. Due to the fact that the Council could demonstrate a five-year housing land supply, the policies for the supply of land were not automatically deemed to be out of date. Nevertheless, the Inspector gave them reduced weight due to their age, and their lack of consistency

---

[29]   [2014] EWHC 754 (Admin); [2017] PTSR 1283.

[30]   In line with the identification of material planning considerations being a matter of law: *Newbury District Council v Secretary of State for the Environment* [1981] AC 578.

[31]   [2016] EWHC 3028 (Admin); [2017] PTSR 408.

[32]   [2014] EWHC 3374 (Admin).

[33]   [2015] EWHC 3459 (Admin); [2016] JPL 578.

[34]   [2016] EWCA Civ 1146; [2017] JPL 402. Permission to appeal to the Supreme Court was refused.

with the aim in the NPPF of boosting significantly the supply of housing.

4.41 Lang J, and the Court of Appeal, found that the Inspector had failed to apply the approach in NPPF 213. Indeed, apart from one erroneous reference (where he meant in fact to refer to another paragraph), there was no reference to NPPF 213 at all, even though that was the paragraph which set out the correct approach for the Inspector to take when determining whether a policy was out of date.

4.42 At para. 40, the Court of Appeal noted that mere age alone does not cause a policy to cease to be part of a development plan, and it continues to be entitled to priority. Weight to be given to different policies may vary with changing circumstances over time. The Court of Appeal went so far as to say, when it came to assessing consistency with the NPPF, the chronological age alone of a policy is "irrelevant for the purposes of assessing its consistency with policies in the NPPF". Even for an old development plan, there is considerable public interest in the maintenance of a plan-led system. Where policies are not deemed to be out of date, due to a lack of housing land supply, this does not mean that the policies cannot be out of date due to the application of NPPF 213.

4.43 Following the decision of the Supreme Court in *Hopkins Homes*, it seems clear that policies which are found in a development plan the period of which has expired, will *ipso facto* be out of date. In the *Willaston* appeal, the development plan extended to 2011. Lord Carnwath found that, for this reason, the development plan was out of date (para. 63).

4.44 Where a local planning authority lacks the required supply of housing land, the effect of the decision in *Hopkins Homes* is that the tilted balance will apply. NPPF 11(d) now states that the key question is whether the "policies which are most important for determining the application are out of date". One would assume that the same approach would apply to the new NPPF as under *Hopkins Homes*. According to the decision of the Supreme Court, the important matter is not so much whether particular policies are out of date, but whether the tilted balance applies.

4.45 Footnote 6 applies to NPPF 11(b)(i), and provides:

> "The policies referred to are those in this Framework (rather than those in development plans) relating to: habitats sites, (and those sites listed in paragraph 176) and/or designated as Sites of Special Scientific Interest; land designated as Green Belt, Local Green Space, an Area of Outstanding Natural Beauty, a National Park (or within the Broads Authority) or defined as Heritage Coast; irreplaceable habitats; designated heritage assets (and other heritage assets of archaeological interest referred to in footnote 63); and areas at risk of flooding or coastal change."

4.46 Whilst Footnote 6 is the broad equivalent of Footnote 9 to the old NPPF, there are a number of key differences. Most significantly, Footnote 6 is an exclusive list. Whilst Footnote 9 used to be a list of examples of specific policies which indicate that development should be restricted, Footnote 7 is a complete list.

4.47 The new wording of Footnote 6 provides a greater level of certainty, although not complete certainty. There will still be potential argument about what constitutes "irreplaceable habitats" (which are different to "habitats sites". Additionally, the cross-reference to Footnote 63 may give local planning authorities a certain level of judgment. Footnote 63 states: "Non-designated heritage assets of archaeological interest, which are demonstrably of equivalent significance to scheduled monuments, should be considered subject to the policies for designated heritage assets". It may be that developers and local planning authorities will have a level of debate as to whether a particular non-designated heritage asset is of "equivalent significance" to a scheduled monument.

4.48   The new wording of NPPF 11 states that the policies in Footnote 7 apply in the decision-taking context only where the application of the policies provides a clear reason for refusing development. Likewise, the policies in Footnote 7 mean that assessed needs need not be met only where the application of the policies provides a strong reason for restricting the overall scale, type of distribution of development in the plan area.

4.49   This avoids the debate which arose in the old NPPF,[35] as to how to approach the presumption in favour of sustainable development where the development was within the scope of, but satisfied, restrictive policies (i.e., where development affected designated heritage assets, but satisfied the tests in policy and law: could the presumption in favour of sustainable development still apply?).

4.50   The difference in wording between a "clear reason" and a "strong reason" can be assumed to be intentional. A reason which is strong will inevitably be clear, but a reason which is clear will not necessarily be strong. Therefore, there is an argument that it will be easier for a local planning authority to rely upon the Footnote 7 policies at the decision-taking stage than it will be at the plan-making stage.

4.51   The NPPF states that a planning application which conflicts with an up-to-date development plan should normally be refused permission (NPPF 12). However, in line with the statutory requirements in section 38(6) PCPA, NPPF 12 goes on to say that it is open to local planning authorities to take decisions which depart from the development plan, but only if material considerations indicate that the plan should not be followed.

4.52   The NPPF no longer includes the twelve core planning principles (formerly in para. 17 of the old NPPF). Some of the principles can now be found in Chapter 11, Making Effective Use of Land. It was not obvious how the core planning principles fitted into the framework of plan-making and decision-taking, and their removal is likely to constitute an improvement to the drafting of the NPPF. On one occasion, the Court of Appeal had to consider the consistency of the core planning principles

---

[35] The Court of Appeal declined to resolve this question, considering it unnecessary to do so, in *Watermead Parish Council v Aylesbury Vale DC* [2017] EWCA Civ 152; [2018] PTSR 43, para. 45. The Court of Appeal accepted the Secretary of State's position, that where the policy was satisfied, then the presumption in favour of sustainable development can still apply, in *East Staffordshire*, at para. 22(2). This understanding is now made explicit in the amended NPPF.

with the substantive principles in the NPPF (*Dartford BC v SSCLG*).[36]

Habitats Assessment

4.53　NPPF 177 excludes the presumption in favour of sustainable development in planning or determining an application for development which requires appropriate assessment because of its potential impact upon a habitats site. This reflected previous policy in the NPPF. Notwithstanding the fact that policy has remained the same, the consequence of this policy has recently dramatically changed as a result of the decision of the Court of Justice of the European Union ("CJEU") in Case C-323/17 *People Over Wind v Coillte Teoranta*.[37]

4.54　The context of *People Over Wind* were works required to lay a cable connecting a wind farm to the electricity grid. The Irish legal regime provided for such connections to be permitted without the need for a separate planning application, unless an appropriate assessment was required under Article 6(3) of the Habitats Directive 92/43/EEC.

4.55　In English law, it has been established since the decision of Sullivan J in *R (Hart DC) v SSCLG*[38] that, when screening for likely significant effects on the environment (a preliminary stage to carrying out an appropriate assessment), it is acceptable to take into account aspects of the development which seek to mitigate the effect of the development on the environment. When considering whether there would be a likely significant effect on the environment, the whole of the proposed development (including measures to protect the environment) should be considered. It is not necessary to carve up the development and consider only the harmful aspects, without also considering the protective aspects, at the screening stage. If, taking into account the mitigation, there would be no significant effects, then Sullivan J held that there was no need for a decision-maker to carry out an appropriate assessment. Applying this approach to the policy in NPPF 177, the presumption in favour of sustainable development could also apply.

4.56　In a brief judgment, in which the CJEU proceeded without the benefit of an Opinion from the Advocate General, the CJEU rejected such an approach. It held that mitigation (or 'protective') measures could be taken into account only at the stage of an appropriate assessment. They were not matters which could be considered by a decision-maker when taking the earlier step of considering whether the development may have likely significant effects on the protected site. This appears to have been because the CJEU feared that taking into account mitigation at the earlier stage would have reduced the protection given to protected habitats sites, as the approach would avoid the full rigour of appropriate assessment.

4.57　The CJEU's decision in *People Over Wind* is poorly reasoned and reaches an impractical result. It was however repeatedly cited by the CJEU in its later decision Case C-164/17 *Grace and Sweetman v An Bord Pleanála*.

---

[36]　[2017] EWCA Civ 141; [2017] PTSR 737.
[37]　[2018] PTSR 1668.
[38]　[2008] EWHC 1204 (Admin); [2008] 2 P&CR 16.

4.58   In terms of the application of the effect of *People Over Wind* on the application of NPPF 177, the most obvious result is that mitigation will have to be ignored when considering likely significant effects. Therefore, the presumption in favour of sustainable development will not apply in circumstances even where, if the mitigation was taken into account, likely significant effects could in fact be ruled out.

4.59   It may be that the domestic courts of England and Wales seek to restrict the application of *People Over Wind*. They may seek to permit the application of the presumption in favour of sustainable development where an appropriate assessment would not have been required under the approach in *Hart DC*. The scope for doing so since *People Over Wind* is limited. One way, however, that the courts may seek to do so is by focusing on the phrase "potential impact" in NPPF 177. If a developer can satisfy the decision-maker (and, subsequently, a court) that, due to proposed mitigation measures, there is in fact no potential impact upon a habitats site, then there is an argument that this would take the proposal outside the scope of NPPF 177.

4.60   This is not a natural meaning of NPPF 177. Furthermore, the revised NPPF was published since the decision of the CJEU in *People Over Wind*. The drafters of the NPPF can be assumed to have been aware of it. It may be said that, if it was intended to exclude the reasoning of *People Over Wind* from the policy expressed in NPPF 177, then this would have been clearly done on the face of the paragraph.

Chapter 5

Principles of Plan-making and Decision-taking

Introduction

5.01　In the original NPPF, the principles of plan-making and decision-taking were relegated behind sections relating to policy advice concerning specific sectors (such as housing) and particular sensitivities (such as the Green Belt). Plan-making and decision-taking did not fall within the broad ambit of achieving sustainable development, instead being categories of their own.

5.02　The structure of the new NPPF is clearly different. Plan-making falls within Chapter 3; Decision-making in Chapter 4. These come immediately after the Introduction (Chapter 1), and Achieving Sustainable Development (Chapter 2). Government guidance on making plans and how individual decisions should be made is at the forefront of what the NPPF is seeking to achieve. Given the significance of viability to residential development, viability is dealt with in that chapter [see Chapter 6].

5.03　This chapter will not seek to express every aspect of Government policy in relation to these issues, but to extract matters of particular significance. There have been recent amendments to the PPG, with the addition of a new section on plan-making, changes to the section on local plans, and updates to the guidance on neighbourhood planning.

Plan-making

General Comments and Objectives

5.04　The NPPF sets out some general comments and objectives for plans at NPPF 15-16. These include the desire that the "planning system should be genuinely plan-led". It is a notable feature of the NPPF that the NPPF is not itself a plan, but merely a material consideration which may override the requirements of the development plan, according to the judgment of the decision-maker.[1] The NPPF notes the statutory priority of the development plan, and seeks that development control be plan-led. However, it provides policies which may be contrary to existing development plans (including, for instance, in relation to the provision of affordable housing). How such matters are to be balanced in the context of individual decisions is a matter for the decision-maker, but it does introduce an element of unpredictability in the process. This is exacerbated by the fact that an applicant (and indeed an objector to an application) may have to consider not only the approach of the local planning authority, but also a Planning Inspector, or possibly the Secretary of State, if the matter proceeds to an appeal.

5.05　Notwithstanding the desire for proposals to be genuinely plan-led, the NPPF seeks

---

[1]　This is the effect of section 38(6) PCPA [see Chapter 2: The Nature and Status of National Planning Policy].

that plans should be "succinct".[2] No definition is provided for succinctness; presumably no more could be said than that a plan should be no longer than it needs to be. Of particular relevance in this regard is NPPF 16(f), which states that plans should "[avoid] unnecessary duplication of policies that apply to a particular area (including policies in this Framework, where relevant)". The indication that local policies should not seek to duplicate the NPPF raises two questions:

- Are local planning authorities comfortable with relying on the existence of national planning policy in place of local planning policy, in circumstances where they have no control over the terms of such policy and it can be changed by the Government, including where there is a change in political control of the Government?

- Given that the legal status of the NPPF is merely as a material consideration, lacking the primacy of the statutory development plan, is it adequate to say that potential important policy controls can be left to the NPPF, rather than included within the development plan?

5.06 The answer may be that NPPF 16(f) does not state that all duplication of policy should be avoided; it instead refers to "unnecessary duplication". This possibly contemplates that there may be situations in which there is legitimate duplication of policies.

5.07 Perhaps bearing in mind the number of legal challenges which can arise from unclearly worded policies, NPPF 16(e) indicates that policies should be "clearly written and unambiguous". However, experience tends to suggest that it is not possible to contemplate every possible scenario against which a policy may be tested, and therefore ambiguity may potentially arise, even with careful drafting. Furthermore, the aim that policies be unambiguous may be in tension with guidance that the policies should be succinct. In *Redhill Aerodrome Ltd v SSCLG*,[3] Sullivan LJ considered the aim of the original NPPF to reduce the length of national planning policy, and held at para. 22, "[v]iews may differ as to whether simplicity and clarity have always been achieved, but the policies are certainly shorter". Sir David Keene considered the relationship between simplicity and clarity in *St Albans v Hunston Properties Ltd*,[4] holding at para. 4, "[u]nhappily, as this case demonstrates, the process of simplification has in certain instances led to a diminution in clarity".[5]

---

[2] Draft Planning Practice Guidance, Ministry of Housing, Communities and Local Government, March 2018, quoted at p.44 the Local Plan Expert Group, in stating that "communities are turned off by the length, slow pace and obscure nature of many local plans". Local Plan Expert Group, Report to the Communities Secretary and to the Minister of Housing and Planning, March 2016, S3. The PPG, Section on Plan-making, para. 030 states that local planning authorities "are expected to be mindful of the need to produce concise, visual evidence, written in plain English to help ensure that it is easily accessible to local communities, to avoid them becoming disengaged with the process".

[3] [2014] EWCA Civ 1386; [2015] PTSR 274.

[4] [2013] EWCA Civ 1610; [2014] JPL 599.

[5] Quoted in *Planning Policy* - Richard Harwood QC and Victoria Hutton, Bloomsbury Professional Ltd 2017, para. 4.8.

5.08   Plan-makers should not forget the requirement of NPPF 11(a), which states that the presumption in favour of sustainable development means, in the context of plan-making, that "plans should positively seek opportunities to meet the development needs of their area, and be sufficiently flexible to adapt to rapid change". Again, this requirement for flexibility in new plans may reduce the certainty which the plan-led system can provide.

5.09   The presumption in favour of sustainable development states at NPPF 11(b) that the starting point is that strategic policies in plans should, "as a minimum, provide for objectively assessed needs for housing and other uses". There are, however, limits to this principle. If specific policies, listed in Footnote 6, provide a strong reason for restricting the overall scale, type or distribution of development, or the adverse impacts of meeting objectively assessed needs in full would significantly and demonstrably outweigh the benefits when assessed against the policies in the NPPF taken as a whole, then the NPPF does not require that needs are met in full.[6]

The Framework of Plans: Strategic and Non-strategic Policies

5.10   Noting the legal requirements in section 19 PCPA, NPPF 17 notes that the development plan must include strategic policies which address a local planning authority's priorities for the development and use of land in its area. The strategic policies can be incorporated in a joint plan by authorities working together, or by a local planning authority working individually. A plan containing strategic policies can also include non-strategic policies. In an area with an elected Mayor or combined authority where plan-making powers have been conferred, a spatial development strategy may contain the strategic policies.

5.11   Strategic policies are defined in the Glossary as:

>   "Policies and site allocations which address strategic priorities in line with the requirements of Section 19(1B-E) [PCPA]."

5.12   Non-strategic policies are defined in the Glossary as:

>   "Policies contained in a neighbourhood plan, or those policies in a local plan that are not strategic policies."

5.13   Policies which concern non-strategic matters can be included in a local plan which contains both strategic and non-strategic policies, and/or in local or neighbourhood plans containing just non-strategic policies (NPPF 18).

5.14   The NPPF indicates that plans should make clear which are its strategic policies (NPPF 21). If a plan contains both strategic and non-strategic policies, then they should be "clearly distinguished" (Footnote 13).

Strategic Policies

5.15   Strategic policies are those which meet the long-term strategic priorities of the area

---

[6]   The presumption in favour of sustainable development is dealt with in more detail below [see Chapter 4: Sustainable Development].

(NPPF 21). They should be long-sighted, planning for at least a 15-year period, except in relation to town centre development (NPPF 22). An example given in the NPPF of a matter properly for consideration in strategic policies is major improvement in infrastructure (NPPF 22). However, if detailed matters can be considered more suitably in neighbourhood plans or non-strategic policies, then these should not form part of strategic policies (NPPF 21). Strategic policies should be the "starting point" for non-strategic policies (NPPF 21).

5.16   The definition of strategic policies in the abstract risks being somewhat circular (reducing to a proposition that strategic policies are policies which deal with strategic matters). There will inevitably be a matter of judgment as to whether a particular matter concerns strategic or non-strategic issues.

5.17   The strategic policies should provide a clear strategy for addressing objectively assessed needs over the plan period, "in line with the presumption in favour of sustainable development" (NPPF 23). This introduces the concept that objectively assessed needs do not need to be met where policies protecting areas or assets of particular importance provide a "strong reason for restricting the overall scale, type or distribution of development in the plan area". As stated above, the NPPF 11(b)(i) refers to Footnote 6 which sets out particular areas or assets which require protection. Additionally, NPPF 11(b)(ii) provides that needs do not need to be met where "the adverse impacts of doing so would significantly and demonstrably outweigh the benefits, when assessed against the policies in [the NPPF] taken as a whole".

5.18   NPPF 20 sets out various matters for which strategic policies should make sufficient provision. These include housing, employment, retail, but also infrastructure and community facilities. Provision must be made for conservation of the natural, built and historic environment. This indicates that the provision which must be made by strategic policies is not simply quantitative, but also qualitative (potentially including providing enough policy support and protection for areas with designations). The PPG emphasises that "the plan should...be realistic about what can be achieved and when".[7]

5.19   Section 33A PCPA introduces a duty upon local planning authorities and county councils to cooperate in the preparation of development plan documents, insofar as they relate to a strategic matter.[8] A "strategic matter" is defined by section 33A(4) as:

(a)   sustainable development or use of land that has or would have a significant impact on at least two planning areas, including (in particular) sustainable development or use of land for or in connection with infrastructure that is strategic and has or would have a significant impact on at least two planning areas, and

(b)   sustainable development or use of land in a two-tier area if the development or use -

---

7   PPG, Section on Plan-making, para. 055.

8   A section of the PPG is dedicated to the duty to cooperate.

(i)   is a county matter, or

(ii)   has or would have a significant impact on a county matter.

5.20   It is worth noting that the NPPF does not incorporate this legislative definition of strategic matters into the definition of strategic policies or strategic priorities. The emphasis in section 33A is on matters which require cooperation between authorities.

5.21   Strategic cooperation itself is dealt with in NPPF 24-27. This emphasises what may be unpopular for many authorities; the requirement for plan-making authorities to determine "whether development needs that cannot be met wholly within a particular plan area could be met elsewhere" (NPPF 26). This is given emphasis by NPPF 26 stating that joint working should "[i]n particular" identify meeting needs outside an authority's area, as well as determine the location for new infrastructure.

5.22   NPPF 27 restates the requirement for one or more statements of common ground between strategic policy-making authorities, "documenting the cross-boundary matters being addressed and progress in cooperating to address these". Such statements of common ground should be made publicly available, in the interests of transparency.

Non-Strategic Policies

5.23   The content of non-strategic policies appears to be more set by their scale than their type. NPPF 28 makes clear that non-strategic policies may still allocate sites for development, provide infrastructure and community facilities, establish design principles, conserve and enhance the natural and historic environment, and set out development management policies. However, in these circumstances, these are matters to be dealt with at the local level.

5.24   Neighbourhood plans are able to allocate land for development, but they should not promote less development than as set out in the strategic policies for the area, or undermine the strategic policies (NPPF 29). However, a more recent neighbourhood plan can override previous non-strategic policies in a local plan which cover the neighbourhood area (NPPF 30). The neighbourhood policies will carry precedence until superseded by later strategic or non-strategic policies.

Preparing and Reviewing Plans

5.25   The NPPF places a considerable burden on plan-making authorities. All policies should be underpinned by "relevant and up-to-date evidence".[9] NPPF 31 says that the evidence should be "focused tightly on supporting and justifying the policies concerned". Presumably this means that the evidence should focus on the issues in question, rather than that evidence should be amassed which supports what the Council wishes to do, and ignoring evidence which points the other way. NPPF 32 refers to the requirement of sustainability appraisal of local plans and spatial development strategies.

5.26   NPPF policy concerns not only the initial drafting but also the review of plans.

---

[9] See PPG, Section on Plan-making, paras 029ff.

Footnote 18 refers to Regulation 10A(1) of the Town and Country Planning (Local Planning) (England) Regulations 2012, which states:

> "A local planning authority must review a local development document within the following time periods -
>
> (a)   in respect of a local plan, the review must be completed every five years, starting from the date of adoption of the local plan, in accordance with [section 23 PCPA];
>
> (b)   ..."

5.27   This is likely to be challenging for local planning authorities. According to NPPF 32, reviews should take into account "changing circumstances affecting the area, or any relevant changes in national policy". The changing local circumstances may include the housing need figure. If a housing need figure is not reviewed after five years and found to not require updating, then NPPF 73 provides that housing land supply will not be assessed against the adopted requirement figure, but rather against the objectively assessed need figure. NPPF 33 contemplates that the housing need figure may require review even earlier than every five years, if "local housing need is expected to change significantly in the near future". The PPG gives an example of a situation where early review may be required, being "where new cross-boundary matters arise".[10]

5.28   The effectiveness of the review requirement will depend in large part upon how intensive reviews are: local planning authorities must not merely carry out a rubber-stamping exercise. Even if national planning policy has remained constant, a local planning authority will need to assess the circumstances in its area, to see whether there has been a material change. The recently-amended PPG provides some guidance in relation to the review of plans.[11] Particular emphasis is placed upon "necessary changes" to policies relating to strategic priorities.[12] A list of information which may indicate whether policies should be updated includes "changes to local circumstances; such as a change in Local Housing Need", and the local planning authority's performance as against the Housing Delivery Test.[13]

Development Contributions

5.29   A plan should set out the contributions to be expected from development: NPPF 34. The most controversial of such policies are likely to be those requiring the provision of affordable housing. Specific provision is made for affordable housing policies at NPPF 62-64. NPPF 34 requires that policies setting out contributions from development (generally, not just for affordable housing) should not "undermine the deliverability of the plan". Presumably the reference to the deliverability of the plan refers to the deliverability of the development proposed by the plan.

---

[10] PPG, Section on Plan-making, para. 043.

[11] PPG, Section on Plan-making, paras 042ff.

[12] PPG, Section on Plan-making, para. 042.

[13] PPG, Section on Plan-making, para. 046.

Examining Plans

5.30   The definition of soundness of local plans and spatial development strategies is set out in NPPF 35. This has been changed from the first version of the NPPF:

- <u>Positively prepared</u> - this aspect now includes that objectively assessed needs are merely a minimum. Such needs, as they relate to housing, should be assessed using a clear and justified method (which will usually be the Government's standard methodology).

- <u>Justified</u> - rather than being "the most appropriate strategy" (as was the case with the first NPPF), a local plan needs now be only "<u>an</u> appropriate strategy" (underlining added).

- <u>Effective</u> - this stresses that cross-boundary strategic matters should be dealt with rather than deferred, and should be evidenced by a statement of common ground.

- <u>Consistent with national policy</u> - this definition has materially remained the same.

5.31   NPPF 36 suggests that the tests of soundness will be applied less stringently to non-strategic policies which are contained in a local plan. This is presumably because such non-strategic policies do not need to be contained in a local plan, and could be provided for in a neighbourhood plan.

5.32   Emerging plans which had been substantially prepared prior to the publication of the amended NPPF do not have to start from scratch. They will be examined as against the original NPPF, rather than against the new NPPF.

5.33   The test for soundness is not prescriptive. This was determined by HHJ Belcher, sitting as a Judge of the High Court, in *DB Schenker Rail (UK) Ltd v Leeds City Council.*[14] The claimants brought a challenge to the adoption of a Natural Resources and Waste Local Plan. Specifically, the claimant wished to quash two policies insofar as they related to two sites owned by the claimants. The parties agreed before the Judge that the guidance as to soundness in the NPPF was "not prescriptive" (para. 12), following an earlier decision of Carnwath LJ in *Barratt Developments Plc v City of Wakefield MDC.*[15] Counsel also agreed that the soundness test "does not mean that an Inspector has to adhere slavishly to national planning policy", but that "if an Inspector chooses to depart from the policy when determining whether a development plan document is sound, he must give clear reasons for doing so in order that the recipient of his decision would know why the decision was being made as an exception to the policy" (para. 14). Given that particular limb of the soundness test, namely that the plan be consistent with national policy, has materially remained the same, it appears likely that this approach would apply to the new NPPF as to the old.

---

[14]   [2013] EWHC 2865 (Admin).

[15]   [2010] EWCA Civ 897; [2011] JPL 48.

5.34   Guidance regarding the preparation of a statement of common ground is set out in amendments to the PPG.[16] The PPG explains the concept of a statement of common ground in this context:[17]

> "A statement of common ground is a written record of the progress made by strategic policy-making authorities during the process of planning for strategic cross-boundary matters. It documents where effective co-operation is and is not happening throughout the plan-making process, and is a way of demonstrating at examination that plans are deliverable over the plan period, and based on effective joint working across local authority boundaries. In the case of local planning authorities, it also forms part of the evidence required to demonstrate that they have complied with the duty to cooperate."

5.35   The PPG sets out detail of the contents of the statement of common ground.[18] There are specific references to the housing requirement figures in the relevant area. The statement of common ground should include distribution of needs in the area, or set out a process of agreeing such distribution of need.[19] Whilst the recommended sections of the statement of common ground indicate a certain level of detail (they include "governance arrangements for the cooperation process"), the PPG states that the statement of common ground "is expected to be proportionate to the matters being addressed". Certain activities are expected to be documented in a statement of common ground;[20] these include "working together at the outset of plan-making to identify cross-boundary matters which will need addressing".

5.36   Production of a statement of common ground is not a one-time only event. The PPG states:[21] "[s]tatements should be prepared and then maintained on an on-going basis throughout the plan making process." This is a potentially time-consuming process.

5.37   In a passage which may come as a relief to local planning authorities, the PPG acknowledges that they "are not obliged to accept needs from other areas where it can be demonstrated it would have an adverse impact when assessed against policies in the [NPPF]".[22]

5.38   There are no transitional arrangements for the introduction of a statement of common ground.[23]

5.39   NPPF 37 notes that neighbourhood plans do not have to meet basic conditions before they can come into force, which are tested by independent examination.

---

[16]   PPG, Section on Plan-making, paras 1-20.

[17]   PPG, Section on Plan-making, para. 002.

[18]   PPG, Section on Plan-making, para. 003.

[19]   There is further detail on need in PPG, Section on Plan-making, para. 004.

[20]   PPG, Section on Plan-making, para. 007.

[21]   PPG, Section on Plan-making, para. 012.

[22]   PPG, Section on Plan-making, para. 014.

[23]   As noted by Sam Grange: NPPF - Joint Working at Statements of Common Ground, http://www.shoos-miths.co.uk/client-resources/legal-updates/joint-working-and-statements-of-common-ground-14451.aspx, accessed 3 September 2018.

As Holgate J noted in *R (Crownhall Estates) v Chichester DC*,[24] the test of soundness does not apply to the examination of neighbourhood plans.

Decision-taking

5.40 The original NPPF required local planning authorities to be proactive, and to look for solutions rather than problems. In the new NPPF, NPPF 38 goes further, and requires local planning authorities to approach decision on applications in a "positive and creative" way. It is not clear what creative role is open to local planning authorities once an application has been made to them: essentially, they are reactive to applications which are made, except to the imposition of conditions, but the new NPPF has sought to circumscribe the imposition of conditions. However, the NPPF does stress the role of the local planning authority at the pre-application stage. Perhaps it is at that stage that local authority officers are to exercise their creativity.

5.41 The thrust of the NPPF as it concerns decision-making is that decision-makers should be looking for a way to say 'yes', rather than a way to say 'no': NPPF 38 states that all decision-makers "should seek to approve applications for sustainable development where possible".

5.42 One major change between the original NPPF and the new NPPF is the status of the three objectives in NPPF 8 (called "roles", in the previous NPPF). NPPF 9 makes clear that the objectives are to be delivered through plan-making and the application of specific policies in the NPPF; "they are not criteria against which every decision can or should be judged" [see Chapter 4: Sustainable Development].

Pre-application

5.43 The NPPF suggests that applicants and local planning authorities should seek to do as much work as possible prior to an application being made. As NPPF 40 states, local planning authorities cannot require pre-application engagement, but they should encourage it. Moreover, applicants should be encouraged to engage with the local community, and any relevant consultees, prior to the submission of an application.[25]

5.44 NPPF 41 refers to the benefits of resolving issues pre-application. However, this does not recognise, at least in terms, that matters cannot formally be resolved at the pre-application stage. Pre-application discussions do not constitute a formal decision, and do not give rise to a legally enforceable expectation that any particular result will be reached. The same can be said for NPPF 42 encouraging consideration of whether development "will be acceptable in principle" even where other consents will be required. As those involved in the planning process will be well aware, the significant aspects of an application are so often in the detail of it. More practical perhaps is the suggestion that separate consents processes should, where possible, be encouraged in parallel with the planning process. NPPF 45 provides that, if an

---

[24] [2016] EWHC 73 (Admin).

[25] Indeed, NPPF 128 suggests that "early, proactive and effective engagement" may itself weigh in favour of a grant of planning permission [see Chapter 8: Communities, Transport, Effective Use of Land and Design].

application is to be made for a major hazard site, installation or pipeline, or application around them, then local planning authorities should consult the appropriate bodies (presumably including the Health and Safety Executive). For complex applications, NPPF 46 suggests consideration of a planning performance agreement.

5.45   NPPF 44 requires local planning authorities to publish a list of information required for planning applications, and to update this every two years.[26] The NPPF states that the requirements should be kept to the minimum necessary, and also says that the information must be relevant, necessary and material to the application in question. There is a genuine emphasis on not overburdening applicants.

Determining Applications

5.46   The effect of section 38(6) PCPA is that planning applications must be determined in accordance with the statutory development plan, unless material considerations indicate otherwise. The first entry of the NPPF under the heading "Determining applications" reminds decision-makers of this duty. Whilst the Secretary of State may wish, by the policies in the NPPF, that decisions be made differently than would otherwise be the case under the statutory development plan, it cannot be said that the Secretary of State does not point decision-makers to their legal duties.

5.47   As with the previous version of the NPPF, NPPF 48 permits local planning authorities to take into account the policies of emerging plans, depending on the stage of preparation, the extent of unresolved objections, and the degree of consistency of the emerging plan with the policies in the NPPF. The closer an emerging plan is to adoption, the greater weight can be given to it; the less serious the objections, the greater weight can be given; the closer the polices to the framework, the greater the weight can be given.

5.48   NPPF 214 provides that plans submitted for examination on or before 24 January 2019 should be examined as against the original NPPF, rather than the amended NPPF. Therefore, the degree of consistency with the NPPF, when considered for such emerging plans under NPPF 48, is consistency with the original NPPF.

5.49   The fact that an emerging plan submitted may be considered as against the original NPPF may be confusing. Emerging policies can be given weight, including according to their degree of compliance with the original NPPF. But the new NPPF will presumably be a material consideration for such applications: it remains the Government's expression of planning policy. As such, it may be that decision-makers may have to consider two different versions of the NPPF when determining applications.

5.50   Likewise, where an emerging plan is submitted for examination prior to 24 January 2019, even once adopted, local planning authorities will have to consider applications as against the development plan (examined against the old NPPF), and against the new NPPF, which will be a material consideration. Only decisions made under development plans examined as against the new NPPF will be free

---

[26]   The original NPPF had said at para. 193 that this should be "on a frequent basis", and placed less of an emphasis on minimising required information.

from complexity caused by the changes between the old and new NPPF, and the transitional provisions.

5.51　Having previously been located in the PPG,[27] the NPPF now contains national Government's guidance on prematurity. The concept of prematurity is that a large-scale application should not come forward where there is an emerging local plan, as determination of the application may prejudice the consideration of issues at the plan-making level.

5.52　The application of prematurity arguments on the facts of any specific proposal is highly subjective, and can be difficult to predict. NPPF 49-50 attempt to restrict the scope of prematurity decisions. The circumstances where prematurity justifies the refusal of permission is described as "limited". NPPF 49 states that the development would have to be "so substantial", or its cumulative impact "so significant", that granting permission would undermine the plan-making process "by predetermining decisions about the scale, location or phasing of new development that are <u>central</u> to an emerging plan" (underlining added). Additionally, the emerging plan would have to be at an advanced stage. Regarding the stage of development, NPPF 50 indicates that refusal on the grounds of prematurity will be unlikely to be justified where a draft plan has not been submitted for examination, or the period of public consultation on a neighbourhood plan has not yet finished. In what may be a warning to local planning authorities, if they are to refuse on the grounds of prematurity, they are to "indicate clearly how granting permission for the development concerned would prejudice the outcome of the plan-making process". The implication may be that, if this decision cannot be clearly expressed or is unreasonable, the local planning authority may face liability in costs if there is an appeal against its decision.

5.53　NPPF 51-52 provide support to the use of Local Development Orders, Neighbourhood Development Orders and Community Right to Build Orders. In relation to the latter two, NPPF 52 suggests that local planning authorities should seek to have involvement in the process so as to resolve issues before draft orders are submitted for examination. NPPF 53 indicates that Article 4 directions, which must mean directions under Article 4 of the GPDO by which permitted development rights can be restricted, should be used only in limited circumstances, where necessary to protect local amenity or the well-being of the area. An example which is given for the use of an Article 4 direction is to require planning permission for the demolition of local facilities. Local planning authorities should also be slow to use conditions so as to restrict the permitted development rights; there must be a "clear justification to do so".

5.54　The NPPF provides guidance at NPPF 54-57 on the use of planning conditions and planning obligations. The Glossary defines a planning condition as:

> "A condition imposed on a grant of planning permission (in accordance with the Town and Country Planning Act 1990) or a condition included in a Local

---

[27]　PPG, Section on Determining a planning application, para. 014.

Development Order or Neighbourhood Development Order."

5.55   By contrast, the Glossary defines a planning obligation as:

"A legal agreement entered into under section 106 of the [TCPA] to mitigate the impacts of a development proposal."

5.56   Interestingly, the definition of planning obligation appears to be incorrect. It is not necessary for a planning obligation to be in the form of an agreement. To avoid the situation whereby local planning authorities could justify the refusal of planning permission by refusing to enter into agreements, the planning harm thereby being unmitigated and therefore unacceptable, section 106 TCPA permits applicants to enter into unilateral planning obligations. It might be said that the Glossary gives the definition of the term "planning obligation" as it appears in the NPPF, and therefore that the NPPF, when referring to planning obligations, is not referring to all obligations under section 106. This is unlikely. The definition has been changed from the previous version of the NPPF which used to refer to a "legally enforceable obligation". Presumably the new definition is an attempt to be clear; instead it has introduced an unintentional error.

5.57   NPPF 54 indicates a preference for the use of planning conditions rather than planning obligations: a planning obligation should be used only where it is not possible to address unacceptable impacts of the development via a planning condition. In relation to the use of conditions, NPPF 55 restates existing policy that conditions should be imposed only where necessary, relevant to planning and to the development to be permitted, enforceable, precise and reasonable in all other respects. However NPPF 55 also states that planning conditions "should be kept to a minimum". National policy now stresses that parties should seek to agree conditions, and that pre-commencement conditions should be avoided without a clear justification.

5.58   NPPF 56, on the use of planning obligations, reflects the legislative requirements of Reg 122(2) of the Community Infrastructure Levy Regulations 2010.[28]

5.59   Planning control has teeth only if breaches of planning control risk being enforced against. NPPF 58 refers to the importance of effective enforcement in maintaining public confidence in the planning system. However, whether to take enforcement action is a discretionary decision, and NPPF 58 requires that decisions made in the face of suspected breaches of planning control to be proportionate. The paragraph suggests that local planning authorities prepare a local enforcement plan.[29]

---

[28]   The legislation sets out where a planning obligation may constitute a reason for granting planning permission; NPPF 56 sets out where a planning obligation may be sought.

[29]   The details of enforcement are beyond the scope of this book. The PPG has a lengthy Section on Ensuring effective enforcement. See also *Planning Enforcement* - Richard Harwood QC, Bloomsbury Professional. The third edition is due out in January 2019.

Chapter 6

Residential Development

Introduction

6.01 The interpretation of policies in the original NPPF concerning residential development gave rise to a vast amount of litigation. Whilst some common themes have
been kept between the first and second versions of the NPPF when it comes to
housebuilding, the Government has introduced new concepts, including the standard methodology for assessing housing need and the housing delivery test. These
concepts are likely not to be without controversy.

6.02 This chapter deals with the following matters:

(a) The assessment of housing need;

(b) The calculation of housing land supply, including the buffer;

(c) The provision of affordable housing;

(d) Viability;

(e) Delivery of housing;

(f) Rural housing.

Housing Need

6.03 A major national policy goal is the significant boosting of the supply of homes. The
Government has stated an intention for 300,000 new homes to be built each year.
However, there is frequently controversy about new housing development; often,
those who own their own homes within an area have little desire to support the
construction of new dwellings. The provision of new housing can therefore be an
important issue in local elections.

6.04 Notwithstanding the abolition of Regional Spatial Strategies, local planning authorities have only a limited level of autonomy concerning the amount of housing required
in their area. Failure to establish that there is enough housing land to meet the
area's needs for five years of house building will mean that the 'tilted balance' will
apply in most cases pursuant to the presumption in favour of sustainable development. This in turn may lead to an increase in the proportion of refusals of planning
permission which are overturned on appeal. The calculation of whether there is
sufficient housing land to meet an area's needs is therefore important.

6.05 There are two main elements in calculating whether a local planning authority
has an adequate supply of housing land: calculating how many dwellings the area
needs and calculating how many dwellings the area can count on coming forward
within the next five years. As the amended PPG states:[1]

---

[1] PPG, Section on Housing needs assessment, para. 001. This Section of the PPG has been updated since
the introduction of the new NPPF.

"Housing need is an unconstrained assessment of the number of homes needed in an area. Assessing housing need is the first step in the process of deciding how many homes need to be planned for. It should be undertaken separately from assessing land availability, establishing a housing requirement figure, and preparing policies to address this such as site allocations."

6.06   Under the previous NPPF, if the local planning authority had a recently adopted local plan, then the needs as assessed in that plan would be what the supply had to meet. This figure would take into account constraints on the supply of housing in the area (for instance, if a large amount of the area was covered by Green Belt, or AONB, then the target figure for housing would likely be reduced). If there was no recently adopted plan, then the figure for housing need would be the objectively assessed needs figure. This would not take into account the constraints on housing in the area: *St Albans v Hunston Properties Ltd.*[2]

6.07   Where strategic policies cover the area of more than one authority, then the need figure should "at least be the sum of the local housing need for each local planning authority within the area".[3] The standard methodology cannot be applied in circumstances where strategic policy-making authorities do not align with local authority boundaries.[4] Examples of such areas are given as the National Parks and the Broads Authority. The PPG advises:[5]

"Such authorities may continue to identify a housing need figure using a method determined locally, but in doing so will need to consider the best available information on anticipated changes in households as well as local affordability levels."

Objectively Assessed Needs

6.08   In the regime of the original NPPF, it has been critical for an objectively assessed needs figure to be established in the plan-making process: *Solihull MBC v Gallagher Homes.*[6] In the past, both the calculation of the need for housing, and the supply of homes coming through the pipeline have been complex, and have led to lengthy disputes at planning inquiries.[7] The assessment of the level of objectively assessed needs for housing could be particularly technical, with no set methodology.

6.09   The amended NPPF now refers to a standard methodology for assessing the objectively assessed needs for housing. This methodology must be used, NPPF 60 states, "unless exceptional circumstances justify an alternative approach which

---

[2]   [2013] EWCA Civ 1610; [2014] JPL 599.

[3]   PPG, Section on Housing need assessment, para. 018.

[4]   PPG, Section on Housing need assessment, para. 013.

[5]   PPG, Section on Housing need assessment, para. 013.

[6]   [2014] EWCA Civ 1610; [2015] JPL 713.

[7]   As Gilbert J entertainingly stated in *Dartford BC v SSCLG* [2016] EWHC 649 (Admin), para. 45, "[t]o some, such an exercise is a sojourn in a garden of delights, but one should not underestimate its complexity and substance. Anyone ever instructed or otherwise participating at the time when Development Plan inquiries involved the examination of such topics at public inquiry will know that only too well".

also reflects current and future demographic trends and market signals". "Local housing need" is defined in the Glossary as "the number of homes identified as being needed through the application of the standard method set out in national planning guidance, or a justified alternative approach". A local planning authority should plan not only for its need, but the need figure of a neighbouring area which cannot be met within that area (NPPF 60).

6.10   The PPG provides a link to the standard methodology for assessing housing need.[8] However, at the time of writing, the PPG provides a reference to the Government's response to the consultation on the revision to the NPPF. This essentially states that the concern is that the population projections, which are an input into the standard methodology, were lower than previously forecast, which may in turn mean that the standard methodology requires less housing than was expected. As the Government's aim was that the reforms should lead to an increase in the amount of housing to be built, the Government may alter the standard methodology.

6.11   The standard methodology, as at the time of writing, takes the following steps:[9]

(1)   Setting the baseline - the baseline figure will be taken from household growth projections for the local authority's area, with a projected average annual household growth figure to be calculated.

(2)   Adjustment to take account of affordability - an equation is set out to adjust the baseline figures to take account of the affordability of the area.

(3)   Capping the increase - crudely put, a local planning authority may cap its need figure at 40% above what the need figure would have been before the advent of the standard methodology.

6.12   The third step is controversial. It did not feature in the Local Plan Expert Group's recommendations, which suggested a standard methodology.[10] The standard methodology is to set an objective need figure. It does not constitute a target figure in a local plan. If the objective need figure cannot be met, then that should be taken into account in the plan-making process, and the target figure for housing will be reduced from the objectively assessed needs figure. The objective need figure is a starting point: it is not clear why an arbitrary reduction should be applied at this stage, rather than a context specific reduction. It is inconsistent with the concept of an unconstrained assessment of needs, notwithstanding the approach taken in the PPG to the meaning of housing need.[11] The following explanation for the cap is given in the PPG:[12]

---

[8]   https://assets.publishing.service.gov.uk/government/uploads/system/uploads/attachment_data/file/728247/
How_is_a_minimum_annual_local_housing_need_figure_calculated_using_the_standard_method.pdf,
accessed 30 September 2018.

[9]   In outline only.

[10]   Local Plan Expert Group, *Report to the Communities Secretary and to the Minister of Housing and Planning*,
March 2016, Appendix 6.

[11]   PPG, Section on Housing need assessment, para. 001, quoted above.

[12]   PPG, Section on Housing need assessment, para. 007.

"The standard method may identify a minimum local housing need figure that is significantly higher than the number of homes currently being planned for. The cap is applied to help ensure that the minimum local housing need figure calculated using the standard method is as deliverable as possible.

The cap reduces the minimum number generated by the standard method, but does not reduce housing need itself. Therefore strategic policies adopted with a cap applied may require an early review and updating to ensure that any housing need above the capped level is planned for as soon as is reasonably possible."

Setting a Target Figure

6.13   The aim is to provide for objectively assessed needs.[13] NPPF 11(b) indicates that for plan-making, objectively assessed needs may not be met if the protection given by the NPPF to areas or assets set out in Footnote 6 provide a "strong reason for restricting the overall scale, type or distribution of development in the plan area", or that "any adverse impacts of [meeting objectively assessed needs in full] would significantly and demonstrably outweigh the benefits, when assessed against the policies in [the NPPF] taken as a whole". If there is no policy restriction which should mean that the requirement figure should be reduced from objective needs, then that needs figure should be adopted: *Exeter CC v SSCLG*.[14] NPPF 65 indicates that local planning authorities should aim to meet those objectively assessed needs. Likewise, NPPF 35(a) states that a plan will be sound only if it is positively prepared, which includes seeking to meet objectively assessed needs, and unmet need from neighbouring areas is met where practical to do so,[15] and this is consistent with sustainable development. NPPF 23 states that objectively assessed needs should be met so far as is consistent with the objective of sustainable development.

6.14   NPPF 65 also provides that the local planning authority should also set a specific figure for smaller areas:

"Within this overall requirement, strategic policies should also set out a housing requirement for designated neighbourhood areas which reflects the overall strategy for the pattern and scale of development and any relevant allocations[16]. Once the strategic policies have been adopted, these figures should not need re-testing at the neighbourhood plan examination, unless there has

---

[13]   The PPG suggests that the standard method may not set a high enough figure in certain circumstances. An uplift may be necessary, for instance where there are growth strategies in place. Local planning authorities should consider previous delivery levels, and recent assessments of need: PPG, Section on Housing need assessment, para. 010.

[14]   [2015] EWHC 1663 (Admin).

[15]   PPG, Section on Housing need assessment, para. 014 states that need from a neighbouring authority, as agreed through a statement of common ground "should be added to the need already calculated for that authority to form a new minimum housing need figure."

[16]   Footnote in NPPF: "Except where a Mayoral, combined authority or high-level joint plan is being prepared as a framework for strategic policies at the individual local authority level; in which case it may be most appropriate for the local authority plans to provide the requirement figure."

been a significant change in circumstances that affects the requirement."

6.15 Even if it is not possible to provide a requirement figure for a neighbourhood area, if a neighbourhood planning body requests an indicative figure, then the local planning authority should provide it (NPPF 66).

6.16 A stepped requirement for housing can be used, where justified, as an alternative to an average annual requirement.[17] The PPG indicates that the use of a stepped requirement may be necessary "where there is to be a significant change in the level of housing requirement between emerging and previous policies and/or where strategic sites will have a phased delivery or are likely to be delivered later in the plan period."[18] The use of a stepped requirement will still need to be consistent with meeting the plan requirements in full.[19]

Need for Specific Types of Housing

6.17 The ingredients into the objectively assessed needs exercise were considered by Dove J in *Kings Lynn and West Norfolk BC v SSCLG*,[20] specifically, whether vacancies and second homes should be considered in the objectively assessed needs exercise. Dove J considered the need for different types of housing. In the original NPPF, the needs for affordable housing should be addressed in determining the objectively assessed need, but it was not suggested that affordable housing need had to be met in full when determining that need (para. 32). As Dove J recognised, affordable housing is generally provided as a proportion of open market-led schemes. The delivery of affordable housing is therefore dependent on the delivery of market housing. Turning back to the question before him regarding considering vacancies and second homes, Dove J considered that the Inspector was correct in including second homes and vacancies in his assessment of objectively assessed needs. There was an evidence basis for the conclusion that some of the housing was not used by the "indigenous population", and therefore could not be used to meet housing need. That this trend would continue was a statistical judgment, not an application of policy (which, according to *Hunston Development Ltd*, should not be applied at the point of assessing need). In the amended version of the NPPF, NPPF 61 states that the need for types of housing for different groups, including those who require affordable housing, "should be assessed and reflected in planning policies". However, the fact that there is now a standard methodology for calculating objectively assessed needs, which includes a correction for affordability but not for affordable housing *per se*, means that the need for affordable housing will be considered at a different stage of the process (see further below).

6.18 Within the context of the assessment of the need for housing as a whole, local planning authorities should assess need for particular types of housing, which should be reflected in planning policies (NPPF 61). The NPPF gives examples of different

---

[17] PPG, Section on Housing and economic land availability assessment, paras 033-034.

[18] PPG, Section on Housing and economic land availability assessment, para. 034.

[19] PPG, Section on Housing and economic land availability assessment, para. 033.

[20] [2015] EWHC 2464 (Admin).

groups in the community (omitting footnotes): "those who require affordable housing, families with children, older people, students, people with disabilities, service families, travellers, people who rent their homes and people wishing to commission or build their own homes." However, the standard methodology does not specifically address different types of housing.[21]

6.19 The PPG provides detailed guidance on assessing need more specifically than simply numbers of new homes.[22] In relation to older people, the PPG refers to Census data, as well as projection of population and households by age group. Online toolkits may assist with breaking down the future need for specialist accommodation for the elderly. In terms of provision for those with disabilities, the PPG again refers to Census data, as well as information from the Department of Work and Pensions. Specific sources are suggested for the private rented sector. For self-build and custom housebuilding, information emerging from a local planning authority's duties under the Self-build and Custom Housebuilding (Register) Regulations 2016 will provide information. Dedicated student accommodation is encouraged by the PPG, in terms of taking pressure of the private rented sector and increasing the overall housing stock.[23] Local planning authorities are encouraged to engage with higher educational bodies about accommodation requirements.

6.20 The calculation of current unmet gross need for affordable housing is complex, including (amongst other matters) assessing trends and estimates of the number of homeless households, the number of households in over-crowded housing, and the number of concealed households.[24] This will not be a straightforward exercise. The PPG suggests data sources, including the Census, and emphasises that care should be taken to avoid double-counting. The calculation will also need to take into account newly forming households and existing households which are falling into need.[25] This exercise will involve an assessment of the minimum household income to afford entry level market housing. The PPG indicates that the calculation of affordable housing supply requires assessment of vacation of affordable dwellings, surplus stock, and the committed number of new net affordable homes.[26] The PPG concludes regarding total annual need for affordable housing:[27]

> "The total need for affordable housing will need to be converted into annual flows by calculating the total net need (subtract total available stock from total gross need) and converting total net need into an annual flow based

---

[21] PPG, Section on Housing need assessment, para. 020.

[22] PPG, Section on Housing need assessment, para. 020.

[23] In *Exeter CC v SSCLG*, the local planning authority argued that the Inspector should have taken into account student accommodation as part of the housing supply, irrespective of whether student accommodation forms part of the housing need requirement. Lewis J rejected this argument, finding that it would be irrational as treating a form of accommodation as meeting a need if it did not contribute to the requirement.

[24] PPG, Section on Housing need assessment, para. 023.

[25] The PPG sets out an equation for this: PPG, Section on Housing need assessment, para. 024.

[26] PPG, Section on Housing need assessment, para. 025. This also sets out a simple equation.

[27] PPG, Section on Housing need assessment, para. 026.

on the plan period.

The total affordable housing need can then be considered in the context of its likely delivery as a proportion of mixed market and affordable housing developments, taking into account the probable percentage of affordable housing to be delivered by eligible market housing led developments. An increase in the total housing figures included in the plan may need to be considered where it could help deliver the required number of affordable homes."

The Calculation of Housing Land Supply

The Significance of a Five-year Supply

6.21 NPPF 73 states that local planning authorities should identify a supply of land capable of supplying five years' worth of housing land. This should be assessed against the strategic policies, unless the strategic policies are more than five years old, in which case it should be assessed against local housing need. In *St Modwen Developments Ltd v SSCLG*,[28] Lindblom LJ described at para. 19 the need for a local planning authority to demonstrate a five-year supply of housing as a "fundamental requirement of national planning policy". Lindblom LJ noted at para. 43 that the calculation of housing land supply involves the exercise of planning judgment. The courts should not seek to go behind the conclusion of the Planning Inspector on the basis of the credibility and reliability of the case put to her: this would be to trespass beyond the role of the court in reviewing decisions (para. 51).

6.22 The Supreme Court considered the significance of demonstrating a five-year supply of housing land in *Hopkins Homes Ltd v SSCLG*.[29] Lord Carnwath JSC found at para. 54 that the primary purpose of the policy concerning a lack of five-year supply was to bring the decision within the scope of the "tilted balance" in NPPF 11. In the new NPPF, the effect that the tilted balance applies is made clear not by the policies in Chapter 5, but by a footnote to NPPF 11 itself. However, the effect is the same as that considered by Lord Carnwath. The previous difficulties regarding the definition of "relevant policies for the supply of housing", as resolved by the Supreme Court in *Hopkins Homes*, do not arise in the new NPPF. NPPF 11 provides that the most important policies for determining an application are deemed to be out of date where an application involves the provision of housing, and the local planning authority lacks a five-year supply of housing. Notwithstanding the significance of demonstrating a supply, in some circumstances there will be no single correct answer as to whether there is a five-year supply of housing: *Bloor Homes East Midlands Ltd v SSCLG*,[30] paras 104-105; the assessment of land availability is "not simply an arithmetical process". Notwithstanding the potential different answers, it is essential that the calculation is "robust" (para. 105).

---

[28] [2017] EWCA Civ 1643; [2018] PTSR 746.

[29] [2017] UKSC 37; [2017] 1 WLR 1865.

[30] [2014] EWHC 754 (Admin); [2017] PTSR 1283.

Planning for a Supply

6.23   The strategic policy-making authority should have a clear understanding of the land available in its area through the SHLAA process. In order to encourage the achievement of a five-year supply of housing, planning policies must identify a sufficient supply and mix of sites. NPPF 67 indicates a range of sites which must be provided:

(i)   For the first five years of the plan period, sites must be identified which are specific and deliverable. This figure must include the buffer as set out by NPPF 73 (see below).

(ii)   For years 6 to 10 of the plan, then specific developable sites or broad locations for growth. If possible, the same must be identified for years 11 to 15.

6.24   The concepts of deliverability and developability are considered in detail below.

6.25   NPPF 73 requires the strategic policies of development plans to include a trajectory with the expected rate of housing delivery. Local planning authorities are required to carry out an annual review of sites which it considers deliverable, sufficient to provide a minimum of five years' housing land supply, and calculated against the requirement as set by policy, or by need, depending on whether the policies were adopted within the last five years.[31]

6.26   If assessed against the needs figure, then the local authority will not be able to reduce its target by referring to restrictive policies in the NPPF which indicate that it would not be possible to provide this level of housing (for instance, if the area is heavily constrained by the AONB or Green Belt): *St Albans v Hunston Properties Ltd.*[32] Sir David Keene held at paras 26-27 that a Planning Inspector had erred in using figures for a needs figure which were below the full objectively assessed needs, before a constrained requirement was produced by the local plan process. A shortfall in housing land supply assessed against the objectively assessed needs will not inevitably mean that planning permission is granted, particularly if the area is heavily constrained. At para. 29, Sir David Keene held:

> "A decision-maker would... be entitled to conclude, if such were the planning judgment, that some degree of shortfall in housing land supply, as measured simply by household formation rates, was inevitable. That may well affect the weight to be attached to the shortfall."

Demonstrating a Supply

6.27   Given the consequences of a local planning authority being able to demonstrate a five-year supply of housing, the practical means by which a local planning authority may evidence such a supply are significant. It would be extremely burdensome for local planning authorities (and indeed for objectors or developers) to have to start from scratch the assessment of a five-year supply in relation to every planning

---

[31]   PPG, Section on Housing and economic land availability assessment, para. 048, provides an indication of what such assessments will be expected to include.

[32]   [2013] EWCA Civ 1610; [2014] JPL 599.

application. NPPF 74 therefore permits decision-makers to demonstrate their supply of housing in existing documents. A recently adopted plan may demonstrate the council's supply of housing land.[33] In order to be "recently adopted", Footnote 38 states:

> "a plan adopted between 1 May and 31 October will be considered 'recently adopted' until 31 October of the following year; and a plan adopted between 1 November and 30 April will be considered recently adopted until 31 October in the same year."

6.28 This passage is, unfortunately, not well drafted. It is clear that a plan adopted on 1 June 2019 will be considered recently adopted until 31 October 2020. Likewise, a plan adopted on 1 February 2020 will be considered recently adopted until 31 October 2020. However, the footnote is not clear in relation to the status of plans adopted between 1 November and 31 December. This is because, on a strict reading, these are to be treated as recently adopted until 31 October in the same year. However, this cannot make sense, as that date will have passed. The policy presumably cannot mean that local plans adopted within the last two months of a calendar year will never be treated as recently adopted. Rather, it must be that local plans adopted in those months will be treated as being recently adopted until 31 October in the following year. This can be reconciled with the wording in the following way: "until 31 October in the same year" means not, "in the same year as adoption", but rather "in the same year as falls the date 30 April, at the end of the period 1 November to 30 April". This is the only interpretation which makes sense. However, there is a further difficulty with it: why does the footnote not distinguish between plans adopted between 1 May and 31 December on the one hand, and plans adopted between 1 January and 30 April? The answer to this question seems to be that the 31 October cut-off date is a relevant threshold, as plans adopted between 1 May and 31 October will be deemed to be recently adopted for more than a year.[34] The relevance of 1 November might be that the Secretary of State is to publish Housing Delivery Test results for England in November of each year (see further below).

6.29 The position regarding housing land supply can be fixed, not only by a recently adopted plan, but also by an annual position statement.[35] Such an annual position statement must be produced through engagement with developers "and others who

---

[33] The PPG states "[i]f strategic policy-makers choose to confirm their 5-year supply under paragraph 74 of the NPPF through the examination of a plan, they will need to indicate that they are seeking to do so at Regulation 19 stage, and will need to ensure they have carried out a sufficiently robust assessment of the deliverability of sites. The Inspector's report will provide recommendations in relation to the land supply and will enable the authority, where the authority accepts the recommendations, to confirm that they have demonstrated a 5-year land supply in a recently adopted plan": PPG, Section on Housing and economic land availability assessment, para. 049.

[34] The PPG unfortunately provides no clarification: PPG, Section on Housing and economic land availability assessment, para. 054.

[35] Details regarding the process for achieving this, and the involvement of the Planning Inspectorate, are set out in the PPG, Section on Housing and economic land availability assessment, para. 050.

have an impact on delivery" (NPPF 74(a)).[36] If the position on specific sites cannot be agreed during the engagement process, then the annual position statement must incorporate the recommendation of the Secretary of State (NPPF 74(b)). Detailed guidance regarding the assessment of housing land supply is set out in the PPG.[37] This includes not only details of construction, but also "details of demolitions and planned demolitions which will have an impact on net completions".

6.30   The recently amended PPG states:[38]

> "In principle, an authority will need to be able to demonstrate a 5 year land supply at any point to deal with applications and appeals, unless it is choosing to confirm its 5 year land supply, in which case it need demonstrate it only once per year."

6.31   The recent amendments to the PPG suggest that completions for the purposes of housing land supply calculations "include conversions, changes of use and demolitions and redevelopments".[39] As the figures are to be net figures, demolitions should be offset against such completions. The Amendments also suggest that the completion of student accommodation can be included in the housing requirement, "based on the amount of accommodation it releases in the housing market".[40] Likewise, it is suggested that housing for the elderly, including residential institutions in Use Class C2,[41] can be counted against the housing requirement.[42]

6.32   If the local planning authority wishes to rely on a housing supply figure in a recently adopted plan, or annual position statement, then this means that the 5% buffer will not apply to the housing land supply figure; this will be increased to 10% (unless there has been significant under delivery of housing, in which case the buffer is increased still further). The buffer is considered further below.

6.33   Amendments to the PPG indicate[43] that deficits or shortfalls against assessed housing requirement should be addressed in the first five years of the plan period.[44] If a different approach is to be taken, this should be established at plan-making stage,

---

[36]   This category is left undefined in the NPPF, but guidance is provided in the PPG, Section on Housing and economic land availability assessment, para. 052. This includes relevant consultation bodies, residents of people carrying on business from which the local planning authority "consider it appropriate to invite representations". The PPG suggests "small and large developers; land promoters; private and public land owners; infrastructure providers (such as utility providers, highways, etc); upper tier authorities (county councils) in two-tier areas; neighbouring authorities with adjourning [sic - presumably adjoining] or cross-boundary sites". One group which has an impact upon delivery, but is not mentioned in the PPG, is those who provide funding for development.

[37]   PPG, Section on Housing and economic land availability assessment, para. 048.

[38]   PPG, Section on Housing and economic land availability assessment, para. 038.

[39]   PPG, Section on Housing and economic land availability assessment, para. 040.

[40]   PPG, Section on Housing and economic land availability assessment, para. 042.

[41]   For more detail, see *The Essential Guide to the Use of Land and Buildings under the Planning Acts* - Martin Goodall, Bath Publishing 2017, pp 142-148.

[42]   PPG, Section on Housing and economic land availability assessment, para. 042.

[43]   PPG, Section on Housing and economic land availability assessment, para. 044.

[44]   This is traditionally known as the "Sedgefield" method.

and not "on a case by case basis on appeal". Where there has been over-supply of housing, then "additional supply can be used to offset any shortfalls against requirements from previous years".[45]

6.34   In individual decisions, a developer may attempt to show that a local planning authority does not have a five-year supply, if the requirements of NPPF 74 are not met. In *Oadby and Wigston BC v SSCLG*,[46] the Court of Appeal considered the question of whether housing supply should be considered in such circumstances against objectively assessed needs of the local planning authority's own area, or whether the supply should be considered against the need of the wider housing market area. The Court of Appeal held that the former NPPF did not prescribe either approach: it would be open to the decision-maker. Nevertheless, the assessment must still be objectively assessed needs, and not some sort of redistribution of housing provision between different local authorities.

6.35   The phrase "housing market area" no longer appears in the amended NPPF, but there is still a requirement in plan-making for a local planning authority to consider meeting needs from neighbouring authorities. For the purposes of determining whether a local planning authority lacks a five-year supply of housing, and therefore whether the tilted balance applies, Footnote 7 to NPPF 11 refers to NPPF 73. This requires local planning authorities to identify and update annually a supply of specific deliverable sites, either again the housing requirement set out in policies adopted in the last five years, or where the strategic policies are more than five years old, "against their local housing need". The reference to "their" need suggests that this may not incorporate the need of neighbouring authorities. Likewise, "local housing need" is defined by reference to the standard methodology (unless a different approach can be justified) which itself focusses on a local planning authority's own area. It is possible that the courts, interpreting the new NPPF, will follow the Court of Appeal in *Oadby and Wigston*, but it seems that there is at least an argument that the need figure should now be assessed only by reference to the local planning authority's own area. The position is different where there is a joint plan. The monitoring of the plan may be done on the basis of the whole of the joint planning area, or on a single authority basis.[47]

Deliverability and Developability

6.36   The five-year supply is to be made up of specific, deliverable sites. "Deliverable" is defined in the Glossary as:

> "To be considered deliverable, sites for housing should be available now, offer a suitable location for development now, and be achievable with a realistic prospect that housing will be delivered on the site within five years. Sites that are not major development, and sites with detailed planning permission, should be considered deliverable until permission expires, unless there is clear

---

[45] PPG, Section on Housing and economic land availability assessment, para. 045.

[46] [2016] EWCA Civ 1040; [2017] JPL 358.

[47] PPG, Section on housing and economic land availability assessment, para. 046.

evidence that homes will not be delivered within five years (e.g. they are no longer viable, there is no longer a demand for the type of units or sites have long term phasing plans). Sites with outline planning permission, permission in principle, allocated in the development plan or identified on a brownfield register should only be considered deliverable where there is clear evidence that housing completions will begin on site within five years."

6.37   The requirement of deliverability reflects "the futility of authorities' relying in development plans on the allocation of sites that have no realistic prospect of being developed within the five-year period" (*Hopkins Homes Ltd*, para. 78, Lord Gill). The definition of deliverability in the Glossary is lengthier than the version in Footnote 11 to the previous version of the NPPF. It seems that there are three main parts to the definition:

(i)   A general definition, encompassing availability, suitability of location, and reasonable prospect of housing within five years.

(ii)   A presumption of deliverability for sites which are not major development, and sites with detailed planning permission.

(iii)   A threshold for demonstrating deliverability (the requirement of "clear evidence" of completions within five years) where a site has outline planning permission, permission in principle, allocated in the development plan or on the brownfield register.

6.38   The second main part to the definition of "deliverable" in the Glossary definition (at (ii) above) is different in form to the previous NPPF. It states: "Sites that are not major development, and sites with detailed planning permission, should be considered deliverable until permission expires, unless there is clear evidence that homes will not be delivered within five years (e.g. they are no longer viable, there is no longer a demand for the type of units or sites have long term phasing plans)." The meaning of it is not entirely clear. Certain sites benefit from a presumption of deliverability. However, this is restricted to "[s]ites that are not major development, and sites with detailed planning permission". It is therefore clear that a site which is not major development, according to the definition in the Glossary, and which has detailed planning permission, will benefit from the presumption that it is deliverable, unless there is clear evidence that homes will not be delivered. However, the wording is less clear in terms of major sites which have detailed planning permission. It would seem likely that the intention of the text would be that such sites would benefit from the presumption. However, if this is correct, the reference to "[s]ites that are not major development" would be unnecessary - the passage could merely refer to (any) sites with planning permission. If a site is not for major development, and has only outline planning permission, then it would seem that this would be covered by the final sentence, which imposes a different test.

6.39   In relation to the third part, the PPG gives examples of clear evidence as a statement of common ground "which confirms the developers' delivery intentions and anticipated start and build-out rates", and "a hybrid planning permission for large sites which links to a planning performance agreement that sets out the timescale for conclusion of reserved matters applications and discharge of conditions".[48]

6.40   The question of deliverability was considered by Lindblom LJ in *St Modwen Developments Ltd v SSCLG*.[49] The claimant was refused planning permission for two schemes involving residential development to the west of Hull. Its appeal was dismissed by the Secretary of State. A challenge brought under section 288 TCPA failed before Ouseley J in the High Court. Likewise, the appeal to the Court of Appeal was dismissed. The claimant argued that the Inspector had erred in her approach to the concept of deliverability. The Court of Appeal disagreed. It made the following findings, which although they concerned the previous version of the NPPF, are likely to apply to the new definition as found in the Glossary and quoted above:

(a)   The concept of deliverability is different to the concept of delivery (para. 35).

(b)   That a site is capable of delivery does not mean that it necessarily will be delivered (para. 35).

(c)   Local planning authorities do not control the housing market, which is subject to the decisions of landowners and housebuilders.[50]

(d)   In order for sites to be deliverable, dwellings do not have to be certain to be delivered.

(e)   The concept of a "realistic prospect" of delivery does not mean that, in order for a site to be deliverable, it must be certain or even probable that the dwellings will be delivered.

6.41   The test of whether a site is "developable" is less demanding than the test of deliverability. The Glossary defines "developable" as:

> "To be considered developable, sites should be in a suitable location for housing development with a reasonable prospect that they will be available and could be viably developed at the point envisaged."

Particular Types of Sites: Small/Medium, Large, and Exception Sites

6.42   The new NPPF prioritises small and medium sites by requiring local planning authorities to accommodate at least 10% of their housing requirement on sites no larger than one hectare. The percentage was decreased, and the size of the site was increased, following consultation on the draft of the NPPF.[51] Neighbourhood planning groups are to consider the opportunities for allocation of small and medium-sized sites, pursuant to NPPF 69.

---

[48]   PPG, Section on housing and economic land availability assessment, para. 036.

[49]   [2017] EWCA Civ 1643; [2018] PTSR 746.

[50]   Lindblom LJ said that NPPF policy recognises this lack of control on the part of local planning authorities. However, the new NPPF now takes a more interventionist approach to the delivery of housing, in the form of the Housing Delivery Test, considered in more detail below.

[51]   Government response to the draft revised National Planning Policy Framework consultation, Ministry of Housing, Communities and Local Government, July 2018, p. 23.

6.43   The NPPF recognises that the delivery of large amounts of housing is often best achieved through larger scale development. However, such major extensions or new settlements need to be well located and designed, and supported by infrastructure and facilities.[52] NPPF 72 sets out a number of elements which the local planning authority must take into account. NPPF 72(d) reflects the Government's concerns about rates of delivery from large-scale sites, and requires the assessment of delivery rates from such sites to be realistic, and to consider where rapid implementation may be achieved. Where a new development is of a significant size, NPPF 72(e) suggests consideration is given to establishing Green Belt around or adjacent to the new settlement, reflecting NPPF 135.

6.44   NPPF 71 provides national policy as concerns proposals for entry-level exception sites. This phrase is defined in the Glossary as:

> "A site that provides entry-level homes suitable for first time buyers (or equivalent, for those looking to rent), in line with paragraph 71 of this Framework."

6.45   The development of such sites is to be supported by local planning authorities, unless there is no need for such homes. Entry-level exception sites must support development in addition to that which would otherwise be proposed, and therefore the site should not already be allocated for housing. Such sites should "not be larger than one hectare in size or exceed 5% of the size of the existing settlement" (Footnote 33). Neither should they be permitted in National Parks, the Broads Authority, AONBs, or within Green Belts. The sites must provide affordable housing, and must comply with local design policies and standards. The proposals must not compromise the protection given to areas or assets of particular importance in the NPPF (a footnote refers to Footnote 6 of the NPPF).

The Buffer

6.46   The amended NPPF has provided clarity on the 'buffer' for assessing housing land supply beyond that in the previous version of the NPPF. This constitutes a considerable improvement. The main dispute which arose under the previous NPPF was over the 20% buffer in circumstances of a "persistent under-delivery of housing". The previous wording of the NPPF gave rise to potential disputes both in terms of how great the under-delivery of housing needed to be in order to give rise to the application of the buffer, but also the period over which it should be calculated. In *Cotswold DC v SSCLG*,[53] for instance, a Planning Inspector considered the previous five-year period for delivery of housing, on the basis that if the assessment looks forward to five years' supply, then five years' delivery is a reasonable period to consider. The Council had recommended looking at a four-year period, whereas the Inspector considered the position at a different inquiry, which had looked back for ten years. Lewis J held that the precise period of time during which to consider whether there has been a persistent under-delivery would be a matter of judgment

---

[52]   The PPG, Section on Plan-making, para. 056, states that "strategic policy-making authorities are expected to make a realistic assessment about the prospect of sites being developed (and associated delivery rates)".

[53]   [2013] EWHC 3719 (Admin).

for the decision-maker, and rejected the challenge. As Lindblom J stated in *Bloor Homes East Midlands Ltd v SSCLG*,[54] at para. 122, the NPPF does not elaborate on the concept of "persistent under-delivery of housing".

6.47 Under the new NPPF, the test is whether there has been a "significant under-delivery of housing". The period for assessing such under-delivery is a period of three years. The period is therefore no longer a matter of judgment. The test of significant under-delivery will also not be a matter of judgment from November 2018, as Footnote 39 to the NPPF states that the test "will be measured against the Housing Delivery Test, where this indicates that delivery was below 85% of the housing requirement". The Housing Delivery Test is considered in further detail below. Amendments to the PPG indicate that the 20% buffer will last until the results of the Housing Delivery Test show that delivery exceeds 85% of the identified requirement.[55]

6.48 NPPF 70 broadly reflects the policy of the previous NPPF regarding windfall sites. "Windfall sites" are defined in the Glossary as "Sites not specifically identified in the development plan". However, the new NPPF is more permissive as regards the use of residential gardens for windfall development. Whilst the previous NPPF states that allowance should not include residential gardens, NPPF 70 says that plans "should consider the case for setting out policies to resist <u>inappropriate</u> development of residential gardens, for example where development would cause harm to the local area" (underlining added). This does not rule out the use of residential gardens, but indicates that local planning authorities should consider when the use of such gardens would be inappropriate. This is consistent with the support to be found in NPPF 68(c) for windfall sites both in policies and decisions. Local planning authorities are to give "great weight to the benefits of using suitable sites within existing settlements for homes".

6.49 The further explanation of the 20% buffer is not the only change wrought to the buffer by the new NPPF. Whilst the 5% buffer has been maintained in all cases, the new NPPF has added a further level of buffer, being 10% "where the local planning authority wishes to demonstrate a five-year supply of deliverable sites through an annual position statement or recently adopted plan, to account for any fluctuations in the market during that year". This appears to deal with a situation in which a local planning authority wishes to stop the clock in terms of the calculation of housing land supply. It is not certain (indeed, it is unlikely) that the rate of housing delivery will be smooth. As such, the fact that a local planning authority has had a particular housing supply figure within the past year does not mean that that figure will continue until the next assessment. If the local planning authority does not wish to expend the work of updating the housing land supply figure to the date of the determination of planning permission (or to the date of its evidence, if in an appeal), then the buffer will be increased from 5% to 10%. The source of the housing land supply figure need not be the annual monitoring report; it can be from a recently-adopted plan (the meaning of 'recently adopted' being defined in

---

[54] [2014] EWHC 754 (Admin); [2017] PTSR 1283.

[55] PPG, Section on Housing and economic land availability assessment, para. 066.

Footnote 38, the problems with which are considered above.

Housing Land Supply and Recently-Adopted Neighbourhood Plans

6.50   NPPF 14 makes specific provision for the application of the tilted balance under
        NPPF 11(d) for proposed development including the provision of housing.[56] The
        tilted balance means, in the context of decision-making, that unless the develop-
        ment is contrary to a restrictive policy in Footnote 6, planning permission should be
        refused only if "any adverse impacts of doing so would significantly and demonstrably
        outweigh the benefits, when assessed against the policies in [the NPPF] taken as a
        whole". NPPF 14 provides an indication of a circumstance in which the quoted test
        will be likely to be satisfied.[57] The neighbourhood plan must have become part of
        the development plan[58] within a period of two years prior to the date of decision.
        This protection therefore lasts only for two years, unless the neighbourhood plan
        is modified by way of material modification, and the relevant criteria in NPPF
        14 continue to be satisfied.[59] The neighbourhood plan must contain policies and
        allocations[60] to meet an identified housing requirement.[61] In those circumstances,
        the thresholds of housing land supply and delivery are limited: the local planning
        authority needs to be able to demonstrate only a three-year supply, and the housing
        delivery need be only at least 45% of that required under the Housing Delivery Test
        over the previous three years.

6.51   NPPF 216 includes transitional provisions for NPPF 14. Until 11 December 2018,
        the policy will include neighbourhood plans older than two years at the date of
        decision. From November 2018 to November 2019, the figure required of the
        housing delivery test will be only 25%, rather than 45%.

6.52   Guidance on NPPF 14 is found in the recently-amended PPG.[62]

6.53   A predecessor of this policy was subject to challenge by a large number of housebuilders

---

[56] This would therefore include mixed use development, so long as it includes the provision of some housing.

[57] Presumably not the only circumstance. Presumably the proposal could still be turned down on the basis
      of, for instance, very poor design.

[58] Note that this does not mean that it has to have been made: the language of NPPF 14(a) reflects that
      of section 38(3A) PCPA, whereby a neighbourhood plan becomes part of the development plan after
      a referendum but before the plan is formally made, unless the local planning authority decides not to
      make the plan.

[59] PPG, Section on Neighbourhood planning, para. 099.

[60] The PPG, Section on Neighbourhood planning, para. 097, states that allocations "are sites clearly
      outlined with a site boundary on a policies map with accompanying site allocation policies in the plan
      setting out, as a minimum, the proposed land use and the quantum of development appropriate for the
      site". The policies and allocation must be in the neighbourhood plan itself. Guidance on the allocation
      of sites for development in a neighbourhood plan is set out at para. 098.

[61] The PPG, Section on Neighbourhood planning, para. 097, makes clear that the identified requirement
      must be met by the plan "in full, whether it is derived from the standard methodology for local housing
      need, the housing figure in the area's strategic policies, an indicative figure provided by the local author-
      ity, or where it has exceptionally been determined by the neighbourhood planning body." It suggests
      that reliance on windfall allowance would not be sufficient.

[62] PPG, Section on Neighbourhood planning, paras 096ff.

in *R (Richborough Estates Ltd) v SSCLG*.[63] Dove J considered when the policy applies. In doing so, he had to interpret the meaning of a three-year supply of housing. He considered that this means "a three-year supply in terms of the exercise for assessing a five-year supply of housing" (para. 41). Essentially, if when a housing land supply calculation is carried out the local planning authority is found to have a less than five-year supply, but a more than three-year supply, then this would be sufficient. There was no indication in the policy that all of the technicality of an entirely separate assessment to demonstrate a three-year supply was necessary. This is now put beyond doubt in the new NPPF 14(c), which states that the three-year supply is to be assessed "against its five-year housing supply requirement". Dove J dismissed the challenge to the lawfulness of the policy. On the basis of the decision of the Court of Appeal in *R (West Berks DC and Reading BC) v SSCLG*,[64] the material considerations to which the Secretary of State needed to have regard in formulating policy were limited; the policy was not inconsistent with the statutory scheme, and was not irrational. The Secretary of State had not made an unlawful error of fact. The claimants argued that the policy was inconsistent with the key objective of the NPPF in boosting significantly the supply of housing. Dove J agreed with the Secretary of State that the objective of boosting housing land supply is not an isolated objective of the NPPF, and "is not a policy objective which is to be pursued at all costs and irrespective of the other objectives of the [NPPF]". It is not unusual for policy goals to pull in different directions, and the Secretary of State's approach was not irrational.

Housing Land Supply and Planning Appeals

6.54   When determining a planning appeal where a local planning authority is found to have a shortfall of housing land, with how much specificity must a Planning Inspector (or the Secretary of State, if the appeal is recovered) determine the local planning authority's shortfall? This was the question resolved by the Court of Appeal in *Hallam Land Management Ltd v SSCLG*.[65] The claimant developer argued that the Secretary of State had not assessed the level of housing land supply with adequate specificity. By contrast, the Secretary of State argued that it would not always, or generally, be the role of the Secretary of State to determine the precise level of housing land supply.

6.55   Lindblom LJ noted the decision of the Supreme Court in *Hopkins Homes Ltd v SSCLG*,[66] regarding the primary purpose of policies concerning a housing shortfall being to determine whether the 'tilted balance' in NPPF 11(d) applies. Nevertheless, the weight to be given to policies remains a matter for the decision-maker. Lindblom LJ stated at para. 47 that "[l]ogically…one would expect the weight given to [restrictive policies] to be less if the shortfall in the housing land supply is large, and more if it is small". There was no requirement in law or policy for a decision-maker to

---

[63]   [2018] EWHC 33 (Admin); [2018] PTSR 1168.

[64]   [2016] EWCA Civ 441; [2016] 1 WLR 3923.

[65]   [2018] EWCA Civ 1808.

[66]   [2017] UKSC 37; [2017] 1 WLR 1865.

determine the <u>exact</u> level of any housing requirement. That said, the weight to be given to a shortfall would be likely to depend on factors including "broad magnitude of the shortfall, how long it is likely to persist, what the local planning authority is doing to reduce it, and how much of it the development will meet" (para. 51). On the facts, the Secretary of State had not given adequate reasons regarding his conclusions on the extent of the shortfall in housing land supply. The Secretary of State also failed to give explicit consideration to two decisions of Planning Inspectors to which he had been referred. These gave consideration to the housing land supply figure, and therefore were relevant to the matter the Secretary of State was considering. The description of the shortfall given by these Inspectors[67] was quite different to that given by the Secretary of State.[68] The Secretary of State's decision was therefore quashed.

6.56   The fact that weight is a matter for the decision-maker, even where a local planning authority lacks a five-year supply of housing land is well established, and has been since at least the decision of Lindblom J in *Crane v SSCLG*.[69] In *Edward Ware Homes Ltd v SSCLG*,[70] Holgate J held that if a decision-maker is entitled to consider what weight to give to a policy, that includes the ability for the decision-maker to assess "whether the justification for and terms of that policy continue to be sound" (para. 29). However, since the decision of the Supreme Court in *Hopkins Homes*, the emphasis is less upon whether the weight to be given to housing policies is diminished by virtue of them being out of date, but rather the fact that the tilted balance applies where there is a housing land supply shortfall. This echoes the findings of Holgate J in *Woodcock Holdings Ltd v SSCLG*,[71] in which he said that the mechanism in the previous NPPF, whereby housing land supply policies were deemed to be out of date by virtue of a lack of five-supply was to bring the application within the scope of the presumption in favour of sustainable development.[72] This approach is consistent with the new NPPF, which no longer uses the concept of policies for the supply of housing, but directly feeds a housing land supply shortfall into the tilted balance by Footnote 6 to NPPF 11.

6.57   Whilst the housing land supply which a decision-maker must consider is that of the local authority area, that does not mean that the distribution of housing land supply within parts of sub-areas of the district is necessarily legally irrelevant: *Edward Ware Homes*, para. 36. However, it may be that a Planning Inspector needs to give notice to a party that such a point may be taken in the decision.

The Provision of Affordable Housing

6.58   The needs for affordable housing should be assessed and reflected in planning policy (NPPF 61). The Glossary defines affordable housing at some length. Affordable

---

[67]   "Significant" or "material".

[68]   "Limited".

[69]   [2015] EWHC 425 (Admin).

[70]   [2016] EWHC 103 (Admin); [2016] JPL 767.

[71]   [2015] EWHC 1173 (Admin); [2015] JPL 1151.

[72]   Holgate J restated this position in *Edward Ware Homes v SSCLG*.

housing itself is defined as:

> "housing for sale or rent, for those whose needs are not met by the market (including housing that provides a subsidised route to home ownership and/ or is for essential local workers); and which complies with one of more of the following definitions…"

6.59   The Glossary then sets out separate definitions for four concepts: affordable housing for rent; starter homes; discounted market sales housing; and other affordable routes to home ownership.

6.60   The NPPF includes prescriptive guidance on the detail of affordable housing policies. Where there is a need for affordable housing, this should be reflected in policies in the development plan, and it should generally be expected to be met on site (NPPF 62).

6.61   One major restriction which national planning policy attempts to put on affordable housing requirements is at NPPF 63. This indicates that, generally speaking, the provision of affordable housing should be restricted to major developments, which are defined in the Glossary as relates to residential development:

> "For housing, development where 10 or more homes will be provided, or the site has an area of 0.5 hectares or more."

6.62   In designated rural areas, the NPPF permits policies to set a threshold of five units or fewer. NPPF 63 also requires the reduction in affordable housing contribution required where a vacant building is reused.

6.63   The policy in NPPF 63 has similarities to that introduced by Written Ministerial Statement on 28 November 2014, but deals only with affordable housing. Furthermore, the threshold is worded differently in the NPPF (by reference to the Glossary) as compared to the Written Ministerial Statement. The 2014 WMS was challenged in *R (West Berks DC and Reading BC) v SSCLG*.[73] Although found unlawful in the High Court by Holgate J, the Court of Appeal reversed this decision. In the course of the litigation, it became clear that the Secretary of State's position (and the law) required that the policy not be treated in a blanket fashion. Local circumstances may justify a lower (or no) threshold to the requirement of contribution towards affordable housing. This decision was made in the context of individual applications for planning permission, and therefore section 38(6) PCPA was relevant. In order to be adopted, local plans must be found to be sound; the definition of soundness is in the NPPF, and this includes that the plan is consistent with national policy. However, it would presumably be open to a local planning authority to conclude that there was robust local evidence to justify a lower threshold in its policies. Consideration of local circumstances is encouraged by NPPF 9.

6.64   Not only does the NPPF restrict the circumstances in which affordable housing should be restricted, but it also makes direction as to what type of affordable housing should be provided. NPPF 64 provides that major development which

---

[73]   [2016] EWCA Civ 441; [2016] 1 WLR 3923.

includes the provision of housing should lead (both in terms of policy creation and decision-making) to at least 10% of the dwellings to be available for affordable home ownership. There are various exceptions to this. Such accommodation need not be provided where the 10% figure would exceed the level of affordable housing required in the area, or where it would "significantly prejudice the ability to meet the identified affordable housing needs of specific groups". Certain types of development do not need to meet the 10% affordable home ownership test (development solely for Build to Rent homes;[74] specialist accommodation, such as for the elderly or students; sites proposed to be developed by people building or commissioning their own homes; site exclusively for affordable housing, an entry-level exception site or a rural exception site).[75]

6.65   Build to Rent is defined in the Glossary as:

> "Purpose built housing that is typically 100% rented out. It can form part of a wider multi-tenure development comprising either flats or houses, but should be on the same site and/or contiguous with the main development. Schemes will usually offer longer tenancy agreements of three years or more, and will typically be professionally managed stock in single ownership and management control."

6.66   A new section to the PPG provides further detail regarding build to rent.[76] Local planning authorities should consider specific policies on build to rent if there is a specific need identified.[77] The PPG indicates that the appropriate proportion of build to rent housing which should be affordable private rent is 20%, and this should be maintained in perpetuity,[78] although different types of affordable housing can be provided if appropriate.[79] The level of such rent should be at least 20% below the private market rent, including service charges.[80] The requirement to offer tenancies of three or more years, known as "family friendly tenancies", should be secured by condition.[81]

---

[74] Amendments to the PPG provide further detail regarding build to rent: PPG, Section on Build to rent. Local planning authorities should consider specific policies on build to rent if there is a specific need identified.

[75] Rural exception sites are defined in the Glossary as "Small sites used for affordable housing in perpetuity where sites would not normally be used for housing. Rural exception sites seek to address the needs of the local community by accommodating households who are either current residents or have an existing family or employment connection. A proportion of market homes may be allowed on the site at the local planning authority's discretion, for example where essential to enable the delivery of affordable units without grant funding."

[76] PPG, Section on Build to rent.

[77] PPG, Section on Build to rent, para. 001.

[78] PPG, Section on Build to rent, para. 002.

[79] PPG, Section on Build to rent, para. 004.

[80] PPG, Section on Build to rent, para. 003.

[81] PPG, Section on Build to rent, para. 010.

Viability

6.67   The amount of contributions housing development should make, in some cases to infrastructure but more commonly the provision of affordable housing, has often been the cause of dispute between local planning authorities and developers at appeals before Planning Inspectors. Developers often argue that the providing of affordable housing, when combined with the other costs of development and a reasonable return for the developer, would make the development unviable. The Equality Impact Assessment into the new NPPF states that the "added certainty around viability, created through clear affordable housing requirements in local plans and a preferred standard approach to appraisals, is intended to increase the delivery of affordable housing".[82] The aim in the current national planning policy is to reduce such disputes at the decision-making stage, by having the question of viability largely resolved at the plan-making stage.[83] There does not need to be a specific assessment for every site, which may be done on a sampling basis. Strategic sites should however be specifically assessed. The PPG states:[84]

> "Policy requirements, particularly for affordable housing, should be set at a level that takes account of affordable housing and infrastructure needs and allows for the planned types of sites and development to be deliverable, without the need for further viability assessment at the decision making stage."

6.68   In relation to a principal recent controversy, the PPG makes clear that the "price paid for land is not a relevant justification for failing to accord with relevant policies in the plan".[85] The onus is on site promoters to engage in the plan-making process, to ensure that their proposals would be policy compliant.

6.69   NPPF 34 states that policies setting out the contributions expected from development "should not undermine the deliverability of the plan". If up-to-date policies set out the contributions which development would be expected to provide, then planning applications which comply with them will be assumed to be viable (NPPF 57). The burden is on the applicant to demonstrate that specific consideration needs to be given to the viability of providing contributions at the application stage. The PPG gives examples of when this may be appropriate:[86]

•   Where development is proposed on allocated sites, but the assessment of viability which informed the plan were on sites of a wholly different type;

•   Where further information is required on infrastructure or site costs;

•   Where the development which is proposed is significantly different to standard development for sale (such as Build to Rent or housing for older people);

---

[82]   National Planning Policy Framework: Equality Impact Assessment, Ministry of Housing, Communities and Local Government, July 2018, p.5.

[83]   Hence the PPG states "The role for viability assessment is primarily at the plan-making stage": PPG, Section on Viability, para. 002.

[84]   PPG, Section on Viability, para. 002.

[85]   PPG, Section on Viability, para. 002.

[86]   PPG, Section on Viability, para. 007.

- Where significant economic changes, including recession, have occurred since the entry into force of the plan.

6.70 Viability assessments for specific applications must refer back to the assessment for the plan. NPPF 57 states that such assessments should reflect the approach in national planning guidance. Specific consideration may be given to the Build to Rent sector, which may permit alternatives to the policy set out in the local plan.[87]

6.71 A viability assessment should take into account risk, and therefore the realisation of that risk does not itself necessitate further viability assessment or trigger a review mechanism: developers cannot 'charge' for risk but then avoid that risk by re-assessing if it eventuates.[88]

6.72 Viability assessments must be presented clearly, including clearly stating what assumptions have been made. The assessment should include an executive summary.[89] There was previously controversy over the confidentiality of viability assessments.[90] NPPF 57 now makes clear that all viability assessments must be made publicly available. However, the reference to "all" is somewhat limited by the content of the PPG, which states that viability assessment may not be made publicly available in "exceptional circumstances" (although an executive summary should then be provided).[91] Viability assessment should not normally be based on information specific to the developer, and therefore the information need not be commercially sensitive. If commercially sensitive information is required, then it should be aggregated in published viability assessments and executive summaries.

6.73 A recommended approach for viability assessment is set out in the PPG.[92] This includes guidance on:

- Gross development value, for both area/typology assessment and site/development-specific proposals.[93] In the case of the latter, the PPG reiterates that "[u]nder no circumstances will the price paid for land be a relevant justification for failing to accord with relevant policies in the plan".

- Costs.[94] These are stated to include build costs, abnormal costs (including contamination), site-specific infrastructure costs (including access roads), total costs of all policy requirements, financing costs, professional costs (including legal, sales and project managing), and project contingency when justified in relation to a particular scheme. Of these costs, site-specific infrastructure costs, policy requirement costs and professional site fees should be taken into account when assessing benchmark land value.

---

[87] PPG, Section on Viability, para. 019.

[88] PPG, Section on Viability, para. 009.

[89] PPG, Section on Viability, para. 020.

[90] See, for instance, *R (Perry) v Hackney LBC* [2014] EWHC 3499 (Admin); [2015] JPL 454.

[91] PPG, Section on Viability, para. 021.

[92] PPG, Section on Viability, para. 010.

[93] PPG, Section on Viability, para. 011.

[94] PPG, Section on Viability, para. 012.

- Land value, which should be assessed on the basis of existing use value,[95] plus a premium. The premium "should reflect the minimum return at which it is considered a reasonable landowner would be willing to sell their land".[96] Such a premium will provide a reasonable incentive, whilst allowing a sufficient contribution to allow compliance with policy requirements.[97] Calculations of land value should be based on considerations including market evidence, but such market evidence should be based on developments which comply with policies, including affordable housing. If there is no such evidence, then adjustments should be made to reflect the cost of policy compliance.[98] In the plan-making stage, then the premium should be assessed against the emerging policies in the plan, and any charge under the Community Infrastructure Levy. There is a further reference to the price paid for the land not constituting a relevant justification for failure to accord with relevant policies in the plan, when viability is assessed at the decision-making stage.[99] Alternative use value may be taken into account in limited circumstances (where there is an existing implementable permission for the use, or as set out by plan-makers).[100]

- Developer's return.[101] This is to be accounted for at the plan-making stage; and the onus is on developers (rather than local planning authorities) to mitigate those risks. The PPG suggests a figure of 15-20% of Gross Development Value to be applied as a suitable return, although alternative figures may be brought forward through the plan.

The Delivery of Housing

6.74   The amended NPPF puts additional emphasis upon the delivery of housing, rather than simply having land allocated for housing development. This manifests itself in four ways:

(i)   The application of the Housing Delivery Test so as to require an action plan in cases of a shortfall in housing delivery;

(ii)   The application of the tilted balance in certain cases of a shortfall in housing delivery;

(iii)   The application of the 20% buffer for housing land supply;

(iv)   Local planning authorities considering shorter deadlines for the implementation of the grant of planning permission.

---

[95] Existing use value is further explained in PPG, Section on Viability, para. 015.

[96] PPG, Section on Viability, para. 013.

[97] The premium is further explained in PPG, Section on Viability, para. 016.

[98] The controversy regarding the regard to be had to policy compliance is clear from *Parkhurst Road Ltd v SSCLG* [2018] EWHC 991 (Admin).

[99] PPG, Section on Viability, para. 014.

[100] This is more fully explained in PPG, Section on Viability, para. 017.

[101] PPG, Section on Viability, para. 018.

6.75   The Housing Delivery Test is defined in the Glossary as:

> "Measures net additional dwellings provided in a local authority area against the homes required, using national statistics and local authority data. The Secretary of State will publish the Housing Delivery Test results for each local authority in England every November."

6.76   The Government has published a Housing Delivery Test Measurement Rule Book.[102] Despite its somewhat daunting name, the Measurement Rule Book contains only seven pages of guidance. The main equation is that the total net number of homes delivered over a three-year period is divided by the total number of homes required over the three-year period, and this is expressed as a percentage.

6.77   The Housing Delivery Test does not apply to all planning authorities: the PPG makes clear that it does not apply to "National Park Authorities, the Broads Authority and development corporations without (or not exercising) both plan-making and decision-making functions".[103]

6.78   Specific explanation is provided of the concept of the net provision of homes, based on the National Statistic for net additional dwellings, with an addition to take into account the net increase in bedrooms in student communal accommodation, as well as the net increase in bedrooms in other communal accommodation.

6.79   The Measurement Rule Book sets out details in terms of the requirement figure for the calculations[104]. Essentially, where housing requirement policies are less than five years old, the requirement figure will be the requirement figure adopted in the policies, or the minimum annual local housing need figure produced by the standard methodology, if lower. Where housing requirement policies are more than five years old, then the figure will generally be the minimum annual local housing need figure from the standard methodology. If there is a stepped requirement, then this will be used; if there is no stepping, then the annual average housing requirement will be applied. Where a housing requirement is set as a range, the lower end of the range will apply.[105]

6.80   If a new housing requirement is adopted, then that figure will be <u>used</u> for the purposes of the Housing Delivery Test calculation from the date that it becomes part of the development plan.[106] For the purposes of <u>carrying out that calculation</u>, the requirement will apply from the start of the plan period, even if this is before the date on which the strategic policies are adopted.

6.81   The standard methodology for the assessment of housing did not apply prior to the adoption of the new NPPF. Therefore, it is not used for the calculation of the

---

[102] https://assets.publishing.service.gov.uk/government/uploads/system/uploads/attachment_data/file/728523/HDT_Measurement_Rule_Book.pdf, accessed 30 September 2018.

[103] PPG, Section on Housing and economic land availability assessment, para. 057.

[104] Which are summarised at Table 2 of the Measurement Rule Book, on p.9.

[105] PPG, Section on Housing and economic land availability assessment, para. 060.

[106] In the case of a neighbourhood plan, this can be before the formal making of the plan: PCPA s.38(3A)-(3B).

need figure up to and including the financial year 2017-18. Instead, an average is taken of years taken from household projections.[107]

6.82   If the delivery of housing according to the Housing Delivery Test falls by even a small margin, then the local planning authority will need to prepare an action plan. The threshold is set at delivery falling below 95% of the local planning authority's housing requirement over the previous three years. The action plan is to assess the causes of the under-delivery, and to identify actions to increase delivery.[108] The PPG sets out various stakeholders, who may be involved in the process, although it is up to the local planning authority to decide whom to involve.[109] The PPG suggests various matters which could be considered in the analysis of problems with delivery of housing. This includes not only the grant of sufficient permissions, but also determination periods, infrastructure provision, engagement with stakeholders, and barriers to delivery on sites which are identified within the five-year supply of housing.[110] The PPG suggest a number of potential actions to boost delivery.[111] The PPG suggests that the action plan should be published no later than six months after the publication of the result of the Housing Delivery Test.[112]

6.83   Potentially more concerning for local planning authorities is the fact that under-delivery of housing can lead to the application of the tilted balance. Footnote 7 to NPPF 11 provides that the tilted balance applies where "the Housing Delivery Test indicates that the delivery of housing was substantially below (less than 75% of) the housing requirement over the previous three years". Extensive transitional provisions are set out at NPPF 215. The Housing Delivery Test does not apply immediately on publication of the NPPF, but only from the publication of the Housing Delivery Test results in November 2008. There is a stepped application of the "substantially below" test. Delivery is substantially below the requirement where the November 2018 results indicate delivery below 25% of housing required over the previous three years; where the November 2019 results indicate delivery below 45% of housing required over the previous three years; where the November 2020 and subsequent results indicate delivery below 75% of housing required over the previous three years.

6.84   As stated above, the application of the 20% buffer is more specifically circumscribed by the new NPPF than was the case with the previous version. From November 2018, the test of a significant under-delivery of housing over the previous three years will apply where the Housing Delivery Test indicates that delivery was below 85% of the housing requirement.

---

[107] This is set out at Table 1 of the Measurement Rule Book, on p.8.

[108] Proposed details of the action plan, including suggestions of what could be reviewed, are set out in PPG, Section on housing and economic land availability assessment, paras 068-075.

[109] PPG, Section on Housing and economic land availability assessment, para. 070. Formal consultation is not mandatory in every case: PPG, Section on Housing and economic land availability assessment, para. 074.

[110] PPG, Section on Housing and economic land availability assessment, para. 071.

[111] PPG, Section on Housing and economic land availability assessment, para. 072.

[112] PPG, Section on Housing and economic land availability assessment, para. 073.

6.85   Sections 91 and 92 TCPA set out a default condition applying to the grant of full or outline planning permission, whereby development must be begun prior to the expiry of that period, or the permission will be lost. NPPF 76 requires local planning authorities to "consider imposing a planning condition providing that development must begin within a timescale shorter" than that period, so long as that requirement would "expedite the development without threatening its deliverability or viability". This is not an onerous requirement: essentially, the local planning authority has only to consider taking such steps, and they should do so only if it would be helpful and not harmful to the prospect of the development coming forward.

Rural Housing

6.86   Local planning authorities are to respond to the local circumstances and the needs of rural areas. The NPPF supports rural exceptional sites which bring forward affordable housing to meet local needs (and even consider market housing on such sites to facilitate this). The Glossary defines rural exception sites as:

> "Small sites used for affordable housing in perpetuity where sites would not normally be used for housing. Rural exception sites seek to address the needs of the local community by accommodating households who are either current residents or have an existing family or employment connection. A proportion of market homes may be allowed on the site at the local planning authority's discretion, for example where essential to enable the delivery of affordable units without grant funding."

6.87   As with the previous version of the NPPF, the new NPPF recognises that development in a village may support services in a nearby village (NPPF 78). The Court of Appeal has noted that there is no definition in the NPPF of "settlement" or "village" (*Braintree DC v SSCLG*, para. 32).[113] Lindblom LJ stated:

> "The NPPF contains no definitions of a "community", a "settlement", or a "village". There is no specified minimum number of dwellings, or population. It is not said that a settlement or development boundary must have been fixed in an adopted or emerging local plan, or that only the land and buildings within that settlement or development boundary will constitute the settlement. In my view a settlement would not necessarily exclude a hamlet or a cluster of dwellings, without, for example, a shop or post office of its own, or a school or community hall or a public house nearby, or public transport within easy reach. Whether, in a particular case, a group of dwellings constitutes a settlement, or a "village", for the purposes of the policy will again be a matter of fact and planning judgment for the decision-maker. In the [third sentence of NPPF 32] the policy acknowledges that development in one village may "support services" in another. It does not stipulate that, to be a "village", a settlement must have any "services" of its own, let alone "services" of any specified kind."

6.88   NPPF 79 indicates that by their policies and decisions, local planning authorities

---

[113] [2018] EWCA Civ 610; [2018] 2 P&CR 9.

should seek to avoid the development of isolated dwellings in the countryside, unless particular circumstances apply. Previously these were examples; the new NPPF sets these out as a closed list. Otherwise, the circumstances in sub-paragraphs (a)-(e) reflect those in para. 55 of the original NPPF, except that:

- Sub-paragraph (a), dealing with a dwelling for a rural worker now explicitly refers to those rural workers "taking majority control of a farm business".

- Sub-paragraph (d) is new, referring to development which would involve the subdivision of an existing residential dwelling.

6.89   A key question for the purposes of this aspect of national planning policy is whether proposed development is isolated. This question was recently considered by the Court of Appeal in *Braintree DC*. A developer had been refused planning permission for two dwellings in a village but outside the settlement boundary in an emerging development plan. Its appeal to a Planning Inspector was successful. A company subject to an enforcement notice also successfully appealed against the notice. Whilst none of the development was within a settlement boundary, the Inspector found that it was not isolated as there were dwellings nearby. The local planning authority challenged the Inspector's decision, arguing that the term "isolated" could mean physically isolated, functionally isolated, or isolated from services. This argument was rejected. The context of NPPF 79 has changed slightly since the previous version of the NPPF (which was similar to the combination of NPPF 78 and 79), but it seems likely that the same reasoning will apply. The true meaning of "isolated" "simply connotes a dwelling that is physically separate or remote from a settlement" (para. 31). Whether this was so was a matter of fact and planning judgment for a decision-maker in each individual case. NPPF 79 is not prescriptive in its terms, and should not be read as creating a "presumption" (para. 28). The Court of Appeal approved the comment of Lewison LJ in *Dartford BC v SSCLG*,[114] to the effect that a new dwelling within the curtilage of an existing residential dwelling will not be "isolated" for the purposes of NPPF 79.

6.90   Whilst the meaning of "isolated" is likely to be the same as in the original NPPF, the new NPPF is more prescriptive. The previous NPPF contemplated development in "special circumstances", of which the bullet points were examples. By contrast, NPPF 79 indicates that policies and decisions should avoid development of isolated dwellings in the countryside unless one or more of the sub-paragraphs apply. In the new NPPF, the sub-paragraphs are not examples; they are the only circumstances in which national planning policy contemplates development of isolated dwellings in the countryside.

6.91   The policy in the NPPF is less restrictive than that in pre-NPPF national planning policy. In *R (Embleton Parish Council) v Northumberland CC*,[115] HHJ Behrens held that policy in the original version of the NPPF was "significantly less onerous" than that in previous planning policy (para. 29), and noted that there was no requirement

---

[114] [2017] EWCA Civ 141; [2017] PTSR 737.
[115] [2013] EWHC 3631 (Admin); [2014] Env LR 16.

that the proposal is economically viable (para. 44).

Chapter 7

Business, Economy, Retail and Town Centres

Introduction

7.01   Reading about the publication of the NPPF in the Government's words, one may be forgiven for thinking that the NPPF concerns only the delivery of housing, and does not concern other development. The Statement made to Parliament on 24 July 2018, introducing the new NPPF, was entitled "Housing Policy", and started with the words: "Fixing our broken housing market is one of the Government's top domestic priorities". The Statement concerns the delivery of housing, design, the environment and the Green Belt. It is only in the penultimate paragraph that there is any reference to buildings other than dwellings, and even this appears to refer to the protection of existing development rather than supporting new proposals:[1]

> "[The amended NPPF] introduces new protections for churches, community pubs and music venues that play such a vital role in communities and can support the local economy."

7.02   However, it was an aim of the amended NPPF to make clear how important it is to support business growth and improved productivity.[2] Whilst not placed at the centre of the Government's publicity regarding the amended NPPF, there has been some change in policy.

The Economy

7.03   Whilst the economy was given a degree of attention in the first version of the NPPF, the policy wording has been strengthened. The reference to significant weight to supporting economic growth has now been bolstered in NPPF 80 to include a reference to productivity, and also a reference to "taking into account both local business needs and wider opportunities for development". NPPF 80 requires plans and decision to "allow each area to build on its strengths, counter any weaknesses and address the challenges of the future". The policy refers to the 2017 *Industry Strategy: Building a Britain fit for the future*.

7.04   The requirements for planning policies in NPPF 81 now include that the economic vision and strategy should have regard to Local Industrial Strategies and other local policies for economic development and regeneration. Flexibility is a matter which remains a requirement for policies (it is also mentioned in the presumption in favour of sustainable development regarding plan-making at NPPF 11). That particular sectors may have locational requirements is given more status in the new NPPF (NPPF 82), and there is new reference to storage and distribution operations.

---

[1]   This sentence appears to be referring to NPPF 182, which concerns ensuring that "new development can be integrated effectively with existing businesses and community facilities".

[2]   National Planning Policy Framework: Consultation proposals, Ministry of Housing, Communities and Local Government, March 2018, p.15.

7.05   There was little judicial interpretation of the equivalent of NPPF 80-82 in the original NPPF. In *R (Tesco Stores Ltd) v Forest of Dean DC*,[3] Patterson J noted that the policy in the NPPF was to support economic growth; this has obviously continued. On the facts of *Tesco Stores Ltd*, it was not irrational to impose a condition on the grant of planning permission which had an aim of supporting economic growth.

7.06   The previous NPPF had a paragraph discouraging the retention of long-term allocations of land for employment purposes where there was no reasonable prospect of a site being used for that purpose. This policy has been removed from the new NPPF. However, a similar result may be achieved by NPPF 120, which requires the review of land allocations.

The Rural Economy

7.07   Protecting the rural economy was formerly a separate section of the NPPF; it is now incorporated into Chapter 6. The guidance in NPPF 83 now applies not only to the creation of local plans, but also planning decisions. In relation to rural tourism, a sentence has been removed which was in the original NPPF which concerned tourist and visitor facilities where identified needs are not met by existing facilities in rural service centres. This could be included in NPPF 83(c), and so it may have been thought that the sentence was unnecessary; the change does not necessarily represent a substantive change in policy.

7.08   Policy recognises the special needs of the rural economy, whilst balancing this with a requirement that development is sustainable. The breadth of the support is demonstrated by encouragement of sustainable growth and expansion of "all types of business in rural areas", whether this is by changes of use or by new buildings. Diversification of agricultural holdings is encouraged, as is rural tourism, and the retention and development of accessible local services. The latter policy may serve to discourage applications seeking permission to change the use of buildings currently used as local shops, pubs, places of worship and other local community facilities.

7.09   Rural policy in the original NPPF was considered by the High Court in *R (Sienkiewicz) v South Somerset DC*.[4] This was a judicial review challenge to a decision to grant planning permission for industrial development in the countryside; the developer produced human and animal health care products. The company had grown since moving to the site, and was looking to increase its production facilities. The proposal would increase the number of employees. In one ground of the claim, the claimant argued that the local planning authority had assumed that the policies of the NPPF superseded those in the development plan, despite the primacy of the development plan. Although the planning permission was quashed, this ground of challenge was not made out. In the course of considering the relationship between the NPPF and the development plan, Lewis J observed that the NPPF "would support the grant of planning permission for even a large scale expansion of a business in a rural area assuming, of course, that any adverse effects of the proposed development were

---

3   [2014] EWHC 3348 (Admin).

4   [2013] EWHC 4090 (Admin); [2014] JPL 620.

considered acceptable and the proposed development was otherwise acceptable in planning terms" (para. 28).

7.10   After the first grant of planning permission was quashed on the basis of the imposition of an unlawful condition, the local planning authority once again granted permission to the developer. The same claimant brought a challenge to the new permission: *R (Sienkiewicz) v South Somerset DC*.[5] Ouseley J found that there had been errors in the way in which the Council had made the decision, but as the planning committee would have made the same decision, notwithstanding the errors, he declined to quash the grant of planning permission. In the course of his decision, Ouseley J made comments regarding the policy of the NPPF towards rural development. He stated that the "NPPF is positive, supportive, welcoming, not restricted to small-scale expansion or business" (para. 46).

7.11   NPPF policy concerning the rural environment was considered by Holgate J in *Dignity Funerals Ltd v Breckland DC*.[6] The challenge was to the third attempt by the local planning authority to grant planning permission for the erection of a new crematorium, car park, gardens of remembrance and associated development. The claimant, a commercial rival to the developer, had previously challenged a grant of planning permission which was quashed with the consent of the council; a local resident had challenged the second grant of permission, which was also quashed by consent. In the course of dismissing the challenge, Holgate J accepted the proposition that the NPPF distinctly encourages a positive approach to sustainable new development in rural areas, and does not require need to be shown for such development. Whilst this decision concerned the previous version of the NPPF, this description would also apply to NPPF 83.

7.12   New policy can be found in NPPF 84. This policy recognises the realities of rural development, in that local businesses or community facilities "may have to be found adjacent to or beyond existing settlements", and such locations may not be "well served by public transport". It goes on to say that "it will be important to ensure that development is sensitive to its surroundings, does not have an unacceptable impact on local roads and exploits any opportunities to make a location more sustainable…". Whilst the effect of the paragraph could be more clearly expressed, the policy seems to recognise that it may be necessary to permit development which would be unacceptable in other contexts.[7] However, in considering whether to grant permission, it is still necessary to consider the impacts, and there should be limits on the acceptable impacts. The policy finishes by encouraging the use of previously developed land, and development on sites that are "physically well-related to existing settlements".

---

5   [2015] EWHC 3704 (Admin); [2016] PTSR 815.

6   [2017] EWHC 1492 (Admin).

7   This appears to be the implication of the Ministry of Housing, Communities and Local Government's Equality Impact Assessment, at p. 6 (National Planning Policy Framework: Equality Impact Assessment, Ministry of Housing, Communities and Local Government, July 2018).

Town Centres

7.13   Changes in shopping patterns, including the rise of online retail, has put pressure on the dynamism of many town centres. As with the previous version of the NPPF, Chapter 7 of the new NPPF has emphasised the need to protect town centres. Whilst there have been some changes in emphasis,[8] the core policy of keeping town centre uses within the town centre itself, and the sequential test to encourage this, has remained.

7.14   Town Centre is defined in the Glossary as:

> "Area defined on the local authority's policies map, including the primary shopping area and areas predominantly occupied by main town centre uses within or adjacent to the primary shopping area. Reference to town centres or centres apply to city centres, town centres, district centres and local centres but exclude small parades of shops of purely neighbourhood significance. Unless they are identified as centres in the development plan, existing out-of-centre developments, comprising or including main town centre uses, do not constitute town centres."

7.15   Primary Shopping Area has a brief definition in the Glossary, being a "Defined area where retail development is concentrated".

7.16   Edge of Centre is likewise defined in the Glossary as:

> "For retail purposes, a location that is well connected to, and up to 300 metres from, the primary shopping area. For all other main town centre uses, a location within 300 metres of a town centre boundary. For office development, this includes locations outside the town centre but within 500 metres of a public transport interchange. In determining whether a site falls within the definition of edge of centre, account should be taken of local circumstances."

7.17   The definition of Out of Centre makes clear that the "centre" is different to the "urban area". Out of Centre is defined in the Glossary as "[a] location which is not in or on the edge of a centre but not necessarily outside the urban area".

7.18   The general aim of Chapter 7 is expressed in the first sentence of NPPF 85:

> "Planning policies and decisions should support the role that town centres play at the heart of local communities, by taking a positive approach to their growth, management and adaptation."

7.19   There follows a list of aims for town centres, including strategic aims (setting out a network and hierarchy of town centres) and spatial tools (defining the extent of town centres and the primary shopping area). As was explained in *Performance Retail Ltd Partnership v Eastbourne DC*,[9] the reference to a network and hierarchy of centres means that a plan must not only provide for centres, but that the relationship

---

[8]   The Equality Impact Assessment suggests that amendments have been made "to ensure a more flexible approach" (p.6).

[9]   [2014] EWHC 102 (Admin).

between centres, and their relative importance, should be set out. At para. 37, CMG Ockelton, sitting as a Judge of the High Court, held that "[t]o suggest that applications for development in any centre are to be considered on the same basis is to ignore the concept of a hierarchy".

7.20   The goal of ensuring that suitable town centre use can be located within the town centre means that town centre boundaries should be kept under review where necessary. The boundaries should be dictated by needs (including retail, leisure and office use), so that a lack of sites does not prevent such development from taking place in the town centre. When considering the requirement for a suitable range of sites, a local planning authority must look "at least ten years ahead" (NPPF 85(d)).

7.21   Whilst the previous NPPF did refer to the potential for residential development to play an important role in town centres, the significance of residential development has been somewhat increased. Rather than stating that residential development "can play an important role", NPPF 85(f) now states that residential development "often plays an important role in ensuring the vitality of centres". NPPF 85(a) refers to a mix of uses, including housing, being promoted through the planning process.

7.22   The PPG sets out indicators which are relevant in assessing the health of town centres:[10]

- diversity of uses

- proportion of vacant street level property

- commercial yields on non-domestic property

- customers' views and behaviour

- retailer representations and intentions to change representation

- commercial rents

- pedestrian flows

- accessibility

- perception of safety and occurrence of crime

- state of town centre environmental quality

The Sequential Test

7.23   The sequential test discourages out of centre development if there are suitable and available sites at the edge of centre or in the town centre. However, in one respect, it is less restrictive than pre-NPPF policy: it is no longer necessary for additional retail development outside a town centre to demonstrate quantitative or qualitative need. This had been extant policy under Planning Policy Statement 6 - Planning for Town Centres, from March 2005 to December 2009 (when it was replaced): see *Warners Retail (Moreton) Ltd v Cotswold DC*,[11] para. 29. The policy of the sequential

---

[10]   PPG, Section on Ensuring the vitality of town centres, para. 005. At the time of writing, this Section is yet to be updated following the publication of the new NPPF.

[11]   [2016] EWCA Civ 606.

test applies to planning applications (NPPF 87), and therefore it does not need to be incorporated into a local plan before it is a matter a decision-maker needs to take into account.[12] The PPG indicates that it is for an applicant to demonstrate compliance with the sequential test, and that failure to carry out a sequential assessment may justify a reason for refusing planning permission.[13] Conversely, compliance with the sequential test does not necessitate a grant of planning permission,[14] which may be unacceptable for non-retail reasons (including, for example, transport). One change made by the new NPPF is that a sequentially preferable site does not need to be available immediately – it is sufficient for the site to be available within a reasonable period. The Government's Consultation Response (p.31) states that advice on the meaning of "reasonable period" will be set out in updated planning guidance, presumably in the PPG. A proposal made in the draft amended version of the NPPF was that primary and secondary frontages need to be defined; this requirement has been removed from the final version "to encourage a more positive and flexible approach to planning for the future of town centres".[15]

7.24   *Warners Retail* concerned the grant of planning permission for an Out of Centre retail site. The claim was brought by the owners of a store which was at an Edge of Centre site (which was therefore sequentially superior. The claimants had obtained planning permission for an extension of their Edge of Centre store. The claimants argued that their site should not have been viewed as unavailable simply because it was owned by them (and not by the applicants). They argued in relation to suitability of the site, the local planning authority should have considered what need was intended to be met by the proposed new store, and whether the claimants' extended store could have met that need. It was also argued that the local planning authority had erred in relying upon the decision of the Supreme Court of *Tesco Stores Ltd v Dundee City Council*[16] regarding the suitability of a site.

7.25   The fact that there was no need test in modern national planning policy did not mean that the need for increased food retail provision was necessarily irrelevant to the planning balance: para. 32.

7.26   The Court of Appeal considered the need for flexibility, as is referred to in NPPF 87. If there were no such requirement for flexibility, then "the sequential approach would likely become a merely self-fulfilling activity, divorced from the public interest" (para. 31). A site would not meet the exact proposed design for an application, and would therefore not be suitable. On the facts before the local planning authority, it was legitimate to conclude that the applicant had not imposed inflexible requirements in testing the suitability of sites:

> "The only site said to have been a sequentially preferable alternative to Minton's

---

[12]   See *Performance Retain Ltd Partnership*, para. 39.

[13]   PPG, Section on Ensuring the vitality of town centres, para. 010.

[14]   PPG, Section on Ensuring the vitality of town centres, para. 010.

[15]   Government response to the draft revised National Planning Policy Framework consultation, Ministry of Housing, Communities and Local Government, July 2018, p.32.

[16]   [2012] UKSC 13; [2012] PTSR 983.

[i.e. the applicant's] is the site of the Budgens store [i.e. the Claimant's]. It is not suggested that that site could have accommodated an additional food store of the kind assumed by Minton for the purposes of the sequential test, even if the permitted extension to the Budgens store were not built."

7.27 In those circumstances, the Court of Appeal rejected the claimant's argument that the local planning authority should have considered the extent to which the claimant's site (as extended) could meet the need for food retail provision in the area. This would be to resurrect a test of need, which is no longer found in national planning policy. If the claimant's extension had been built-out by the time of the applicant's application, then (even on the claimant's case), there would have been no argument that there was a sequentially preferable site. This, if correct, would have left the application of the sequential test down to the commercial decision of the claimant, whether or not to build-out the planning permission. Lindblom LJ found that such an approach would be "hard to reconcile" with the policy to meet the need for retail development "in full". Whilst the exact phrase "in full" can no longer be found in the NPPF, it seems likely that the same policy intention motivates the new NPPF.

7.28 The Court of Appeal considered that, when applying the sequential test, it would be an error for a local planning authority to discount a site's availability on the basis that it is owned by a commercial rival (para. 39).[17] However, the local planning authority had not fallen into that error: they had lawfully concluded that there was no suitable site which could accommodate a foodstore of the type proposed.

7.29 The Court of Appeal also considered the decision of the Supreme Court in *Tesco Stores Ltd v Dundee City Council* regarding the suitability of a site. The Supreme Court had considered that the suitability of a site must be assessed in relation to the suitability for the development proposed, not for any development which would meet deficiencies of provision in the area. To take the latter approach would resurrect a test of need, which no longer features in national planning policy. However, Lindblom LJ was keen to point out that the policies being considered in *Tesco Stores* are not identical to those now found in the NPPF. It was not appropriate to simply read across from the Supreme Court's decision to the NPPF. However, on the facts, the local planning authority had not erred: it was clear that the requirement of flexibility in the NPPF had been lawfully considered.

7.30 Whilst the interpretation of the meaning of suitability and availability will be a matter of law for the courts, whether, on the facts of a particular application, a site is suitable or available is a matter for the decision-maker. Lindblom J noted the role of the decision-maker in *R (CBRE Lionbrook (General Partners) Ltd) v Rugby BC*.[18] This was a judicial review of a planning permission granted for major shopping development on the outskirts of Rugby. The claim was brought by the owner of a shopping centre in the town centre. Lindblom J described at para. 164 the sequential test as having been "an essential part of government policy for retail

---

[17] This appears to be reflected in the PPG, Section on Ensuring the vitality of town centres, para. 011.

[18] [2014] EWHC 646 (Admin).

development for some time". He went on to make clear that "[s]uitability and avail-ability are matters of planning judgment. They are not matters on which the court will substitute its own view for that of the decision-maker. The decision-maker's exercise of judgment upon them will not be vulnerable to challenge except on *Wednesbury* grounds".[19] The approach set out by national policy is not supposed to be "a uniform and inflexible approach".

7.31   The Court of Appeal rejected without hesitation[20] a challenge to an Inspector's decision granting planning permission on appeal, where the grounds of challenge before the court were detailed disagreements with the Inspector's decision: *Telford and Wrekin Council v SSCLG*.[21] The Court of Appeal's decision is however helpful for making clear that, if a decision-maker lawfully concludes that a (potential) alternative site is not sequentially superior to an application site, then it is not strictly necessary to consider issues of suitability, availability and viability of the alternative site (paras 40-41). The Inspector had however not erred in reaching conclusions on matters which had been subject to detailed consideration and argument at a lengthy inquiry before her. The consideration of sequential superiority includes giving preference to "accessible sites which are well connected to the town centre" (NPPF 76).

7.32   In *CBRE Lionbrook*, it was a material consideration in applying the sequential test on the facts that there was a particular concern regarding the retail provision leaving the borough altogether. This "lent a degree of urgency to the Council's application of the sequential test in this case" (para. 170). The appropriate timescale for con-sidering the sequential test was a matter for the Council to consider. The Council took a period of five years for the assessment, and there was nothing unlawful about this (paras 171-173). The Council's decision reflected the "pragmatism called for in the application of the sequential test".

7.33   Ouseley J considered an interesting question in *Aldergate Properties Ltd v Mansfield DC*:[22] when considering the sequential test, could a local planning authority take into account the fact that a sequentially preferable location would compete with the applicant's own stores in the town centre? The claimant challenged a grant of planning permission which would be used for an Aldi store. There were already Aldi stores in the town. The claimant argued that the applicant's lack of desire to compete with its own stores could not rule out sites in the town centre, and this approach failed to apply the requirement of flexibility. Ouseley J held at para. 35:

> "I have no doubt but that [Leading Counsel for the claimant's] essential argument is correct, for a variety of reasons. In my judgment, "suitable"

---

[19]   A reference to *Associated Provincial Picture Houses Ltd v Wednesbury Corporation* [1948] 1 KB 223: a decision will be challengeable if it is not within the statutory powers of the decision-maker, it ignores relevant considerations or takes into account irrelevant considerations, or it makes a decision which is so unrea-sonable that no reasonable decision-maker could have made it.

[20]   Indeed, the decision appears to have been given "unreserved", i.e. Sullivan LJ delivered judgment on the same day as oral argument.

[21]   [2014] EWCA Civ 507.

[22]   [2016] EWHC 1670 (Admin).

and "available" generally mean "suitable" and "available" for the broad type of development which is proposed in the application by approximate size, type, and range of goods. This incorporates the requirements of flexibility in [NPPF 87], and excludes, generally, the identity and personal or corporate attitudes of an individual retailer. The area and sites covered by the sequential test search should not vary from applicant to applicant according to their identity, but from application to application based on their content."

7.34   Ouseley J relied on the use of the word "required" in para. 24 of the old NPPF. Nevertheless, it seems likely that his reasoning would apply, despite the lack of this wording in the new NPPF: NPPF 90 provides that an application which fails the sequential test "should be refused". The decision in *Aldergate Properties* is sensible. Whilst the courts are generally slow to quash decisions made under the sequential test, allowing the individual requirements of the applicant to take precedence would be contrary to the general principle of planning law that planning permission should be blind as to the identity of the applicant. The imposition of a condition tying the development to a particular occupant would not save the process. Ouseley J based his decision on the further consideration of availability, another requirement within the sequential test:

"A town centre site may be owned by a retailer already, to use itself for retailing, who is not going to make it available to another retailer. It is plainly available for retailing, though only to one retailer. That does not mean that another retailer can thus satisfy the sequential test and so go straight to sites outside the town centre. "Available" cannot mean available to a particular retailer but must mean available for the type of retail use for which permission is sought."

7.35   The claimant in *R (Midcounties Co-operative Ltd) v Forest of Dean DC*[23] sought to persuade the court that the local planning authority had, in that case, made the same mistake as in *Aldergate Properties*, in finding that the site was too small for the developer, rather than the broad type of development which was contemplated. The difficulty with this argument was that the council's resolution did not make that error: it referred to whether a potential alternative site "was not comparable or suitable for the broad type of development". The court did not agree with the claimant that the discussions of Councillors as recorded in the minutes showed that the resolution did not reflect the true basis of the decision.

7.36   NPPF 88 replicates the policy in the previous version of the NPPF that the sequential test does not apply to "applications for small scale rural offices or other small scale rural development".

The Retail Impact Test

7.37   NPPF 89 sets out a retail impact test. The test applies where applications for retail and leisure development are assessed for sites outside town centres, "which are not in accordance with an up-to-date plan". It no longer includes office development,

---

[23] [2017] EWHC 2056 (Admin).

which featured in the original NPPF.[24] An application may not be in accordance with an up-to-date plan for one of two reasons: it may be that there is an up-to-date plan, but the application is not in accordance with it, or it may be that there is no up-to-date plan. NPPF 89 requires a proportionate, locally-set threshold (in default of which, a threshold of 2,500m² gross floorspace applies)[25] for assessment of the impact of the development. The assessment should consider the impact of the proposal of investment, both public and private, and whether existing, committed or planned, in centre(s) in the catchment area of the proposal, and the impact upon vitality and viability of the town centre, including local consumer choice and trade in the town centre, as well as the wider retail catchment.[26] The PPG has stressed that impact should be assessed in relation to all town centres potentially affected by the proposed development, not just those closest to the proposal; it may affect town centres in other local planning authority areas.[27]

7.38   Even if the application succeeds on the sequential test, if it would be likely to have significant adverse impact on one or more of investment, vitality or viability of the town centre, then NPPF 90 provides that planning permission should be refused.

7.39   The planning permission under scrutiny in *Midcounties Cooperative Ltd* was ultimately quashed for a failure on the part of the local planning authority to consider the question of impact on the town centre. It was not clear what decision would have been made if impact had been taken into account, which would require the exercise of planning judgment (para. 117).

---

[24]   The Government's proposals, set out in the Consultation proposals for the NPPF, March 2018 (p.16) explained the reasons for the change: "the Government considers that the approach to offices is covered sufficiently by the sequential approach, and is aware that there is no generally accepted or used method for assessing office impacts". The former reason is perhaps more robust than the latter: if the Government's sole concern was a lack of methodology for assessing office impacts, then presumably it could devise one and promote it through the PPG.

[25]   The PPG explains gross floorspace: "Gross retail floorspace (or gross external area) is the total built floor area measured externally which is occupied exclusively by a retailer or retailers, excluding open areas used for the storage, display or sale of goods": PPG, Section on Ensuring the vitality of town centres, para. 016.

[26]   The PPG provides detailed guidance on carrying out the impact test, including a checklist: Section on Ensuring the vitality of town centres, paras 017-018.

[27]   PPG, Section on Ensuring the vitality of town centres, para. 013.

Chapter 8

Communities, Transport, Effective Use of Land and Design

Introduction

8.01   This chapter deals with four chapters of the NPPF:

- Chapter 8: 'Promoting healthy and safe communities'

- Chapter 9: 'Promoting sustainable transport'

- Chapter 11: 'Making effective use of land'

- Chapter 12: 'Achieving well-designed places'

8.02   These chapters concern important matters in terms of making development work for the communities it is intended to serve. However, the aims are often quite broad, and the concepts subjective. This makes them less likely to give rise to hard-edged questions of interpretation which are the main focus of this book.

Promoting Healthy and Safe Communities

8.03   NPPF 91-92 set out a number of aims for policy-making and decision-taking. The planning system should promote safe interaction, make safe and accessible places, and enable and support healthy lifestyles. There is support for shared spaces, community facilities and local services, and local strategies to improve the health, social and cultural well-being for all sections of the community. Valued facilities and services should not be lost unnecessarily, and established shops and services should be given the support to make the changes necessary to ensure that they survive. An integrated approach should be taken to housing, economic uses and community facilities.

8.04   These paragraphs suggest that proposals for residential led development should not merely seek to maximise the quantity of housing which can be placed on a site at the expense of the aspects of a settlement which allow it to perform as a well functioning community. NPPF 92(b) stresses the interests of "all sections of the community". Section 149 of the Equality Act 2010 provides that regard should be had to the need to eliminate discrimination, harassment, victimisation and other conduct prohibited under the Equality Act, to advance equality of opportunity between persons who share a relevant characteristic protected under the Equality Act, and those who do not share it, and to foster good relations between persons who share such a relevant protected characteristic and persons who do not share it.

8.05   NPPF 93 gives the support of national planning policy to estate regeneration, and notes the "social, economic and environmental benefits" which it can provide. The provision of estate regeneration should be to a high standard, being achieved through the use of a local authority's planning powers.

8.06   The availability of sufficient school places is dealt with in NPPF 94. Not only should local planning authorities seek to ensure that there are enough school places in a numerical sense, but should be proactive, positive and collaborative in seeking development that will "widen choice in education". NPPF 94(a) makes specific provision regarding weight: great weight should be given to the need to create, expand or alter schools. This applies both in the preparation of plans and decisions on individual applications. The pre-application stage is identified as important in NPPF 94(b): local planning authorities should seek "to identify and resolve key planning issues before applications are submitted".

8.07   NPPF 95 recognises that particular consideration will need to be given to public safety, wider security concerns and defence requirements, in certain circumstances. In areas where large numbers of people congregate, particular consideration should be given to the risk from both natural and malicious sources. In policy creation, this will involve consultation with the police and other agencies. Development for operational defence and security purposes is to be supported, and where such facilities already exist, they should not be prejudiced by further proposed development.

Open Spaces and Recreation

8.08   NPPF 96-101 is headed "Open space and recreation". Of these, NPPF 99-101 concern Local Green Spaces. "Open Space" is defined in the Glossary as:

> "All open space of public value, including not just land, but also areas of water (such as rivers, canals, lakes and reservoirs) which offer important opportunities for sport and recreation and can act as a visual amenity."

8.09   The NPPF promotes access to open spaces, and opportunities for sport and physical activity. When making plans, NPPF 96 requires local planning authorities to consider "robust and up-to-date assessments of the need for open space, sport and recreation facilities". New provision should be supported through plans as the assessments indicate is necessary. A high level of policy protection is given to <u>existing</u> open space, sports and recreational buildings by NPPF 97. Land used as open space or for playing fields should not be built upon, and recreational buildings should not be lost, unless one of three tests is satisfied:

(a)   The open space, buildings or land are surplus to requirements according to an assessment; or

(b)   The loss would be replaced by equivalent or better provision, both in terms of quantity <u>and</u> quality, and this must be in a suitable location; or

(c)   Where development is proposed for alternative sports or recreational provision, the benefits clearly outweigh the loss or the current or former use.

8.10   The Court of Appeal stressed in *R (Loader) v Rother DC*[1] that the tests in NPPF 97 are disjunctive, in that if one of them is satisfied, then the others do not need to be. The local planning authority accepted that NPPF 97(b) was satisfied. This did not require an assessment to be carried out, and therefore it was irrelevant that there

---

[1]   [2016] EWCA Civ 795; [2017] JPL 25.

had been no such assessment. As the new sports facilities would be an improvement on what had been present, this was more than sufficient to satisfy compliance with NPPF 97(b), and therefore with the test as a whole. The definition of "open space" includes a reference to "public value". Lindblom LJ considered the relevance of visual amenity, bearing in mind the definition of open space, in *Loader*, and held at para. 24:

> "Tests framed in terms of open space, buildings or land being "surplus to requirements" and alternative or equivalent or better "provision" of such facilities are not, I think, germane to a site's "visual amenity". However, in so far as "visual amenity" and "the social well-being or social interests of the community" contributed to the "public value" of the open space on the site, their protection was, in my view, inherent in the application of the [local policy] and [NPPF 97] tests, and were dealt with appropriately in this case by the application of those tests. To the extent that these considerations went beyond the ambit of those tests, they were taken into account and given due weight in the council's decision."

8.11　Lindblom LJ therefore did not need to reach a definitive view on the relevance of visual amenity to the requirements of the NPPF, since it was undoubtedly otherwise taken into account in the decision. A possible answer may be that visual amenity may be relevant to the assessment of a proposal under NPPF 97, but only to the extent to which visual amenity is relevant to the site's role in its capacity as an open space, sports or recreational building or land. If visual amenity would not be relevant to the purpose of a site as, for instance, a hockey pitch, then it need not be taken into account in the NPPF 97 exercise.

8.12　If an assessment is to be carried out of the need for sports and recreation facilities, the PPG points authorities and developers to Sport England's Guidance.[2]

8.13　Notwithstanding the reference to quantity and quality being maintained in NPPF 97(b), this need not be applied mechanistically. In *Turner v SSCLG*,[3] Collins J rejected an argument that quantity would necessarily have to be preserved in circumstances where existing open spaces were largely unused by the public. At para. 37, he considered that a "requirement in such circumstances for equivalent quantity is too restrictive and would, if applied to the letter, prevent sensible development when in reality there has been no overall loss". Whether this is strictly speaking a matter of the interpretation of the NPPF, or its application in the particular facts of this case, is not entirely clear.

8.14　Public rights of way are the subject of NPPF 98: policies and decisions should protect and enhance such rights of way and access. The local planning authority should take into account the possibility of adding links to existing rights of way networks.

2　http://www.sportengland.org/facilities-planning/planning-for-sport/planning-tools-and-guidance/, accessed 30 September 2018.

3　[2015] EWHC 375 (Admin); [2015] JPL 936.

Local Green Spaces

8.15   A designation of land as Local Green Space is significant, as NPPF 101 provides that policies for development within Local Green Spaces "should be consistent with those for Green Belts". Such policy is amongst the most restrictive in national planning policy. The restrictive nature of the designation is clear from the PPG, which states "Local Green Space designation is a way to provide special protection against development for green areas of particular importance to local communities".[4]

8.16   As with the Green Belt, Local Green Space should be designated only when a plan is prepared or updated. The designation should be capable of lasting beyond the end of the period of the plan being prepared or updated. NPPF 99-100 are concerned to ensure that designation of Local Green Space is not too extensive, and should not prejudice the provision of sufficient homes, jobs and essential services. Furthermore, the Local Green Space must meet certain characteristics: it must be reasonably close to the community it serves, it must be "demonstrably special to a local community and hold particular local significance", and must be "local in character and...not an extensive tract of land".

8.17   The interpretation of NPPF policy concerning Local Green Space was in issue in *R (Legard) v RB Kensington and Chelsea*.[5] This claim concerned a challenge to a local planning authority permitting a neighbourhood plan to proceed to referendum. The controversy concerning the NPPF concerned whether the site "served" the local community. The claimant stated that the public has no access to the site, and views of it were limited. Dove J rejected the argument. He considered that the requirement that the Local Green Space "serve" the community is met through consideration of whether the site is "demonstrably special", and holds a "particular significance" for the local community. That the land must serve the community added nothing further to these requirements. The tests in NPPF 100 overlap; they are not completely distinct. Dove J referred to a passage from the PPG, which states that "the proximity of the Local Green Space to the community it serves will depend on local circumstances, including why the Green Area is seen as special, but it must be reasonably close".[6]

8.18   The PPG indicates that Local Green Space designation "will rarely be appropriate where the land has planning permission for development", but a designation may nevertheless be appropriate if the development would not be inconsistent with the reasons for designating land as Local Green Space, or where the planning permission could no longer be implemented. Interestingly, the PPG suggests that Local Green Space can be designated in new communities;[7] it is implied that the area could hold

---

[4]   PPG, Section on Open space, sports and recreation facilities, public rights of way and local green space, para. 005. At the time of writing, this Section of the PPG is yet to be amended following the new NPPF..

[5]   [2018] EWHC 32 (Admin); [2018] PTSR 1415.

[6]   PPG, Section on Open space, sports and recreation facilities, public rights of way and local green space, para. 014.

[7]   PPG, Section on Open space, sports and recreation facilities, public rights of way and local green space, para. 012. At the time of writing, this is yet to be updated following the new NPPF.

"particular local significance" notwithstanding the fact that the community is yet to come into existence, but it seems that this would be relatively unusual.

Promoting Sustainable Transport

8.19   Notwithstanding the title of Chapter 9, most of the Chapter concerns ensuring that proposals for development have access to suitable transport options, rather than development for transport infrastructure itself.

8.20   The NPPF is clear that transport should be considered at an early stage, not only in plan-making, but also in decision-taking (NPPF 102). This helps ensure that the design of the project is consistent with sustainable transport, that an adequate assessment of the impact upon transport networks can be assessed (as can the environmental impact of the use of such transport) and that the full potential for use of proposed transport infrastructure, and opportunities to promote walking, cycling and public transport can be realised. Policies may have a positive impact upon transport, without relating to transport directly themselves: a mixed-use development may be more sustainable in transport terms, as it may minimise the number and length of journeys (for instance, if a residential-led development also includes a supermarket, then residents would not need to travel out of the development in order to shop for their groceries). As with the previous version, the new NPPF recognises that what may be achievable in terms of sustainable transport will differ as between urban and rural areas.

8.21   The Glossary defines sustainable transport modes as:

> "Any efficient, safe and accessible means of transport with overall low impact on the environment, including walking and cycling, low and ultra low emission vehicles, car sharing and public transport."

8.22   Plans should set out "high quality walking and cycling networks", and cycle parking (NPPF 104(d)). Any large scale transport facilities should be planned for, which may involve collaboration with other bodies (NPPF 104(e)).

8.23   NPPF 105 sets out guidance for parking standards for residential and non-residential development. Maximum parking standards are to be provided only in the limited circumstances set out in NPPF 106 (including there being a clear and compelling justification). NPPF 107 sets out a new policy regarding providing adequate overnight lorry parking facilities, which did not appear in the previous version of the NPPF. However, the specific policy provision regarding appropriate provision for motorcycles in town centres no longer appears in the new version of the NPPF.

8.24   When assessing sites for policies, or specific applications for development, the decision-maker must ensure that opportunities to promote sustainable transport modes are taken up, that all users can access the site safely and by suitable access, and that any significant impacts on the transport network or on highway safety can be "cost effectively mitigated to an acceptable degree" (NPPF 108). The requirement for a developer seeking planning permission for a proposal generating significant amounts of movement to produce a travel plan has been maintained (NPPF 111). A transport statement or assessment still needs to be produced, so that the likely impacts of the development in travel terms can be assessed.[8]

8.25 Transport assessment is defined in the Glossary as:[9]

> "A comprehensive and systematic process that sets out transport issues relating to a proposed development. It identifies measures required to improve accessibility and safety for all modes of travel, particularly for alternatives to the car such as walking, cycling and public transport, and measures that will be needed [to] deal with the anticipated transport impacts of the development."

8.26 Transport statement is defined in the Glossary as:

> "A simplified version of a transport assessment where it is agreed the transport issues arising from development proposals are limited and a full transport assessment is not required."

8.27 Presumably the agreement referred to is agreement between the applicant for planning permission and the local planning authority.

8.28 Travel plan is defined in the Glossary as:

> "A long-term management strategy for an organisation or site that seeks to deliver sustainable transport objectives and is regularly reviewed."

8.29 In the previous version of the NPPF, it was the case that proposals should be turned down on transport grounds only "where the residual cumulative impacts of development [were] severe". Whilst a severe impact on the road network has remained a ground for refusing development in NPPF 109, the new version of the NPPF makes clear that an unacceptable impact on highway safety would also justify a refusal on highways grounds. NPPF 109, in full, states:

> "Development should only be prevented or refused on highways grounds if there would be an unacceptable impact on highway safety, or the residual cumulative impacts on the road network would be severe."

8.30 The decision of the Court of Appeal in *Redhill Aerodrome Ltd v SSCLG*[10] mainly related to the policies of the previous version of the NPPF concerning the Green Belt. However, the claimant had argued that the NPPF should be interpreted as a whole, and that NPPF highways policies affected the way in which the court should approach Green Belt policies. This led the Court of Appeal to consider the test of severe residual cumulative impacts.

8.31 Sullivan LJ explained the meaning of "residual cumulative impacts" as "those traffic impacts which would remain after any highway improvement to limit the significant impacts of the development have been carried out" (para. 27). He considered that the policy is unusual in providing for the only basis on which permission may be

---

[8]   The PPG has a specific Section which deals with Travel Plans, Transport Assessments and Statements.

[9]   Whilst not relevant to its interpretation, it is striking that this definition appears to include a grammatical mistake; the second sentence needs the word in square brackets adding.

[10] [2014] EWCA Civ 1386; [2015] PTSR 274.

refused (i.e. severe cumulative impacts).

8.32   It is not entirely clear how the NPPF 109 safety/severity test fits with the require-ments in NPPF 108, which apply at both plan-making and decision-taking stage. It may be that the requirements of NPPF 108, including in relation to significance of impact (or highway safety) being cost-effectively mitigated is used as a means of considering how the NPPF 109 test will apply to the facts of a particular application. Likewise, if safe and suitable access to the site cannot be achieved for all users, this <u>may</u> mean that there would be an unacceptable impact on highway safety. However, whilst NPPF 110 is expressly within the context of NPPF 109, NPPF 108 is not.

8.33   Proposals for development should give priority to pedestrian and cycle movements, "both within the scheme and with neighbouring areas" (NPPF 110(a)).[11] The second objective, in terms of priority, is to facilitate access to high quality public transport. This should be achieved both through layout to maximise the catchment of public transport facilities, and there should be appropriate facilities to encourage public transport use (the latter may include bus shelters).

8.34   Whilst the duty under section 149 of the Equality Act 2010 requires the needs of those with disabilities to be taken into account, NPPF 110(b) requires the "needs of people with disabilities and reduced mobility in relation to all modes of transport" to be <u>addressed</u>. On its face, this is a potentially onerous duty. It is broad, given that it relates to all modes of transport. It is also strict, given that it requires the needs to be addressed. It goes beyond the duty in the former NPPF to "consider the needs of people with disabilities".[12]

8.35   The places which are created by developments are required to minimise the scope for conflicts between those travelling by different modes. Unnecessary street clutter should be avoided, and should "respond to local character and design standards" (NPPF 110(c)). Convenient charging points for low-emission forms of transport should be provided (NPPF 110(e)).

Achieving Well-designed Places

8.36   Whether a proposal is well-designed is quintessentially a matter of judgment for the decision-maker. Moreover, the concepts which express the quality of design are generally open-textured and non-prescriptive. The scope for the courts to intervene in decisions concerning the design of development is therefore limited.[13] However, perhaps in order to ensure that the subjective nature of design assessment is mini-mised, the NPPF promotes the use of design guides and codes. "Design code" is defined in the Glossary as:

---

[11]   Presumably this does not require a developer to achieve this on an area outside its control by some sort of *Grampian* condition.

[12]   This was in para. 35 of the former NPPF; it is not entirely clear whether this related only to plan-making or also decision-taking.

[13]   In *Horsham DC v SSCLG* [2015] EWHC 109 (Admin), Lindblom J held at para. 41 that judgments on design "are among the most difficult to upset in proceedings such as these, because widely differing views on the quality of a particular design can fall within the range of reasonable judgment".

"A set of illustrated design requirements that provide specific, detailed parameters for the physical development of a site or area. The graphic and written components of the code should build upon a design vision, such as a masterplan or other design and development framework for a site or area".

8.37 Design is about more than simply the architecture of individual buildings. NPPF 127(b) refers to "good architecture, layout and effective designing". Likewise, ensuring good or consistent design is about more than just the materials which are used for the facing of a building. NPPF 127(d) refers to the arrangement of streets, spaces, building types and materials.

8.38 The weight to be given to design has been emphasised by the Government in the amendments to the new NPPF. Although the new NPPF seeks to emphasise the delivery of housing development, it does not seek to do so at the expense of design quality. It is now said that creating high quality buildings and places "is fundamental to what the planning and development process should achieve" (NPPF 124).[14] According to NPPF 130, a decision-maker should refuse permission for a proposal which "fails to take the opportunities available for improving the character and quality of an area and the way it functions". The requirement to secure improvement, rather than merely preservation of the area is a weighty burden. This may in part explain the importance which the NPPF places on engagement in relation to design (see below); engaging with the community will assist a developer in designing development to improve the way it works.

8.39 Lindblom J considered in *Horsham DC v SSCLG*[15] whether the requirement to refuse planning permission for poorly designed development which does not improve the area meant that planning permission had to be refused in circumstances where a proposal with a lesser impact upon views may come forward in due course. Lindblom J rejected this argument. He held that design which fails to take a particular opportunity for improvement is one kind of poor design. But he held at para. 39 that the requirement in the NPPF does not mean "that a proposal which does not take every conceivable opportunity to improve the character and quality of an area, or which does not do as well in this respect as some alternative proposal might have done, must therefore automatically be rejected". Design needs to be assessed in the round, and the weight to be given to the various factors in considering design is a matter for the decision-maker. It seems likely that, if the decision-maker has applied his or her mind to the policy at NPPF 130, then it will be difficult to overturn the decision on such grounds.

8.40 Despite the weight which the NPPF places on good design, this is not to be an excuse to refuse acceptable planning permission. In a passage which is perhaps more relevant to a developer making a costs application in an appeal to a Planning Inspector than to a High Court challenge to a decision, NPPF 130 states that "where the design

---

[14] This is similar to the PPG, which states that "[g]ood quality design is an integral part of sustainable development": PPG, Section on Design, para. 001. In *Horsham DC v SSCLG* [2015] EWHC 109 (Admin), Lindblom J held at para. 11 that the guidance in the PPG "amplifies the policy in the NPPF".

[15] [2015] EWHC 109 (Admin).

of a development accords with clear expectations in plan policies, design should not be used by the decision-maker as a valid reason to object to development".

8.41   Particularly for large scale development proposals, it is common for a developer to have to amend the proposal between the grant of planning permission, and the development being built out. NPPF 130 requires local planning authorities to be wise to the risk that such amendments may lead to a diminution in design quality, stating:

> "Local planning authorities should...seek to ensure that the quality of approved development is not materially diminished between permission and completion, as a result of changes being made to the permitted scheme (for example through changes to approved details such as the materials used)."

8.42   The NPPF emphasises the significance of design being a matter which involves the local community. Engagement between the developer and other stakeholders (the local planning authority, the community, and other interests)[16] is important. Engagement can be a means of reconciling local and commercial interests (and, less optimistically, "clarifying expectations"). In a striking passage, NPPF 128 states:

> "Applications that can demonstrate early, proactive and effective engagement with the community should be looked on more favourably than those that cannot."

8.43   This would appear to indicate that engagement with the community is a matter which weighs in the planning balance. It is independent of the merits of what is actually proposed: positive engagement is a matter which should be taken into account as a reason to grant planning permission. In theory,[17] therefore, if there were two identical applications which were close to the line in terms of whether they should be granted planning permission, if the developer were to engage in a positive way, and the other were not to engage at all, this could be a justification for granting planning permission for the former despite refusing the latter.

8.44   There are a number of reasons why engagement may be capable of tipping the balance in terms of an application for planning permission:

- This is a means for national planning policy to encourage applicants to engage prior to making applications, which itself is positive in terms of increasing the quality of development and the prospect that proposed development would be acceptable to the community.

- If a developer has properly engaged with other stakeholders, then it is more likely that the proposal will have taken whatever steps are available to resolve

---

[16]   Presumably including Historic England, for developments which may have an impact upon designated heritage assets.

[17]   Such an example would never arise: if the applications were simultaneous then the engagement for the one would presumably count towards engagement for the identical other proposal. If the applications were not simultaneous, then the situations would likely not be identical (the housing land supply in the area would be likely to have changed, and the grant or refusal of the first application would be a matter to take into account in the consideration of the second application).

the matters which weigh against the development in the planning balance.[18] This may reflect the requirement that the engagement be effective.

8.45   The previous version of the NPPF stressed that policies should not attempt to be too prescriptive regarding design. The amended NPPF appears less concerned about this as an issue. Indeed, NPPF 125 indicates that the design vision in the plan should be clear, seeking that "applicants have as much certainty as possible about what is likely to be acceptable". The new NPPF indicates that neighbourhood plans may play an important role in making clear what is special about an area, and how development should reflect that special feature. Some areas will require a greater level of prescriptiveness in design guidance than others (NPPF 126). Some variety may be justified in proposals.

8.46   Perhaps as part of the compromise (or, some might say, marriage)[19] between good design and the delivery of residential development, the NPPF does not indicate that good design requires low density. NPPF 127(c) specifically contemplates that increased density may be an appropriate innovation or change which should not be prevented or discouraged by planning decisions and policies. Likewise, NPPF 127(e) requires decision-makers and policy-makers to "optimise the potential" of the site, including in relation to the amount of development.

8.47   As in the previous NPPF, great weight should be given to outstanding or innovative designs, if they help to raise the standard of design more generally in the area (NPPF 131). However, the new version of the NPPF makes clear that the designs must still "fit in with the overall form and layout of their surroundings".

8.48   The NPPF's policy for the control over advertisements is found in NPPF 132. The previous version of the NPPF restricted which advertisements should be subject to detailed assessment, limiting it to where advertisements "will clearly have an impact upon a building or on their surroundings". This aspect has been removed from the new NPPF.

Making Effective Use of Land

8.49   Chapter 11 of the new NPPF is a new chapter: it was not found in the previous version of the NPPF. Some of the principles found in Chapter 11 were previously found in the now-removed twelve core planning principles, which had previously been found in para. 17 of the original NPPF. The main purpose of Chapter 11 is to promote the appropriate use of brownfield and underdeveloped land, to ensure that appropriate development is not held back by an inappropriate historic development plan designation, and to ensure that development is of appropriate density.

8.50   NPPF 118 notes that development of land can have multiple benefits, but also that land which is left undeveloped can perform multiple functions. The re-use of

---

[18] Planning permission should not be refused for acceptable development for the sole reason that a preferable proposal could be contemplated: *Horsham DC v SSCLG* [2015] EWHC 109 (Admin), para. 1. However, that is different to saying that, if there is planning harm which could practically be avoided, then the possibility of avoiding the harm should be ignored.

[19] Some others may say that the two are synonymous.

brownfield land, the development of under-utilised land and buildings, and the use of airspace and upward extensions are all supported by NPPF 118.

8.51 The NPPF wishes to avoid land being tied up by designations which are no longer appropriate. NPPF 120 provides that, if land has been allocated for a use for which there is no reasonable prospect of an application coming forward, then the local planning authority should reallocate the land for a use for which there is a more deliverable use which can help to address identified needs. Until such time, applications for alternative uses should be supported, if the proposed use would contribute to meeting an unmet need. NPPF 121 supports alternative changes of use, which would help meet unmet needs. This includes in particular the use of retail and employment land for housing development in areas where there is high housing demand (subject to this not undermining key economic sectors and sectors or the vitality and viability of town centres, and where not otherwise inconsistent with the NPPF). Applications should be supported for making more effective uses of sites that provide community services.

8.52 Density is the subject of NPPF 122-123. NPPF 123 in particular deals with circumstances of existing or anticipated shortfall of land. In such areas, low density housing should be avoided in plan-making and decision-taking. Policies should include minimum densities for city and town centres and for other areas well served by public transport. The standards should not serve to continue the *status quo*, but "seek a significant uplift in the average density of residential development within these areas, unless it can be shown that there are strong reasons why this would be inappropriate". It would appear that local planning authorities will struggle to defend policies which do not have an uplift at examination, in the face of the requirement of "strong reasons". Even outside of such areas, minimum density standards should be appropriate. If the use of land is inefficient, then local planning authorities should refuse applications where there is a current or projected shortfall in housing land supply. A flexible approach should be taken to sunlight and daylight policies. In practice, this suggests that the weight to be given to such policies may need to be reduced. However, the development would still need to provide acceptable living standards.

Chapter 9

Supporting High Quality Communications

Introduction

9.01　The NPPF has a short chapter on communications. The importance of a high quality communications network is stressed in national policy. However, the Government is keen to avoid a proliferation of communications masts, and to avoid interference with existing infrastructure and services. The NPPF specifies what evidence should be included with applications.

The Support for Infrastructure

9.02　High quality communications infrastructure is, says NPPF 112, "essential for economic growth and social well-being". Policy support is given to enabling access to services from a range of providers (NPPF 112), and local planning authorities in determining applications should not "seek to prevent competition between different operators" (NPPF 116). Local planning authorities should not select certain areas for a ban on new electronic communications development, or impose directions under Art 4 of the GPDO restricting permitted development rights over a wider area or for a wide range of electronic communications development. Minimum distances between new electronic communications development and existing development should not be sought (NPPF 114).

9.03　The use of existing masts, buildings and other structures for new electronic communications capability should be encouraged (NPPF 113).

9.04　The NPPF indicates that local planning authorities "should not seek to prevent competition between different operators" (NPPF 116). This requirement, as it existed in the previous NPPF, was considered by Hickinbottom J in *Infocus Public Networks Limited v SSCLG*.[1] The claimant was a provider of telephone kiosks.[2] Some of its applications for prior approval under the GPDO were refused, and it appealed to the Secretary of State; the appeals were dismissed by a Planning Inspector. The claimant challenged that decision before the High Court. The Inspector had found that the proposed telephone kiosks were close to other telephone boxes, and found that the proposals would look incongruous and the perceived size would be emphasised by this proximity. The claimant alleged that this was contrary to the principle that decision-makers should not seek to prevent competition. Hickinbottom J rejected this argument at para. 34:

> "Of course, by refusing the Claimant's appeal, it may mean that, in fact the… operators who already have a telephone box in the area will have or may have a commercial advantage over the Claimant who will not have a kiosk in that

---

[1]　[2013] EWHC 4622 (Admin).

[2]　It would be an interesting question whether Hickinbottom J's opening comments, made in late 2013, would be repeated in 2018: "The advent of the mobile telephone did not bring the era of the telephone box to an end".

area. However, that is not to the point. The Inspector was here simply and quite properly commenting on matters of siting and an [sic] appearance as planning considerations, which was his central remit. ...."

9.05 Simply put, the rejection of planning permission may have the effect of reducing competition, but that does not mean that the decision-maker was illegitimately seeking to prevent competition.

9.06 In *Infocus*, it was also argued that the Inspector had found that a telephone kiosk was not supported by NPPF policies on high quality communications. This argument was rejected on the facts; the Inspector had not so found. He had said that "much of the detailed advice in the NPPF is directed at other communications infrastructure". This was a legitimate approach to the NPPF policy: there is policy within the Section which "expressly relates to masks [sic], base stations and other specific structures than kiosks" (para. 37).

9.07 The need for an electronic communications system is not to be questioned in the determination of planning applications. Local planning authorities should not adopt health safeguards which are different to International Commission guidelines for public exposure.

9.08 Local planning authorities should consider the possibility that new buildings or structures could interfere with broadcast and electronic communications services (NPPF 114(b)). Presumably this is at the stage of considering applications for planning permission for such proposals (or, potentially, at the plan-making stage), and may give rise to a justification for refusing planning permission for them.

Restrictions upon Communications Development

9.09 NPPF 113 states that the number of masts for radio and electronic communications, and the number of sites for such masts "should be kept to a minimum". However, this policy objective is expressly subject to "the needs of consumers, the efficient operation of the network and providing reasonable capacity for future expansion". As previously stated, the use of existing sites is supported. If new sites are found to be necessary, then NPPF 113 indicates that "equipment should be sympathetically designed and camouflaged where appropriate".

Evidence Required

9.10 According to NPPF 114(a), a local planning authority should ensure that it has evidence suggesting that there will not be a certain level of interference with "other electrical equipment, air traffic services or instrumentation operated in the national interest". What is notable is the threshold which is set; the NPPF refers to the development being "expected to cause significant and irremediable interference...". This would appear to be a high threshold.

9.11 NPPF 115 sets out further requirements for evidence. NPPF 115(a) concerns consultations with organisations which may be affected by the proposed development (giving examples of masts installed near a school or college, within a safeguarding zone for an aerodrome, or a technical site or military explosives storage area).

Where an application is to add to an existing mast or base station, the application should include a statement self-certifying that "the cumulative exposure, when operational, will not exceed International Commission guidelines on non-ionising radiation protection" (NPPF 115(b)). The same self-certification applies to applications for a new mast or base station in NPPF 115(c)); in such circumstances, there must also be evidence "that the applicant has explored the possibility of erecting antennas on an existing building, mast or other structure".

Chapter 10

The Green Belt

Introduction

10.01　The Green Belt has a special place in the English national psyche.[1] However, the nature of the Green Belt is not always understood. Green Belt is a formal (and highly restrictive) designation of particular areas of land, particularly around major urban centres. It has specific purposes. Those purposes are largely spatial, rather than environmental. The protection of the Green Belt is therefore a different concept to the protection of greenfield sites (i.e. open sites which have not been built upon), or sites which have some specific designation due to their attractiveness. Such sites are considered in relation to the conservation of the natural environment [see Chapter 12: Conserving and Enhancing the Natural Environment].

10.02　The Green Belt is protected both in plan-making and in decision-taking. In the case of an authority's development plan, the boundaries of the Green Belt can be altered only through a review of the local plan, and, even then, only in exceptional circumstances. The approach to reviewing the boundaries of the Green Belt has been tightened up in the new version of the NPPF, in line with the Government's Housing White Paper, *Fixing Our Broken Housing Market*, published in February 2017.

10.03　In decision-taking, the level of protection is also high. Unless an application falls within specified categories, development will constitute inappropriate development in the Green Belt. Inappropriate development in the Green Belt can be justified only where there are very special circumstances to override the harm to the Green Belt by reason of inappropriateness, and any other harm caused by the proposed development.

10.04　Notwithstanding these restrictions, given the national shortage of housing, the Green Belt continues to find itself under pressure. Perhaps for this reason, and given the strength of feeling regarding the Green Belt, the amount of litigation concerning the interpretation of national planning policy relating to the Green Belt has been high. Indeed, in *Calverton Parish Council v Nottingham CC*,[2] Jay J stated at para. 3 that "[d]evelopment within Green Belt is never without controversy". Whilst many of the major questions of interpretation of the policy were resolved under the first version of the NPPF, the amendment to the wording may well mean that there will be further litigation challenging the interpretation of the new NPPF.

Structure of Green Belt Policy

10.05　The NPPF's policy regarding Green Belt land is found largely in Chapter 13, "Protecting Green Belt Land". Chapter 13 opens by recording the "great importance"

---

[1]　An (unattributed) quotation on the website of the Campaign to Protect Rural England states, "Green Belt makes me and my family who we are": http://www.cpre.org.uk/what-we-do/housing-and-planning/green-belts, accessed 15 August 2018.

[2]　[2015] EWHC 1078 (Admin).

which the Government attaches to Green Belts (NPPF 133). The paragraph explains two aspects of policy:

- <u>Fundamental aim of Green Belt policy</u> - which is expressed as preventing urban sprawl, by keeping land permanently open;

- <u>The essential characteristics of Green Belts</u> - openness and permanence.

10.06 In addition to the fundamental aim and essential characteristics, NPPF 134 sets out five purposes, which the Green Belt serves:[3]

(a) to check the unrestricted sprawl of large built-up areas;

(b) to prevent neighbouring towns merging into one another;

(c) to assist in safeguarding the countryside from encroachment;

(d) to preserve the setting and special character of historic towns; and

(e) to assist in urban regeneration, by encouraging the recycling of derelict and other urban land.

10.07 NPPF 135 explains that Green Belts are already established across the policy, and therefore sets out a restrictive policy for the creation of new Green Belts. NPPF 136 explains the policy regarding the amendment of the boundaries to existing Green Belts. The new NPPF, at NPPF 137, places considerable weight on the existence of alternatives when consideration is given to the alteration of the Green Belt. NPPF 138 provides that, when considering Green Belt boundaries during the plan process, decision-makers will need to take into account sustainable patterns of development. NPPF 139 sets out a number of requirements of well-defined Green Belt boundaries. The correct approach to the inclusion of villages in the Green Belt is set out at NPPF 140. NPPF 141 concerns seeking the beneficial use of the Green Belt at the plan-making stage. The National Forest and Community Forests are considered at NPPF 142, and are given protection in line with the Green Belt.

10.08 NPPF 143-147 concern proposals for development which affects the Green Belt. The principle that inappropriate development is, by definition, harmful to the Green Belt is set out at NPPF 143. Substantial weight must be given to any harm to the Green Belt in the consideration of any planning application: NPPF 144. NPPF 144 also explains the 'very special circumstances' test, which is considered in detail further below. The construction of new buildings is dealt with at NPPF 145; the general principle is that new buildings will be inappropriate in the Green Belt, but limited exceptions are set out. NPPF 146 sets out certain other forms of development which will not be inappropriate development in the Green Belt, provided that they preserve the openness of the Green Belt and do not conflict with the purposes of including land within it. Chapter 13 concludes with NPPF 147, which concerns renewable energy projects in the Green Belt.

---

[3] The fundamental aim in NPPF 133 is of "Green Belt policy". NPPF 134 sets out the five purposes of "Green Belt", rather than Green Belt policy. It is likely that little turns on this, and arguments based on this distinction may be considered by decision-makers - and the courts - to be overly legalistic.

10.09   There are a number of significant concepts in the law as it relates to the Green Belt. The discussion follows this structure:

(a)   Green Belts in Development Plans

(b)   Exceptional Circumstances and Alternatives

(c)   Development to Improve the Green Belt

(d)   Villages

(e)   Inappropriate Development

(f)   The Very Special Circumstances Test

(g)   Openness and Consistency with Green Belt Objectives

(h)   New Buildings in the Green Belt

(i)   Other Development in the Green Belt

(j)   Renewable Energy in the Green Belt

Green Belts in Development Plans

10.10   The Green Belt has a long history.[4] It is therefore not surprising that the NPPF considers that the general extent of Green Belt protection should be already established (NPPF 135). As such, it will be very rare that entirely new Green Belts are created.

10.11   An example of when such exceptional circumstances might arise is suggested in national policy as when a new settlement or major urban extension is being planned for. New risks of urban sprawl or the encroachment of settlements arise where major new development is proposed. However, even in those circumstances, strategic policies are required to provide a number of justifications for the new designation (NPPF 135).

10.12   More common than the creation of entirely new Green Belts will be the amendment of existing Green Belt boundaries. However, even this should not be common: amendments should take place only in exceptional circumstances, only through the plan-making process, and the new boundaries should last beyond the period of the plan. In line with the NPPF's distinction between strategic and non-strategic policies, NPPF 136 provides that the decision as to whether to change the Green Belt is a decision for the strategic policy stage; but detailed amendments to the boundaries of the Green Belt may be carried out through non-strategic policies, including neighbourhood plans.

Exceptional Circumstances and Alternatives

10.13   The amendments to the NPPF in 2018 have made it more difficult for a local planning authority to justify changing the boundaries of a Green Belt. The new NPPF includes NPPF 137, which requires a local planning authority to examine fully "all

---

[4]   See generally *Green Belts: a greener future* - Natural England and the Campaign to Protect Rural England, 2010, pp 10-11 and Figure 1 - Key dates in Green Belt history.

other reasonable options" prior to concluding that exceptional circumstances exist to justify a modification of Green Belt boundaries.

10.14   "Exceptional circumstances" to justify the amendment of the Green Belt has historically been a high threshold, as the term itself suggests. Jay J noted in *Calverton Parish Council v Nottingham CC*[5] that the term is undefined, and considered that this was a deliberate policy decision on the part of central Government. In *Solihull MBC v Gallagher Homes*,[6] the Court of Appeal held that the inclusion of land within the Green Belt had not been justified. Laws LJ held at para. 36:

> "The fact that a particular site within a council's area happens not to be suitable for housing development cannot be said without more to constitute an exceptional circumstance, justifying an alteration of the Green Belt by the allocation to it of the site in question."

10.15   The land had not been brought into the Green Belt, and the Inspector had not thought it necessary to do so, in a Report in 2005. The same Inspector reached the opposite conclusion in 2013. The text of the plan did not purport to return the sites to the Green Belt for any reason relating to the Green Belt. This echoes the decision of Hickinbottom J at first instance,[7] who said that the Inspector applied the wrong test, simply balancing the various factors as a matter of planning judgment, rather than applying the exceptional circumstances test. The very fact that a new local plan was being prepared does not, of itself, constitute an exceptional circumstance.

10.16   *Gallagher Homes* concerned a situation where it was said that land was not suitable for housing development; this did not of itself constitute an exceptional circumstance. The converse question arose in *Calverton Parish Council*. A Parish Council sought to quash, in part, the Greater Nottingham - Broxtowe Borough, Gedling Borough and Nottingham City - Aligned Core Strategies. The Parish Council sought to rely on the decision of Laws LJ in *Gallagher Homes*, but to "turn [it] through 180 degrees", and argue that the fact that a site is suitable for housing development does not, of itself, constitute an exceptional circumstances. Jay J agreed with the claimant (para. 42):

> "insofar as this goes, but in my view there is not a precise symmetry here. The issue in Solihull was whether land could be allocated to Green Belt: in other words, the point was addition, not subtraction. The mere fact that a particular parcel of land happens to be unsuitable for housing development cannot be a Green Belt reason for expanding the boundary. In a case where the issue is the converse, i.e. subtraction, the fact that Green Belt reasons may continue to exist cannot preclude the existence of countervailing exceptional circumstances - otherwise, it would be close to impossible to revise the boundary. These circumstances, if found to exist, must be logically capable of trumping the purposes of the Green Belt; but whether they should not in

---

[5]   [2015] EWHC 1078 (Admin).

[6]   [2014] EWCA Civ 1610; [2015] JPL 713.

[7]   [2014] EWHC 1283 (Admin); [2014] JPL 1117, para. 135.

any given case must depend on the correct identification of the circumstances said to be exceptional, and the strength of the Green Belt purposes."

10.17 Jay J considered that suitability alone was not sufficient to constitute an exceptional circumstance, but that suitability <u>and</u> availability may do so.

10.18 At para. 51, Jay J set out what he described as an ideal approach to considering the release of land from the Green Belt on the basis of housing land supply. It will need to be added to in the light of NPPF 137, but Jay J held that a local planning authority should identify and grapple with:

(i) the acuteness/intensity of the objectively assessed need (matters of degree may be important);

(ii) the inherent constraints on supply/availability of land *prima facie* suitable for sustainable development;

(iii) [on the facts of *Calverton Parish Council*] the consequent difficulties in achieving sustainable development without impinging on the Green Belt;

(iv) the nature and extent of the harm to [the Green Belt in question] (or those parts of it which would be lost if the boundaries were reviewed); and

(v) the extent to which the consequent impacts on the purposes of the Green Belt may be ameliorated or reduced to the lowest reasonably practicable extent.

10.19 There is not a set point at which the alternative reasonable options to Green Belt release should necessarily be considered, which NPPF 137 now requires. Indeed, Jay J was in fact considering an alternative to the release of Green Belt land, namely the local planning authorities not meeting their objectively assessed needs for housing.

10.20 The decision of the High Court in *IM Properties Development Ltd v Lichfield DC*[8] reveals the extent to which policy has being changed by the insertion of NPPF 137 regarding the assessment of alternatives. Patterson J in fact found that she did not have jurisdiction to consider the claim under the statutory provisions for bringing a challenge to the adoption of a development plan document under section 113 PCPA. However, she nevertheless went on to consider the substance of the claim.[9] At para. 96, she held that the question of whether the exceptional circumstances test is met is a matter of planning judgment. She did not find there to be a test that release of land from the Green Belt has to be a matter of last resort. There was no "falsification doctrine", such that a proposal to revise the Green Belt cannot be brought forward unless the fundamental basis for exclusion of the land from the Green Belt was "subsequently falsified". The local planning authority had not erred in removing land from the Green Belt.

---

[8] [2014] EWHC 2440 (Admin); [2014] PTSR 1484.

[9] This consideration would therefore be *obiter dicta*, and therefore not formally binding.

10.21 Patterson J's decision now needs to be seen in the context of the amendments to the NPPF. Since the introduction of NPPF 137, the exceptional circumstances test is not simply a matter at large for the judgment of the decision-maker. All other reasonable options for meeting need for development must have been examined prior to releasing land from the Green Belt. Furthermore, the assessment of whether the local planning authority has demonstrated that it has examined all other reasonable options must take into account the considerations at NPPF 137(a)-(c), namely whether the strategy:

(a) makes as much use as possible of suitable brownfield sites and underutilised land;

(b) optimises the density of development in line with the policies of chapter 11 of [the NPPF], including whether policies promote a significant uplift in minimum density standards in town and city centres and other locations well served by public transport; and

(c) has been informed by discussions with neighbouring authorities about whether they could accommodate some of the identified need for development, as demonstrated through the statement of common ground.

10.22 The wording of NPPF 137 strictly speaking requires the local planning authority to demonstrate only that it has examined all other reasonable options. This does not, in terms, state that the local authority cannot amend the boundary of the Green Belt notwithstanding whatever conclusion it reaches about the reasonable options; put another way, it might amend the Green Belt even if there are reasonable alternatives. However, in considering whether to amend the boundaries of the Green Belt, or to take one of the other reasonable options for meeting need, the local planning authority would need to be clear that the test that they were applying remained one of exceptional circumstances. It seems likely that the principle that the exceptional circumstances test does not make amendment of the Green Belt a matter of last resort may need to be revisited. Furthermore, NPPF 138 refers to release of Green Belt land being "necessary". This supports an approach beyond merely taking into account the desirability of avoiding amendments to Green Belt boundaries.

10.23 NPPF 138 sets out that decision-makers, in drawing up or reviewing Green Belt boundaries, must take into account the need to promote sustainable patterns of development. In relation to the predecessor of NPPF 138, Jay J held in *Calverton Parish Council* that this paragraph does not shed light on the meaning of "exceptional circumstances", or dilute that test. Whilst the wording of NPPF 138 has been expanded since the previous wording, there is no reason to think that this would change Jay J's conclusion on this precise point.

10.24 NPPF 138 says that, if it is concluded that release of Green Belt land is necessary, then "plans should give first consideration to land which has been previously-developed and/or is well-served by public transport". On a close reading of this phrase, there is no priority between previously developed land, and land which is well served by public transport (or even previously developed land which is well served by public transport). Presumably, therefore, how to prioritise between these various types of land would be a matter of planning judgment for the decision-maker, and national planning policy does not seek to be prescriptive.

10.25 Specific objectives of Green Belt boundary amendment are set out at NPPF 139. Land which it is not necessary to keep permanently open should not be included. Safeguarded land should be identified (where necessary), which may be needed for longer term development beyond the end of the plan period. However, such safeguarded land should not be treated as allocated for development, and the fact that it is safeguarded should not be treated as encouragement for speculative applications for windfall development. The boundaries for the Green Belt should be defensible, and should make use of physical features "that are readily recognisable and likely to be permanent". NPPF 139(a) indicates that plans should "ensure consistency with the development plan's strategy for meeting identified requirements for sustainable development". This presumably does not mean that Green Belt boundaries have in every case to be reviewed to ensure that a local planning authority can meet its objectively assessed need for housing. Local planning authorities which are heavily constrained by the Green Belt commonly use this as a reason not to plan for their full objectively assessed need.[10] Indeed, the wording of the presumption in favour of sustainable development in NPPF 11(b) indicates that objectively assessed needs do not need to be met by strategic policies where protective policies in Footnote 6 of the NPPF provide a strong reason for restricting the overall scale, type or distribution of development in the plan area, or any adverse impacts of meeting needs in full would significantly and demonstrably outweigh the benefits, when assessed against the policies in the NPPF taken as a whole.

Development to Improve the Green Belt

10.26 NPPF 138 refers to offsetting the impact of the loss of Green Belt land through "compensatory improvements to the environmental quality and accessibility of remaining Green Belt land". This is similar to the approach required in NPPF 141 after Green Belts have been defined: councils should plan to positively enhance the beneficial use of Green Belts (including by retaining and enhancing landscapes, visual amenity and biodiversity). This is an interesting aspect of national planning policy, carried over from para. 81 of the original NPPF. The Green Belt is not an environmental designation, but rather a spatial designation. Neither the fundamental aim in NPPF 133, nor the purposes in NPPF 134, of the Green Belt include improving access or improving the environmental status of Green Belt land. However, this remains an aspect of national planning policy; there is no indication

---

[10] In *City and District Council of St Albans v Hunston Properties Ltd* [2013] EWCA Civ 1610; [2014] JPL 599, Sir David Keene stated at para. 6 that it "seems clear, and is not in dispute in this appeal, that… a Local Plan could properly fall short of meeting the "full objectively assessed needs" for housing in its area because of the conflict which would otherwise arise with policies on the Green Belt or indeed on other designations hostile to development such as those on Areas of Outstanding Natural Beauty or National Parks". The Court of Appeal was considering the previous NPPF, but the text of the relevant policy was materially identical.

that it is unlawful and it should not be neglected. However, if planning permission is needed for a change of use, or any operational development to support these aims, then presumably such applications would have to be assessed against the policies for proposals affecting the Green Belt, in NPPF 143-144.

Villages

10.27   The inclusion of villages in the Green Belt is considered at NPPF 140. There are two types of villages considered:

- villages which have an open character, which make an important contribution to the openness of the Green Belt;

- villages whose character should be protected for other reasons.

10.28   According to NPPF 140, which reflects the policy of the previous NPPF,[11] only the first type of village should be included in the Green Belt; the second type of village should be excluded. Protection of the character of the second type of village should be achieved via other means, whether by designation as a conservation area, or the application of non-Green Belt development control policies.

10.29   Into which category a particular village falls will depend on the particular facts and circumstances, and will require an exercise of planning judgment. However, whilst it is possible to imagine a village which has an open character, possibly due to a large village square, it seems likely that more villages will fall into the second category than the first.

Inappropriate Development

10.30   It is established that the word "development" as it is used in Chapter 14 of the NPPF has the same meaning as the term in section 55 TCPA.[12] In *Fordent Holdings Ltd v SSCLG*,[13] HHJ Pelling QC, sitting as a Judge of the High Court applied the meaning of section 55 when considering whether development is inappropriate; Ouseley J did likewise in *Europa Oil and Gas Ltd v SSCLG*[14] at para. 53 when considering the meaning of "engineering operation".

10.31   If development constitutes inappropriate development, then the applicant would need to demonstrate very special circumstances before permission is granted. Inappropriate development is not expressly defined in Chapter 13, or in the Glossary. However, NPPF 145 and NPPF 146 set out some indications of the meaning of inappropriate development. NPPF 145, which is considered in detail below, establishes that the construction of new buildings in the Green Belt is generally inappropriate, subject to certain exceptions. Likewise, NPPF 146 states that other forms of development (provided that they do not harm openness or conflict with the purposes of the

---

[11]   But not national planning policy prior to the NPPF: *Redhill Aerodrome Ltd v SSCLG* [2014] EWCA Civ 1386; [2015] PTSR 274, para. 16(1).

[12]   For detailed analysis of the meaning of this word, see P55.01-P55.64 in Vol 2 of the *Encyclopedia of Planning Law and Practice*, Sweet & Maxwell.

[13]   [2013] EWHC 2844 (Admin); [2013] 2 P&CR 12.

[14]   [2013] EWHC 2643 (Admin); [2014] 1 P&CR 3.

inclusion of land within the Green Belt) are not inappropriate.

10.32   This tends to suggest that development within the Green Belt will be inappropriate unless it falls within the categories in NPPF 145-146. This was the approach taken by HHJ Pelling QC in relation to the previous version of the NPPF in *Fordent Holdings Ltd*: he considered that development in the Green Belt was inappropriate "by necessary implication", unless it was found to be not inappropriate (para. 19). He expressed no view on the question of whether there is a distinction between development which is "not inappropriate", and development which is appropriate (the terminology used by, for instance, Ouseley J in *Europa Oil and Gas Ltd*). This was resolved by Lindblom LJ in *R (Lee Valley Regional Park Authority) v Epping Forest DC*,[15] para. 8, in which he held that there was no distinction between development being not inappropriate, and development being appropriate.[16]

10.33   In *R (Lee Valley Regional Park Authority) v Epping Forest DC*, Lindblom LJ considered, and rejected, an argument on the part of the claimant that questions of openness are relevant whether or not development is inappropriate. The development in question was for buildings for the purpose of agriculture, which is not inappropriate development, by virtue of NPPF 145(a). As the development is not inappropriate, then they are "not to be regarded as harmful either to the openness of the Green Belt to the purposes of including land in the Green Belt" (para. 17). The requirement in NPPF 144 to give "substantial weight" to harm in the Green Belt does not require such weight to be given to harm to openness when proposals are within NPPF 145. Such proposals are deemed, as a matter of policy, not to harm openness or the purposes of including land in the Green Belt. Lindblom LJ quoted Richards LJ in *R (Timmins) v Gedling BC*,[17] that there is "no general test that development is appropriate provided it preserves the openness of the Green Belt and does not conflict with the purposes of including land within the Green Belt". Lindblom LJ went on to state (para. 18):

> "The distinction between development that is "inappropriate" in the Green Belt and development that is not "inappropriate" (i.e. appropriate) governs the approach a decision-maker must take in determining an application for planning permission. "Inappropriate development" in the Green Belt is development "by definition, harmful" to the Green Belt - harmful because it is there - whereas development in the excepted categories in [NPPF 145 and NPPF 146] is not."

10.34   Lindblom LJ went on to summarise the position at para. 24:

> "…development appropriate in - and to - the Green Belt is regarded by the

---

[15]   [2016] EWCA Civ 404; [2016] Env LR 30.

[16]   Confusingly, there are two important cases in relation to planning policy for the Green Belt, both brought by Lee Valley Regional Park Authority: Ouseley J's decision in *R (Lee Valley Regional Park Authority) v Broxbourne BC* [2015] EWHC 185 (Admin), and the decision of the Court of Appeal, in which Lindblom LJ gave the leading judgment, in *R (Lee Valley Regional Park Authority) v Epping Forest DC* [2016] EWCA Civ 404; [2016] Env LR 30.

[17]   [2015] EWCA Civ 10; [2015] PTSR 837.

Government as not inimical to the "fundamental aim" of Green Belt policy "to prevent urban sprawl by keeping land permanently open", or to "the essential characteristics of Green Belts", namely "their openness and their permanence" [NPPF 133] or to the "five purposes" served by the Green Belt [NPPF 134]. This is the real significance of a development being appropriate in the Green Belt, and the reason why it does not have to be justified by "very special circumstance"."

10.35 Even if proposed development is not inappropriate development in the Green Belt, that does not mean that it must be granted planning permission. It may be unacceptable in planning terms, when assessed against non-Green Belt development control policies, including policies on the protection of the countryside (*R (Lee Valley Regional Park Authority) v Epping Forest DC*, para. 26). An agricultural building in the Green Belt, which is treated as appropriate development, and harm cannot therefore be considered to arise by reason of the loss of openness; nevertheless, such a building may be viewed as having an adverse impact upon rural character or visual amenities of the Green Belt (para. 33).

10.36 NPPF 147 states that, if falling within the Green Belt, "elements of many renewable energy projects will comprise inappropriate development". This seems to suggest that there will be elements which would not compromise inappropriate development, but this may be explained by such aspects of the proposals falling within NPPF 145 or NPPF 146 (for instance, the re-use of buildings to house elements of a renewable energy project).

10.37 There is no indication that, simply because harm is temporary, it cannot be inappropriate development in the Green Belt: *Europa Oil and Gas Ltd*, per Ouseley J, para. 56.

The Very Special Circumstances Test

10.38 What needs to be taken into account when carrying out the very special circumstances test in NPPF 144? This was considered by the Court of Appeal in *Redhill Aerodrome Ltd v SSCLG*.[18] A Planning Inspector had dismissed an appeal, refusing planning permission for the replacement of grass runways with a hard runway at an aerodrome in the Green Belt. In doing so, the Inspector had considered whether there were very special circumstances to justify the grant of permission notwithstanding it constituted inappropriate development in the Green Belt. The test in NPPF 144 states that "'[v]ery special circumstances' will not exist unless the potential harm to the Green Belt by reason of inappropriateness, and any other harm resulting from the proposal, is clearly outweighed by other considerations".[19]

10.39 The meaning of this phrase had been considered in a decision interpreting Planning Policy Guidance Note 2, national planning policy on Green Belt predating the

---

[18] [2014] EWCA Civ 1386; [2015] PTSR 274.

[19] The words "resulting from the proposal" are insertions to the new NPPF and were not in the previous version. However, this is unlikely to affect the approach to the Court of Appeal's decision.

NPPF: *River Club v SSCLG*.[20] Frances Patterson QC, sitting as a Deputy High Court Judge, had held that "any other harm" referred to any other harm whatsoever; it was not restricted to any other harm <u>to the Green Belt</u> itself.

10.40 In *Redhill Aerodrome*, the Planning Inspector was considering the (old) NPPF, rather than PPG2. However, she considered that the meaning of the phrase was the same as that decided in *River Club*. This conclusion formed the basis of Redhill Aerodrome's challenge. The Aerodrome argued that, notwithstanding that the wording of the tests were the same in PPG2 as in the NPPF, the context of the NPPF as a whole was different, such that the meaning of "any other harm" was different in the NPPF to that in the PPG. The argument ran that, if the *River Club* approach were taken, then this would mean that the bespoke tests in the NPPF concerning certain types of harm would be disregarded.

10.41 This argument persuaded the High Court.[21] However, the Court of Appeal reversed the High Court's decision. The meaning of "any other harm" has remained consistent. It refers to any other harm whatsoever, and is not restricted to harm to the Green Belt. The approach of the High Court would have made it easier for applicants to satisfy the very special circumstances test (para. 15). Had there been such a major change in Government policy, one would have expected there to be a clear statement to that effect (para. 16). On the wording of the policy itself, there was no explicit reference to harm being only to the Green Belt. Furthermore, to take such an approach would constitute a policy imbalance as it would mean that non-Green Belt benefits were taken into account in the very special circumstances analysis, but non-Green Belt harms would not. The Court of Appeal did not accept that national planning policy had changed in such a way that the meaning of "any other harm" had also changed.

10.42 The Court of Appeal stressed the <u>context</u> of the test in NPPF 144, when considering it in *R (Lee Valley Regional Park Authority) v Epping Forest DC*.[22] The planning permission under challenge was the construction of a very large glasshouse in the Green Belt, so as to extend a nursery. The glasshouse was to be used for the growing of tomatoes and peppers. The claimant argued that, even for new buildings for the purposes of agriculture or forestry, the decision-maker had to take into account the impact on openness. The Court of Appeal rejected that argument. Lindblom LJ held at para. 17:

> "I think it is quite clear that "buildings for agriculture and forestry", and other development that is not "inappropriate" in the Green Belt, are not to be regarded as harmful either to the openness of the Green Belt or to the purposes of including land in the Green Belt. This understanding of the policy in the first sentence of [NPPF 144] does not require one to read into it any additional words. It simply requires the policy to be construed objectively in its full context—the conventional approach to the interpretation of policy…"

---

[20] [2009] EWHC 2674 (Admin); [2010] JPL 584.

[21] [2014] EWHC 2476 (Admin): remarkably, Patterson J, who had decided *River Club*.

[22] [2016] EWCA Civ 404; [2016] Env LR 30.

10.43   Ouseley J considered in *R (Lee Valley Regional Park Authority) v Broxbourne BC*[23] at
           para. 68 that the effect of *Redhill Aerodrome* is that "[i]t is not necessary to go through
           the process of considering whether a factor is not a very special circumstance but
           nonetheless falls to be taken into account in favour of the development as another
           relevant material consideration". All factors which are in favour of a grant of plan-
           ning permission for inappropriate development in the Green Belt are capable of
           contributing towards the assessment of very special circumstances.

10.44   Whether the very special circumstances test is met, on the facts of a particular
           proposal, is a matter for the decision-maker. As Sir David Keene held at para. 10
           of *Hunston Properties*, the NPPF "does not seek to define further what "other con-
           siderations" might outweigh the damage to the Green Belt". He goes on to suggest
           that there is no reason in principle why, "in certain circumstances", a shortfall in
           the supply of housing land may not do so.

10.45   The question of policy in relation to unmet need for housing land arose in *Copas
           v SSCLG*.[24] The claimants had applied for planning permission for 23 affordable
           housing units within the Green Belt. Their application for planning permission had
           been turned down by Windsor and Maidenhead RLBC, and their appeal (determined
           by way of hearing) was dismissed by a Planning Inspector. The Inspector referred
           to a Ministerial Statement of 1 July 2013, summarising it to the effect that "unmet
           demand for housing is unlikely to outweigh the harm to the Green Belt and other
           harm so as to constitute the very special circumstances justifying inappropriate
           development in the Green Belt". The Inspector found that the threshold of very
           special circumstances was not met.

10.46   The claimants argued that the Inspector had misunderstood the policy expressed
           in the Ministerial Statement, arguing that it applied only where the single issue
           was one of unmet demand for housing. The claimants then argued that there was
           more than a single issue in the appeal: the appeal did not concern a proposal for
           standard housing, but rather for affordable housing. The issue was not therefore
           housing need *simpliciter*, but the need for affordable housing. Additionally, the
           claimants argued that the Inspector had failed to have regard to the aspect of the
           Ministerial Statement which indicated that "each case will depend on its facts".

10.47   Supperstone J found that the Ministerial Statement clarified, rather than amended,
           policy as expressed in the NPPF. He referred to the decision of *Connors v SSCLG*,[25]
           in which Lewis J held at para. 165 that there was "nothing intrinsically unlawful"
           about an approach on the part of the Secretary of State that "unmet need alone is
           unlikely to justify the grant of planning permission in the Green Belt".

10.48   Regarding the argument that the policy applied only where unmet need for housing
           is the single issue, Supperstone J held at para. 34, "the third paragraph of the Written
           Statement means what it says, namely that although each case will depend on its

---

[23]   [2015] EWHC 185 (Admin).

[24]   [2014] EWHC 2634 (Admin); [2015] JPL 83.

[25]   [2014] EWHC 2358 (Admin); [2015] JPL 196.

facts, the Secretary of State wishes to make clear that, of itself, unmet demand will not constitute the very special circumstances necessary to justify Green Belt development".

10.49 Although the Ministerial Statement had not been referred to at the Hearing, it was not procedurally unfair for the Inspector to consider it in reaching her conclusion.

10.50 Ouseley J set out the relationship between housing need and very special circumstances at para. 68 of *R (Lee Valley Regional Park Authority) v Broxbourne BC*:[26]

"A shortfall in housing land supply can, as a matter of policy, be a very special circumstance, although the occasions when it is likely to suffice by itself to warrant the grant of permission for housing development in the Green Belt are expected to be few and far between. That is in effect what the NPPF and the Ministerial statement say. So there is nothing unlawful in the committee treating it as one of a number of very special circumstances."

10.51 In a somewhat prescriptive passage, Ouseley J suggests that, in order for the design of a development to constitute very special circumstances, there would need to be something to suggest that it goes beyond compliance with normal development control policies (para. 71). The design of the buildings did not indicate anything which could constitute very special circumstances, but the layout of the development could have potentially fallen into that bracket.

10.52 When considering whether the very special circumstances test is met, a decision-maker may take into account the extent of any shortfall in housing land supply (*Hunston Properties*, para. 28). However, on the other side of the balance may lie the fact that a district or borough is heavily constrained: indeed, it would be irrational for a decision-maker to have to "close his or her eyes to the existence of those constraints when making a development control decision" (para. 30). Sir David stated at para. 32:

"There may be nothing special, and certainly nothing "very special" about a shortfall in a district which has very little undeveloped land outside the Green Belt. But ultimately that is a matter of planning judgment for the decision-maker."

10.53 The role of the decision-maker's judgment was stressed by Patterson J in *R (Khan) v Sutton LBC*,[27] para. 80. She also noted that the approach of Carnwath LJ in *Wychavon DC v SSCLG*[28] applies in the era of the NPPF: rarity is not essential to meet the very special circumstances test; "[t]he word "special" connotes not a quantitative test, but a qualitative judgment as to the weight to be given to the particular factor for planning purposes" (*Wychavon DC*, para. 21). Carnwath LJ considered that the potential considerations which may be taken into account in the very special circumstances analysis are not restricted, and they may even include

---

[26] [2015] EWHC 185 (Admin)

[27] [2014] EWHC 3663 (Admin).

[28] [2008] EWCA Civ 692; [2009] PTSR 19.

personal circumstances (para. 23). In *Khan*, Patterson J rejected an argument that, as compliance with policy is commonplace, it could not constitute a very special circumstance, Patterson J finding that proposition to be too simplistic.

10.54   The Court of Appeal considered the very special circumstances test in *R (Luton BC) v Central Bedfordshire Council*.[29] Central Bedfordshire Council had decided to change the boundaries of the Green Belt, so as to remove a site (HRN1) from it. It considered that there were exceptional circumstances to justify doing so. In parallel, Central Bedfordshire Council also considered an application for planning permission for development of HRN1. It found that very special circumstances existed, and so granted planning permission. Luton BC challenged the grant of planning permission. One ground of challenge, maintained before the Court of Appeal, was that Central Bedfordshire Council had erred in relation to the interpretation of the NPPF concerning amendment of Green Belt boundaries (despite the fact that the challenge was to the grant of planning permission).

10.55   The Court of Appeal explained that the Green Belt boundary review process was different to the consideration of very special circumstances on an application for inappropriate development in the Green Belt (paras 53-54). At para. 54, Sales LJ found that the very special circumstances test is stricter than the test for changing the boundaries in the local plan. There is no requirement, or even a presumption, that the boundaries of the Green Belt must be changed to exclude a site prior to development within that site. Neither was there a presumption that the plan must be amended first, prior to determination of an application, in circumstances where there was a parallel local plan process and planning application. Therefore, in an application for planning permission, there was no legal error in failing to refer to NPPF 136. Given that the planning committee had considered the issue of prematurity, there was no error.

10.56   It remains to be seen whether Sales LJ's comment (perhaps not necessary for him to determine the challenge) that the very special circumstances test is a higher threshold than the exceptional circumstances test, will survive the amendments to the NPPF. Sales LJ's comment was made in relation to the old NPPF, but there have been changes to the exceptional circumstances test made in the new version. Notably, NPPF 137 emphasises the consideration of reasonable alternatives to the release of Green Belt land (considered above). In these circumstances, it may well be the case that Sales LJ's comments no longer hold good. However, Sales LJ's comment was to compare two evaluative thresholds, the application of which would be a matter of planning judgment, to each other. It will be rare for a decision-maker in fact to apply both tests,[30] and so a direct comparison between the two tests is unlikely to be common in practice.

10.57   The very special circumstances test must not be confused with a simple balancing exercise. If the proposal is viewed as inappropriate development, then the very

---

[29]   [2015] EWCA Civ 537; [2015] P&CR 19.

[30]   Possibly when considering the weight to be given to unresolved objections to a policy of an emerging plan under NPPF 48(b), when determining a planning application.

special circumstances need to be set out: *R (Lee Valley Regional Park Authority) v Broxbourne BC*,[31] para. 65.

10.58 Objectors challenged the grant of planning permission for a noise-attenuating bund for a motocross track in the Green Belt in *Atkins v Tandridge City Council*.[32] The claimants argued that the local planning authority's conclusion, that there were very special circumstances to justify the development, was irrational. Dove J noted that it was necessary to show that the harm caused by the proposal (both Green Belt harm, and any other harm) was <u>clearly outweighed</u> by the matters put forward as very special circumstances. However, the Judge noted that the exercise for the decision-maker remains a balance (para. 45). The decision was neither irrational, nor inadequately reasoned.

10.59 How should a decision-maker approach the very special circumstances test, where the best interests of the child would be for permission to be granted for inappropriate development in the Green Belt? This was a matter considered by HHJ Belcher, sitting as a Judge of the High Court, in *Dear v SSCLG*.[33] The Judge applied the decision of the Supreme Court in *ZH (Tanzania) v Secretary of State for the Home Department*.[34] The best interests of children must be a primary consideration, although this was not the same as being <u>the</u> primary consideration, or <u>the</u> paramount consideration (para. 42). The Secretary of State accepted before HHJ Belcher that "inherently the best interests of the children must carry no less weight than other factors". The Judge agreed with Hickinbottom J in *Stevens v SSCLG* that,[35] even in the context of the best interests of the child, weight was still a matter for the decision-maker. Additionally, what matters in the decision is substance, rather than form. HHJ Belcher held at para. 47, "provided the decision-maker ascribes the correct weight at the outset, in carrying out any adjustment to the weighting when considering the individual circumstances of the case, it matters not whether he reduces the weight on one side of the balance, or increases the weight on the other. The effect will be the same".

Openness and Consistency with Green Belt Objectives

10.60 The tests of openness and consistency with the objectives of including land within the Green Belt do not have to be determined in circumstances where a proposal falls within the types of new building listed in NPPF 145(a)-(g), unless those sub-paragraphs themselves incorporate the openness tests. This is the implication of the decision of Lindblom LJ in *R (Lee Valley Regional Park Authority) v Epping Forest DC*.[36]

10.61 As held by Jefford J in *Euro Garages Ltd v SSCLG*,[37] at para. 21, the relevant openness is the openness of the Green Belt, rather than the "site as such".

---

[31] [2015] EWHC 185 (Admin).

[32] [2015] EWHC 1947 (Admin); [2016] LLR 19.

[33] [2015] EWHC 29 (Admin).

[34] [2011] UKSC 4; [2011] 2 AC 166.

[35] [2013] EWHC 792 (Admin); [2013] JPL 1383.

[36] [2016] EWCA Civ 404; [2016] Env LR 30.

[37] [2018] EWHC 1753 (Admin).

10.62   The significance of openness depends on which paragraph of the NPPF is being considered. As Ouseley J noted in *Europa Oil and Gas* (para. 66),[38] a new house and a new sports pavilion will be treated differently in the Green Belt analysis. The house will constitute inappropriate development by virtue of its nature.[39] There need be no analysis of the effect on openness when considering whether the house is inappropriate.[40] The effect on openness may be relevant to the analysis of whether any harm other than by reason of inappropriateness is clearly outweighed by other considerations in the "very special circumstances" test in NPPF 144. The sports pavilion, by contrast, may not be inappropriate in the first place. It would constitute inappropriate development only if it fails to preserve the openness of the Green Belt, or conflicts with the purpose of including land within it. If not inappropriate development, then the proposal would not have to satisfy the "very special circumstances" test.

10.63   Ouseley J considered in *Europa Oil and Gas* (para. 67) that the duration of development and the reversibility of the effects of development is a factor which affects appropriateness, the preservation of openness and conflict with Green Belt purposes. Furthermore, Ouseley J appears to suggest at paras 72-73 that local development plan policies might be relevant to the question of how consistency with the purposes of the Green Belt should be approached.

10.64   Planning permission was quashed in *R (Lee Valley Regional Park Authority) v Broxbourne BC*,[41] in part on the basis that the officer report had provided no explanation of the conclusion it had reached in relation to openness. There would need to be some consideration of comparing the proposed development with the *status quo*. Even though Ouseley J accepted that the assessment of the effect of a proposal on openness "may involve questions of degree", there would still need to be some analysis of the question.

10.65   The relationship between the concept of openness, and that of visual impact, has caused some confusion and controversy. In *R (Lee Valley Regional Park Authority) v Epping Forest DC*,[42] Lindblom LJ referred to pre-NPPF caselaw (*R (Heath and Hampstead Society) v Camden LBC*)[43] to the effect that the concept of openness "means the state of being free from built development, the absence of buildings - as distinct from the absence of visual impact" (para. 7). Lindblom LJ also cited, to this effect, the decision of Green J in the High Court in *Timmins v Gedling BC*.[44]

10.66   Openness as a concept, and the relationship between openness and visual impact,

---

[38]   [2013] EWHC 2643 (Admin); [2014] 1 P&CR 3.

[39]   Unless it falls within one of the limited categories in NPPF 145, such as replacement of a building, limited infilling, or limited affordable housing for local community needs.

[40]   Lindblom LJ approved this passage in *R (Lee Valley Regional Park Authority) v Epping Forest DC* [2016] EWCA Civ 404; [2016] Env LR 30, para. 25.

[41]   [2015] EWHC 185 (Admin).

[42]   [2016] EWCA Civ 404; [2016] Env LR 30.

[43]   [2007] EWHC 977 (Admin); [2007] 2 P&CR 19.

[44]   [2014] EWHC 654 (Admin).

was considered by the Court of Appeal in *Turner v SSCLG*[45]. On the site was a mobile home and a substantial commercial storage yard, which had the benefit of a certificate of lawfulness. The claimant sought to argue that the development he proposed, that the mobile home and the storage yard be replaced with a bungalow with residential curtilage, constituted "limited infilling" under NPPF 145(g). Planning permission was refused by the local planning authority and a Planning Inspector dismissed the applicant's appeal. The Inspector compared the *status quo* with the proposed development, which he found would have a detrimental impact upon openness. A permanent dwelling would have a greater impact on openness than moveable chattels such as caravans and vehicles. He found no very special circumstances, and therefore refused planning permission. The claimant challenged the Inspector's decision before the High Court, which rejected his appeal, and he appealed against that decision to the Court of Appeal.

10.67 The claimant argued that the sole matter which was relevant to the assessment of openness was a volumetric exercise: would the new dwelling be greater in volume than what was being replaced? The Court of Appeal rejected this approach. Sales LJ said about the term "openness" at para. 14:

> "The concept of "openness of the Green Belt" is not narrowly limited to the volumetric approach suggested... The word "openness" is open-textured and a number of factors are capable of being relevant when it comes to applying it to the particular facts of a specific case. Prominent among these will be factors relevant to how built up the Green Belt is now and how built up it would be if redevelopment occurs (in the context of which, volumetric matters may be a material concern, but are by no means the only one) and factors relevant to the visual impact on the aspect of openness which the Green Belt presents."

10.68 Concerning visual impact, Sales LJ held at para. 15 that this is "implicitly part of the concept of "openness of the Green Belt"". There are aspects of visual impact which go beyond the visual aspect of openness, but this does not mean that visual impact is irrelevant to the question of openness (para. 16). Sales LJ disagreed with Green J in the High Court in *Timmins*, who had said that it was an error to reach a specific conclusion on openness by reference to visual impact. Whilst it is true that openness has a spatial aspect (and therefore, that the absence of visual effect does not rule out an impact on openness), that does not mean that openness does not also have a visual aspect.

10.69 Openness is not confined to the visual impact arising from buildings: *Smith v SSCLG*,[46] para. 30. Where there are features which affect visual impacts which do not arise from development, they should still be taken into account, as the "NPPF does not require an inspector to disaggregate the impacts of non-development features from the impacts of proposed development more generally".

---

[45] [2016] EWCA Civ 466; [2017] 2 P&CR 1.

[46] [2017] EWHC 2562 (Admin).

10.70   A further development in the law concerning openness and visual impact came in the form of the Court of Appeal's decision in *Samuel Smith Old Brewery (Tadcaster) v North Yorkshire CC.*[47] The local planning authority granted planning permission for an extension to a limestone quarry. The claimants sought to challenge the Council's decision on the grounds of misapplying the NPPF. The claim was unsuccessful before Hickinbottom J in the High Court, but the claimants successfully appealed to the Court of Appeal.

10.71   In the officer report put before the planning committee of the Council, there was consideration of visual impact of the development. When considering Green Belt impact, the officer expressed her view that the development did preserve the openness of the Green Belt. She stated that openness "is not defined, but it is commonly taken to be the absence of built development".

10.72   The claimant persuaded the Court of Appeal that the officer report contained an error regarding the interpretation of Green Belt policy. Lindblom LJ held at para. 37:

> "Different factors are capable of being relevant to the concept [of openness] when it is applied to the particular facts of a case. Visual impact, as well as spatial impact, is, as Sales LJ said, "implicitly part" of it. In a particular case there may or may not be other harmful visual effects apart from harm in visual terms to the openness of the Green Belt. And the absence of other harmful visual effects does not equate to an absence of visual harm to the openness of the Green Belt."

10.73   However, Lindblom LJ went on to find that it will be necessary for a decision-maker to consider whether it is possible to determine the impact on openness merely by having regard to the existence of the proposed development, or whether it would be necessary also to consider visual impact. NPPF 146 does not exclude consideration of visual impact. Lindblom LJ held at para. 38, a "realistic assessment will often have to include the likely perceived effects on openness, if any, as well as the spatial effects". A decision-maker will need to make a judgment as to whether there are likely to be visual impacts on the openness of the Green Belt, and whether those impacts will be harmful or benign.

10.74   Lindblom LJ proceeded to consider the meaning of development which would "preserve" the openness of the Green Belt. This cannot require the openness of the Green Belt to be left "entirely unchanged" (para. 39). Rather, the meaning of "preserve" in this context is that the "effects on openness must not be harmful". He suggested that development for mineral extraction "will often have long-lasting visual effects on the openness of the Green Belt", but whether there would be harm to openness is a matter of planning judgment.

10.75   Lindblom LJ summarised his view of the law at para. 40:

---

[47]   [2018] EWCA Civ 489.

"when the development under consideration is within one of the five[48] categories in [NPPF 146] and is likely to have visual effects within the Green Belt, the policy implicitly requires the decision-maker to consider how those visual effects bear on the question of whether the development would "preserve the openness of the Green Belt". Where that planning judgment is not exercised by the decision-maker, effect will not be given to the policy. This will amount to a misunderstanding of the policy, and thus its misapplication, which is a failure to have regard to a material consideration, and an error of law."

10.76 Lindblom LJ found that there was such an error in the decision of the local planning authority, and therefore the decision was quashed.

10.77 It would be an error to consider openness merely in terms of the absence of built development (openness can also be harmed by a change of use of the land), but this error was not made out on the facts of *Samuel Smith*. In *Euro Garages*, Jefford J held that an impact on openness means more than a change in the environment; there must be a greater impact upon openness. Whether this test is met is a matter of judgment. Reviewing the decision in *Samuel Smith*, Jefford J considered that there is no "check list" which a decision-maker must go through, but "where openness of the Green Belt is in issue, visual impact, as well as spatial impact, requires consideration, subject to a margin of appreciation". On the facts of the decision, the Planning Inspector had erred in assuming that any change will result in a greater impact on openness.

10.78 The precise wording of the different sub-paragraphs for the NPPF referring to the concept of openness may possibly be relevant to the application of the concept of openness. In *Euro Garages*, Jefford J held at para. 24:

"I would not wish to decide, for all purposes, that the concepts of not having a greater impact on the openness of the Green Belt and of preserving the openness of the Green belt are identical. Having said that, there is an obvious reason why the wording in differs paragraphs and bullet points differs [sic]. Where there is no existing development, consideration must be given to whether the development preserves the openness of the Green Belt. Where there is some existing development, the openness of the Green Belt has not been wholly preserved and there will necessarily have been some impact on the openness of the Green Belt already. It makes sense, therefore, to consider whether there will be a greater impact from the contemplated limited infilling. Asking the question whether there is any greater harm is one way of assessing the impact."

New Buildings in the Green Belt

10.79 The list of new buildings which are nevertheless appropriate development in NPPF 145 is a closed list; they are not just examples: *R (Lee Valley Regional Park Authority)*

---

[48] As stated above, an additional category has been added to the new version of the NPPF (material changes of use) which makes the total number of categories in NPPF 146 six.

v Epping Forest DC,[49] para. 18; *Bromley LBC v SSCLG*,[50] paras 25-27.

10.80 Perhaps as something of an expression of the obvious, in order to fall within the policy concerning the construction of a new building, the proposal needs to involve the construction of a new building. In *Gill v SSCLG*,[51] the claimant had applied for planning permission for the change of use of a building from stables to offices. This was refused by the local planning authority and his appeal to the Secretary of State had been dismissed by a Planning Inspector. He then sought to challenge the decision before the High Court. The building had been constructed with planning permission for use as stables. However, the Inspector found that, as constructed, it did not have the appearance of stables, and there was no evidence that it had ever been used as stables.

10.81 Before Rhodri Price-Lewis QC, sitting as a Deputy Judge of the High Court, the claimant argued that the Inspector should have considered whether the proposal constituted the partial or complete redevelopment of previously developed land. The Judge rejected this argument. The proposal was not for the construction of a new building, and therefore it could not fall within NPPF 145.

10.82 Further consideration to the question of what constitutes a "building" was provided by the Court of Appeal in *Lloyd v SSCLG*.[52] The claimant sought planning permission for a log cabin. It was claimed that this was the replacement of a building, the original building having been a mobile home. The Court of Appeal considered NPPF 145 in the context of the planning legislation, including the distinction between operational development (which includes building operations), and material changes of use of land. Sullivan LJ held at para. 45 that the reference to "buildings" in the NPPF does not include mobile homes, stating that a building "is something that is constructed on site. It does not include a moveable structure that is merely stationed on a site". Furthermore, Sullivan LJ held at para. 57 that mobile homes were "inherently of a temporary rather than a permanent nature". The appeal was therefore refused; permission to appeal to the Supreme Court was also refused.

10.83 A point regarding the distinction between the different sub-paragraphs of NPPF 145 was considered by Ouseley J in *R (Lee Valley Regional Park Authority) v Broxbourne BC*.[53] Land had previously housed horticultural buildings. The definition of previously developed land in the Glossary excludes "land that is or was last occupied by agricultural or forestry buildings". The officer report had stated that land was previously developed land. Ouseley J held that the buildings were no longer used for agricultural purposes alone. They could therefore fall within the definition of previously developed land. However, the officer report did err in suggesting that the whole of an area was previously developed land, whereas in fact only part had been developed. Ouseley J held at para. 51:

---

[49] [2016] EWCA Civ 404; [2016] Env LR 30.

[50] [2016] EWHC 595 (Admin); [2016] PTSR 1186.

[51] [2015] EWHC 2660 (Admin); [2016] JPL 262.

[52] [2014] EWCA Civ 839; [2014] JPL 1247.

[53] [2015] EWHC 185 (Admin).

"While I accept… that the flexibility in the NPPF for previously developed land may not require every part of the application site to have been previously developed land, the presence of some previously developed land within an application site does not make the whole site previously developed land either, applying the definition in the NPPF. The NPPF itself draws a limit on whether a site is previously developed land by reference to the curtilage of the buildings."

10.84   Lindblom LJ, in *R (Lee Valley Regional Park Authority) v Epping Forest DC*,[54] described the category of buildings for agriculture and forestry, at NPPF 145(a), as "entirely unqualified". At para. 19, he considered that the consequence of this is that all buildings for agriculture and forestry are "in principle, appropriate development in the Green Belt, regardless of their effect on the openness of the Green Belt and the purposes of including land in the Green Belt, and regardless of their size and location".

10.85   By contrast to agricultural and forestry buildings,[55] all of the other categories in NPPF 145 are subject to some form of restriction. This may be a restriction relating to openness and the purpose of including land in the Green Belt, or in terms of size, or that the development be "limited". The special position of agricultural and forestry buildings is explained by Lindblom LJ at para. 20 of *Lee Valley*:

"Implicit in the policy in [NPPF 145] is a recognition that agriculture and forestry can only be carried on, and buildings for those activities will have to be constructed, in the countryside, including countryside in the Green Belt. Of course, as a matter of fact, the construction of such buildings in the Green Belt will reduce the amount of Green Belt land without built development upon it. But under NPPF policy, the physical presence of such buildings in the Green Belt is not, in itself, regarded as harmful to the openness of the Green Belt or to the purposes of including land in the Green Belt. This is not a matter of planning judgment. It is simply a matter of policy."

10.86   Buildings for a new outdoor sports facility were considered by Supperstone J in *R (Boot) v Elmbridge BC*.[56] The officer report recommended a grant of planning permission, and the planning committee agreed. The officer report stated that there would be an impact on openness, but that this would not be significant. The officer report suggested that the development would therefore not be inappropriate development in the Green Belt, and did not analyse the proposal under the very special circumstances test. The claimant challenged this conclusion, on the basis that NPPF 145(b) refers to preservation of the Green Belt. There was no threshold of less than significant harm. Supperstone J agreed that the Council had erred, and quashed the grant of planning permission. He held that a finding of a limited adverse impact on openness is not a finding that openness has been preserved.

---

[54]   [2016] EWCA Civ 404; [2016] Env LR 30.

[55]   As Lindblom LJ notes in *R (Lee Valley Regional Park Authority) v Epping Forest DC*, para. 19.

[56]   [2017] EWHC 12 (Admin); [2017] 2 P&CR 6.

10.87 It is possible that some doubt is cast on the correctness of the decision in *Boot* by the Court of Appeal's later judgment in *Samuel Smith Old Brewery (Tadcaster) v North Yorkshire CC*.[57] The Court of Appeal was faced with an argument that a planning officer had erred in finding that proposed development preserves the openness of the Green Belt, but elsewhere found that the development would not "materially harm" openness. It was argued that these findings were inconsistent. Lindblom LJ rejected this ground of claim. He stated that preserving the openness of the Green Belt cannot mean making no physical change to it. He then stated (para. 60):

> "In both places [the officer] was effectively saying that in her view, despite the reduction in the "openness of the Green Belt", the development would not fail to "preserve" it. In this respect, therefore, the development was not "inappropriate" under the policy in [NPPF 146]. This might have been, in itself, a surprising conclusion, even untenable. But it did not involve a contradiction in the officer's advice, or a misunderstanding of the verb "preserve" as it is used in the policy."

10.88 It is not entirely clear whether this conclusion is consistent with the decision in *Boot* (Lindblom LJ does not refer to Supperstone J's decision).

10.89 NPPF 145(d), concerning replacement buildings, was the subject of detailed judicial scrutiny in *Tandridge DC v SSCLG*.[58] The claimant local authority argued that a Planning Inspector, on appeal, had erred in reading "the replacement of a building" with "the replacement of buildings". David Elvin QC, sitting as a Deputy High Court Judge, held that this was not an error. He considered the purpose of the policy, which is to protect openness and the purposes of land being included in the Green Belt. In such light, there was no reason why many buildings could not be replaced with a single building under NPPF 145(d). The Judge also noted that "building" is a word which features in (and is defined in) the TCPA. When used in that legislative context, section 6(c) of the Interpretation Act 1978 would apply such that the single word "building" could be read as "buildings". This provided indirect support to the interpretation of NPPF 145(d) which he had taken.

10.90 It was common ground between the parties that the approach to be taken to the replacement building exception was similar to that explained by Carnwath LJ in *R (Heath and Hampstead Society) v Camden LBC*.[59] Carnwath LJ had held at para. 37:

> "The words "replacement" and "not materially larger" must be read together and in the same context. ... Size ... is the primary test. The general intention is that the new building should be similar in scale to that which it replaces. ... some qualification to the word "larger" is needed. A small increase may be significant or insignificant in planning terms, depending on such matters as design, massing and disposition on the site. The qualification provides the necessary flexibility to allow planning judgment and common sense to play a

---

57 [2018] EWCA Civ 489.

58 [2015] EWHC 2503 (Admin).

59 [2008] EWCA Civ 193; [2008] 2 P&CR 13.

part, and it is not a precise formula. However, that flexibility does not justify stretching the word "materially" to produce a different, much broader test."

10.91   The perception of the size of the new building could be relevant to the materiality of a measured increase in size. However, Carnwath LJ held that this is different to substituting a test of the visual impact of the development (which was not legitimate) for the test of size (para. 44). On the facts of *Tandridge DC*, the Inspector's approach was open to him as a matter of law.

10.92   NPPF 145(e), concerning limited infilling in villages, was considered by the Court of Appeal in *R (Tate) v Northumberland CC*.[60] Lindblom LJ held at para. 37 that whether development constitutes "limited infilling" is a matter of planning judgment. The term is not defined in the NPPF. Lindblom LJ referred to characteristics, being "the nature and size of the development itself, the location of the application site and its relationship to other, existing development adjoining it, and adjacent to it". The assessment of such issues was not a matter for the court, which will be slow to interfere with the decision-maker's view. The decision of the planning committee to grant planning permission was quashed, as the officer report had failed to take into account the conclusion a Planning Inspector had previously reached in relation to the question of whether development on the site would constitute limited infilling.

10.93   NPPF 145(f), concerning limited affordable housing for community needs, must be "under policies set out in the development plan". In *R (Robb) v South Cambridgeshire DC*,[61] the claimant argued that the local planning authority had misunderstood this policy when deciding to grant planning permission. The proposal was not fully in accordance with the development plan policy. The claimant therefore argued that the proposal was not made "under" the development plan policy, as "under" should be read as "in accordance with", or "complying with". Ouseley J agreed, rejecting the Council's argument that, so long as there was a policy for limited affordable housing for community needs, then the proposal would be "under" that policy. "Under" means "in accordance with".

10.94   David Elvin QC, sitting as a Deputy Judge of the High Court, considered the predecessor to NPPF 145(g) in *Bromley LBC v SSCLG*.[62] The local planning authority refused planning permission for the redevelopment of previously developed land, to provide a number of dwellings, to retain part of an existing livery business with a new barn, and associated workers' dwellings. The developer successfully appealed. The local planning authority sought to challenge the Inspector's decision, on the ground that NPPF 145(g) does not include changes of use; it relates only to the construction of buildings. The Deputy Judge rejected this argument. Planning policy must be interpreted in the statutory context. Section 75(3) TCPA provides that, where planning permission is granted for operational development, then if no purpose is specified for the grant of permission, the permission "shall be construed as including permission to use the building for the purpose for which it is designed".

---

[60]   [2018] EWCA Civ 1519.

[61]   [2017] EWHC 594 (Admin).

[62]   [2016] EWHC 595 (Admin); [2016] PTSR 1186.

10.95   The argument in *Bromley* would appear not even to be available since the amendments to the NPPF. NPPF 146 now includes material changes of use (so long as they preserve the openness of the Green Belt, and do not conflict with the purposes of including land within it). This change is considered further below. However, at para. 51, the Judge made a finding regarding the nature of "infilling" which will remain of assistance. In rejecting some examples provided by the local authority of when NPPF 145(g) could apply if it did not support planning permission for a change of use, the Judge stated that infilling development "of its nature involves the filling in of gaps in existing development not merely gaps created by former, now derelict uses".

10.96   In *Euro Garages Ltd v SSCLG*,[63] Jefford J considered that the predecessor to NPPF 146(g) "does not entirely make sense" (para. 18), and words needed to be read in, in order to make the policy read properly. However, the defect in the wording which Jefford J identified no longer appears in the amended NPPF. The new NPPF no longer refers to the purposes of including land within the Green Belt. Furthermore, it distinguishes between two types of development: where development re-uses previously developed land, and would contribute to meeting an identified affordable housing need within the area of the local planning authority; and any other development. Unsurprisingly, the test for the former type of development (substantial harm to openness) is easier for a developer to satisfy than for the latter (no greater impact on openness).

Other Development in the Green Belt

10.97   NPPF 146 sets out various other types of development which are "not inappropriate" in the Green Belt, provided that they preserve the openness of the Green Belt, and they do not conflict with the purpose of including land within it.

10.98   In relation to the first NPPF, there was some debate in judicial decisions as to whether the list set out was a "closed list", or not, i.e. whether there could be other types of development which may be not inappropriate (if they were consistent with openness and Green Belt purposes), despite not being mentioned in the list.

10.99   In *R (Timmins) v Gedling BC*,[64] Richards LJ was clear that the list in the predecessor to NPPF 146 was a closed list. The list did not include material changes of use, which had been included in PPG2. Richards LJ stated at para. 31:

> "It is not stated expressly but is implicit that other forms of development apart from those listed in [NPPF 146] are inappropriate. I do not think that the NPPF gives any scope to local planning authorities to treat development as appropriate if it does not fall within [NPPF 145 or NPPF 146]. In particular, there is no general test that development is appropriate provided it preserves the openness of the Green Belt and does not conflict with the purposes of including land within the Green Belt. Had such a general test been intended, in my view it would have been spelled out in express terms and would also

---

[63]   [2018] EWHC 1753 (Admin).

[64]   [2015] EWCA Civ 10; [2015] PTSR 837.

have affected the way in which the specific exceptions were expressed."

10.100 Therefore, although buildings in connection with cemeteries were capable of being appropriate, there was no basis for finding changes of use of land to use as a cemetery as appropriate development.

10.101 Mitting J agreed with Richards LJ on the result, but considered that the predecessor to NPPF 146 could not be a closed list. He was strongly influenced by NPPF 141 concerning putting the Green Belt to beneficial use, including for outdoor sport and recreation. He struggled to see how this could be applied if the effect of policy was that change of use of land for outdoor sport was always inappropriate, even if (say) the use as a cricket pitch did not harm openness and was not contrary to Green Belt purposes. Tomlinson LJ preferred to express no view on the matter of whether the list was closed, given that it was not necessary to resolve the case before the Court of Appeal.

10.102 There has been a major change between the first and second versions of the NPPF in relation to NPPF 146. A new sub-paragraph has been added to include material changes of use. This means that Mitting J's concerns fall away. It therefore appears that NPPF 146 should be treated as a closed list, and that Richards LJ's reasoning should be followed (except to the extent that there is now a class within NPPF 146 of changes of use which maintain openness and are consistent with Green Belt purposes). Indeed, it appeared that, even in relation to the old NPPF, the better view was that the list of other development in the predecessor to NPPF 146 was a closed list (Lindblom LJ in *R (Lee Valley Regional Park Authority) v Epping Forest DC*[65] referring at para. 18 to the predecessors to NPPF 145 and NPPF 146 as "closed lists").

10.103 In *Davis v SSCLG*,[66] HHJ Cooke, sitting as a Judge of the High Court, considered Richards LJ's finding that there was no general test that development is appropriate unless it is inappropriate. A local planning authority had brought enforcement proceedings. The appellant's appeal against the enforcement notice was dismissed, and she appealed to the High Court under section 289 TCPA. One ground of appeal alleged that the Inspector had erred in not expressly finding that an aspect of operational development (hardstanding) did not constitute inappropriate development. It was further alleged that, since the Inspector had stated that the hardstandings did not impact on openness, it could probably be inferred that he did not find the hardstandings to be inappropriate. The Judge held at para. 66:[67]

"Neither Mitting J nor Tomlinson LJ therefore expressed a view as to whether there was any "general test" such as Richards LJ had rejected. But the clear inference must be that they did not consider that there was any such test, since if there had been it would have been relevant to the outcome of the

---

[65] [2016] EWCA Civ 404; [2016] Env LR 30.

[66] [2016] EWHC 274 (Admin).

[67] In a sentence at the end of this paragraph, the Judge contemplates the list of exclusions. This would appear not to be open, on the basis of the subsequent decision in *R (Lee Valley Regional Park Authority) v Epping Forest DC* and (possibly) the amendment to the NPPF.

case. The cemetery had been agreed not to affect openness; if it was to be presumed not to be inappropriate for that reason the appeal should have succeeded. Further, none of the judges in the Court of Appeal disagreed with Green J's conclusion that prima facie all development in the Green Belt is to be regarded as inappropriate unless within the stated exclusions."

10.104 One of the earliest decisions on the interpretation of the NPPF was that in *Europa Oil and Gas Ltd v SSCLG*.[68] The critical question before Ouseley J was whether the exploration for minerals fell within the meaning of "mineral extraction" in NPPF 146(a). The Inspector had found that it did not; the Secretary of State (in defending against the developer's challenge) considered that it did, but that the Inspector's decision was immaterial. Reading the NPPF as a whole, including the support for minerals development, Ouseley J considered that it would be odd if there were more support for the extraction of minerals than the exploration for them, as it would mean that (provided that openness were preserved and the development did not conflict with the purpose of including land within the Green Belt), exploration would require the demonstration of very special circumstances, whereas extraction would not.

10.105 The Inspector had therefore erred in his interpretation of the NPPF, and Ouseley J therefore had to consider whether this error would have made any difference to the outcome. He held that it potentially would have done. In the course of doing so, he considered the nature of NPPF 146(a), including that it contemplates that mineral extraction may, in certain circumstances, be such as to preserve the openness of the Green Belt, and to be consistent with the purpose of including land in the Green Belt (para. 65). Ouseley J stated "[e]xtraction is generally not devoid of structures, engineering works and associated buildings. The policy was not designed to cater for fanciful situations but for those generally encountered in mineral extraction". Indeed, Ouseley J went so far as to say at para. 75 that "the mere fact of the presence of the common structural paraphernalia for mineral extraction cannot cause development to be inappropriate".

10.106 The Court of Appeal upheld Ouseley J's decision,[69] finding his reasoning to be "cogent". In relation to the points concerning whether the Inspector's decision would have been the same, were it not for his misinterpretation of the meaning of "mineral extraction", Richards LJ held that he "agreed with the general thrust of [Ouseley J's] reasoning, without needing to consider every detail of it" (para. 41). Richards LJ specifically reasoned that the exercise is very different once one determines that the development is capable in principle of being appropriate.

10.107 When considering the re-use of buildings under NPPF 146(d), it may be relevant to the assessment of openness that, for instance, domestic use will come with features such as fences, bin storage, car parking and domestic paraphernalia (*Smith v SSCLG*,[70] para. 32).

---

[68] [2013] EWHC 2643 (Admin); [2014] 1 P&CR 3.

[69] [2014] EWCA Civ 825; [2014] PTSR 1471.

[70] [2017] EWHC 2562 (Admin).

Renewable Energy in the Green Belt

10.108 NPPF 147 makes specific provision in relation to renewable energy projects in the Green Belt. The paragraph does not carve out a general exception, for example that renewable energy projects should be treated as appropriate development, and therefore very special circumstances will need to be shown if the development is inappropriate. However, NPPF 147 makes the point that the very special circumstances "may include the wider environmental benefits associated with increased production of energy from renewable sources". The need for renewable energy does not have to be demonstrated in an application for development to produce such energy: NPPF 154(a).

Chapter 11

Climate Change, Flooding and Coastal Change

Introduction

11.01 The Government, through the NPPF, recognises the risk that climate change and adverse weather conditions may cause to development. Making decisions as to whether to grant planning permission is likely to include an element of balance between competing considerations: the risk that new development will be prone to flooding, or will increase the risk elsewhere, or the risk that new development will increase greenhouse gas emissions on the one hand, balanced as against the proposed benefit of the development on the other hand. The NPPF seeks to provide a guide to this balance.

Climate Change

11.02 As with the previous version of the NPPF, the new NPPF provides some trenchant guidance in relation to climate change. NPPF 148 encourages the planning system to "shape places in ways that contribute to <u>radical reductions</u> in greenhouse gas emissions" (emphasis added). Neither developers nor local planning authorities should underestimate the ambition of central Government in using the planning system to combat climate change.

11.03 It was noted at Chapter 4: Sustainable Development that the meaning of sustainable development in United Nations General Assembly Resolution 42/187 referred to in NPPF 7 has not played a major part in court decisions interpreting the previous version of the NPPF. However, the desire that the needs of the present are met, without compromising the ability of future generations to meet their own needs, is perhaps most striking in relation to climate change. NPPF 149 states that policies should ensure that development is future-proofed, even to the point of "making provision for the possible future relocation of vulnerable development and infrastructure".

11.04 Planning for new development should emphasise not only avoiding increased vulnerability of the proposed development, but also the potential to reduce greenhouse emissions (NPPF 150). New development in vulnerable areas should be managed through suitable adaptation measures. The Glossary defines "Climate change adaptation" as:[1]

> "Adjustments made to natural or human systems in response to the actual or anticipated impacts of climate change, to mitigate harm or exploit beneficial opportunities."

11.05 Government policy supports the use and supply of renewable and low carbon energy and heat plans. "Renewable and low carbon energy" is given an inclusive

---

[1] Angus Evers has pointed out that this is a much more far-reaching definition than in the original NPPF: NPPF – Climate Change http://www.shoosmiths.co.uk/client-resources/legal-updates/nppf-climate-change-14469.aspx, accessed 3 September 2018.

definition in the Glossary, which states that it:

> "Includes energy for heating and cooling as well as generating electricity. Renewable energy covers those energy flows that occur naturally and repeatedly in the environment – from the wind, the fall of water, the movement of the oceans, from the sun and also from biomass and deep geothermal heat. Low carbon technologies are those that can help reduce emissions (compared to conventional use of fossil fuels)."

11.06   The PPG has explained the importance of renewable and low carbon energy resources.[2] The benefits are given not only as the reduction in greenhouse gas emissions and hence the reduction of climate change, but also to ensure the security of the UK's energy supply, and to "stimulate investment in new jobs and businesses".

11.07   Whilst the use of environmentally friendly solutions and resources is supported by the NPPF, the NPPF is not blind to the potential adverse impacts of such development (specifically referring to cumulative landscape and visual impacts: NPPF 151(a)).[3] The PPG gives guidance as to technical considerations relating to renewable energy technologies which can affect their siting.[4] Considerations will generally include the proximity of grid connection infrastructure and site size. There are particular considerations for concerning specific forms of development. For biomass, appropriate transport links should be taken into account.[5] For hydro-electric power, sources of water are important for siting.[6] A Flood Risk Assessment is likely to be required for hydropower.[7] Where planning applications are required for active solar technology (photovoltaic and solar water heating), the PPG directs decision-makers to consider: siting systems where they can collect the most energy from the sun; the need for a sufficient area of solar modules; the effect on an area which is designated (specifically referring to the AONB); and the colour and appearance of the solar modules.[8] A number of specific issues are raised in relation to applications for large scale ground-mounted solar photovoltaic farms.[9] For the siting of wind turbines, decision-makers should consider predicted wind resources, considerations relating to air safeguarding, electromagnetic interference and access for large vehicles.[10]

11.08   Support is given to community-led initiatives for renewable and low-carbon energy,

---

[2]   PPG, Section on Renewable and low carbon energy, para. 001. At the time of writing, this Section is yet to be updated following the new NPPF.

[3]   As the PPG states, Section on Renewable and low carbon energy, para. 003, the need for renewable energy does not "automatically [override] environmental protections and the planning concerns of local communities".

[4]   PPG, Section on Renewable and low carbon energy, para. 006.

[5]   PPG, Section on Renewable and low carbon energy, para. 006.

[6]   PPG, Section on Renewable and low carbon energy, para. 006.

[7]   PPG, Section on Renewable and low carbon energy, para. 011.

[8]   PPG, Section on Renewable and low carbon energy, para. 012.

[9]   PPG, Section on Renewable and low carbon energy, para. 013.

[10]   PPG, Section on Renewable and low carbon energy, para. 006. Further policy in the NPPF regarding wind turbines is set out below; there is extremely detailed guidance regarding wind turbine development in the PPG in the Section on Renewable and low carbon energy, paras 015-031.

including, but presumably not limited to, development outside areas identified in plans (NPPF 152).[11]

11.09　NPPF 153 states that local planning authorities should expect new development to comply with development plan policies for decentralised energy supply. However, there is an exception where "it can be demonstrated by the applicant, having regard to the type of development involved and its design, that this is not feasible or viable". This raises the question: in what circumstances can the developer hide behind the design of the scheme to avoid having to comply with development plan policies? The NPPF may be read as indicating that the developer may choose to design the scheme in such a way that it is not practical to comply with the decentralised energy supply policy, even if it would be possible to do so. This would be surprising, and the alternative conclusion is that the reference to the "design" in NPPF 153 relates to an inherent aspect of the scheme, which could not be altered. In any event, it would be open to the decision-maker, under section 38(6) PCPA, to decide that the material consideration of national planning policy was not a sufficient reason to depart from the requirement of the statutory development plan.

11.10　As with previous national planning policy, it is not necessary for applicants for renewable or low carbon energy to demonstrate the need for renewable energy. As the policy says, "even small-scale projects provide a valuable contribution to cutting greenhouse gas emissions". In relation to such development in the Green Belt, NPPF 147 states that the environmental benefits of renewable energy sources may contribute to very special circumstances.

11.11　There is a particular carve-out of policy relating to wind turbines. Footnote 49, which relates to NPPF 154(b), restricts the circumstances in which development for new turbines will be considered acceptable. To be acceptable, such development must:

(a)　be in an area identified for such development in the development plan;

(b)　follow consultation with the local community;[12]

(c)　fully address the planning impacts identified by the local community;

---

[11]　The PPG is optimistic about the role to be played by community initiatives: PPG, Section on Renewable and low carbon energy, para. 004.

[12]　Pre-application consultation is in any event a legal requirement for major wind turbine development, under Article 3 of the DMPO. When required by legislation, the pre-application consultation must meet the requirements of sections 61W and 61X TCPA, and Article 4 DMPO. The PPG states, Section on Renewable and low carbon energy, para. 028, that there "is no one size fits all approach to pre-application consultation and, providing it meets the legislative requirements, decisions on the nature and extent of consultation will need to be made on a case by case basis and in light of the relevant circumstances. Pre-application consultation should be proportionate to the scale and nature of a proposed development, the local context and the people that might be materially affected by the planning impacts of the development". The PPG states that the level of engagement that the local planning authority would normally undertake if a planning application were submitted is a "useful starting point" for determining how and whom to consult.

(d)   have the backing of the local community.[13]

11.12   Given that wind turbines commonly cause harm (including in terms of landscape and visual effects) at the local level, but the benefits are less tangible, less easily observable and less locally-applicable, this policy is likely to constitute a major restriction on the grant of planning permission for wind turbines.[14]

Coastal Change

11.13   National planning policy requires local planning authorities to take into account the UK Marine Policy Statement and marine plans in both making planning policies and decisions. National planning policy aims towards the alignment of terrestrial and marine planning (NPPF 166). NPPF 166 also recommends Integrated Coastal Zone Management, which is explained in the PPG as "a process which requires the adoption of a joined-up and participative approach towards the planning and management of the many different elements in coastal areas (land and marine)", before setting out key principles in implementing an integrated approach.[15]

11.14   The NPPF uses the concept of a Coastal Change Management Area to permit local planning authorities take further control. A Coastal Change Management Area is, according to the Glossary:

> "An area identified in plans as likely to be affected by physical change to the shoreline through erosion, coastal landslip, permanent inundation or coastal accretion."

11.15   NPPF 167 brings in a test of avoiding inappropriate development in vulnerable areas. Development in a Coastal Change Management Area will, according to NPPF 168, be appropriate only where it is demonstrated that: it will be "safe" over the planned lifetime of the development; it will not have an unacceptable impact on coastal change; it will not compromise the character of the coast, including designations of it; the development provides wider sustainable benefits; and it does not hinder the creation and maintenance of a continuous signed and managed route around the coast. The requirement of "wider sustainable benefits" indicates that the concept of appropriate development concerns not only avoiding harm to such areas, but also the provision of benefits. The PPG indicates that different types of development may be appropriate depending on the time horizon for risk from erosion of the coastline.[16]

11.16   The restrictiveness of these policies is combined with the broad scope of application of the definition. NPPF 167 states that "<u>any area</u> likely to be affected by physical changes to the coast" (underlining added) should be identified as a Coastal Change

---

[13] The PPG states that the question as to whether a proposal for wind turbine development has the backing of the affected local community "is a planning judgment for the local planning authority": PPG, Section on Renewable and low carbon energy, para. 033.

[14] Indeed, Angus Evers describes this as an "effective ban": NPPF – Climate Change http://www.shoosmiths.co.uk/client-resources/legal-updates/nppf-climate-change-14469.aspx, accessed 3 September 2018.

[15] PPG, Section on Flood risk and coastal change, para. 070.

[16] PPG, Section on Flood risk and coastal change, para. 073.

Management Area. Whilst it will be a matter of judgment whether this definition is met, it seems that this would be capable of covering much of the coast. The PPG states "[a] Coastal Change Management Area will only be defined where rates of shoreline changes are significant over the next 100 years, taking account of climate change. They will not need to be defined where the accepted shoreline management plan policy is to hold or advance the line (maintain existing defences or build new defences) for the whole period covered by the plan, subject to evidence of how this may be secured".[17] It is not clear that this approach is easily consistent with the wording of the NPPF (the PPG seeming more restrictive in terms of defining a Coastal Change Management Area than the NPPF), although it may be that the courts decide that the NPPF should be read subject to it. At the time of writing, this aspect of the PPG has not been amended following the new NPPF.

11.17   It may be that restricting the lifetime of a development within a Coastal Change Management Area may reduce the unacceptable impact of it. In such circumstances, local planning authorities should limit the planned lifetime of a development.

Flood Risk

11.18   The planning system should seek to avoid new development being at unacceptable risk of flooding itself, and increasing the risk of flooding elsewhere.[18] This is to be achieved through a combination of policy tests in plan-making and decision-taking, and the application of two specific tests: the sequential test, and the exception test. The general aims of national policy concerning flooding are set out at NPPF 155, with the achievement of those aims explained in more detail in subsequent paragraphs. The aims are to avoid inappropriate development in areas at risk of flooding by directing development away from areas at the highest risk of such flooding, and that where development is necessary in such areas, the development should be made safe for its lifetime, without increasing flood risk elsewhere.

11.19   The High Court has made clear that the NPPF proposes different approaches to plan-making and decision-taking, in the context of flooding: *Menston Action Group v City of Bradford MDC*.[19] These matters will therefore be taken separately.

Plan-making

11.20   Strategic policies must be based on a Strategic Flood Risk Assessment (NPPF 156). The PPG defines "Strategic Flood Risk Assessment" as "a study carried out by one or more local planning authorities to assess the risk to an area from flooding from all sources, now and in the future, taking account of the impacts of climate change, and to assess the impact that land use changes and development in the area

---

[17]   PPG, Section on Flood risk and coastal change, para. 072.

[18]   As the PPG notes, the quantification of risk has two dimensions: the prospect of an event occurring, and the harmfulness of that event if it does occur (PPG, Section on Flood risk and coastal change, para. 002).

[19]   [2016] EWHC 127 (QB); [2016] PTSR 466.

will have on flood risk".[20] Expert advice should be taken into account. The policies should consider not only direct impacts, but also cumulative impacts in local areas (or affecting such areas) which are susceptible to flooding.

11.21 The risk of flooding should be avoided, where possible, taking into account the current and future impacts of climate change. This includes not only the flood risk to people, but also to property (NPPF 157). The means for achieving this, as well as managing residual risk,[21] are:

- the application of the sequential test and the exception test, if necessary;

- safeguarding land for development which is, or is likely to be, required for current or future flood management;

- using opportunities from new development to reduce the causes and impacts of flooding;

- seeking opportunities to relocate development, including housing, to more sustainable locations where climate change alters the balance of risk.

11.22 The final bullet point is striking: it indicates that residential development may need to be relocated as a result of flood risk arising from climate change. Presumably in planning terms, this means providing new dwellings as a replacement for existing dwellings which may become uninhabitable due to flooding and flood risk.

Decision-taking

11.23 In any area with a risk of flooding, either now or in the future, an application for planning permission must satisfy the sequential test, or alternatively, the exception test (NPPF 158-159). If a site is allocated in the development plan through the sequential test then, at planning application stage, it will not be necessary to consider the sequential test again at that point. The same is not true of the exception test: if a site is allocated not in satisfaction of the sequential test but the exception test, then this may need to be re-examined at the application stage, in two circumstances (NPPF 162):

- where relevant aspects of the proposal had not been considered at the plan-making stage;

- where more recent information has come to light since the allocation of the site within the plan.

11.24 A local planning authority in determining a planning application should ensure that the development as proposed would not increase flood risk elsewhere. Dove J considered in *Menston Action Group* whether there was a requirement to seek that

---

[20] PPG, Section on Flood risk and coastal change, para. 008. Detailed guidance on the approach to such assessment is set out at paras 011-018.

[21] The concept of residual risk is explained by the PPG, Section on Flooding and coastal change, para. 041, as risk which remains after applying the sequential approach to the location of development and applying mitigation. Examples of residual risk include failure of flood management infrastructure, failure of a reservoir, or a severe flood event exceeding a flood management design standard.

planning applications reduce flood risk in the wider area. He held that there was not. If a proposal would improve the *status quo* regarding flood risk, that would be a positive benefit of the application which could be taken into account, but such improvement was not a policy requirement of the NPPF.

11.25   A flood risk assessment may be required to determine the application (NPPF 163). Footnote 50 states that such an assessment will be required for all development in Flood Zones 2 and 3. Flood zones are designated in order to indicate which areas are likely to be at the most risk from flooding, and therefore what level of assessment will be required.[22] An assessment will be required even for land within Flood Zone 1 if:

- the site is 1 hectare or more;

- the Environment Agency has identified the land as having critical drainage problems;

- land has been identified in a strategic flood risk assessment as being at increased flood risk in future;

- land that may be subject to other sources of flooding, where development would introduce a more vulnerable use.

11.26   If development is to be permitted in areas at risk of flooding, then it must meet criteria set out in NPPF 163. Within the site itself, the elements of the development which would be most vulnerable to flooding must be located in areas at the lowest risk of flooding, unless there are overriding reasons to prefer a different location. An example of this may be residential-led development which has an area for on-site recreation and dog-walking. The dwellings themselves should be placed in the part of the site least susceptible to flooding, and the dog-walking area could be located in the area at a higher risk. The development itself must be appropriately flood resistant and resilient.[23] This may involve architectural elements of the design. Unless there is clear evidence that it would be inappropriate to do so, the development should incorporate sustainable drainage systems. The applicant must be able to demonstrate that residual risk[24] can be safely managed, and that there

---

[22]   The flood zones are explained in Table 1 of the PPG Section on Flood risk and coastal areas, at para. 065.

     Zone 1 has a low probability of flooding, with a less than 1 in 1,000 annual probability of river or sea flooding.

     Zone 2 has medium probability, with probability between 1 in 100 and 1 in 1,000 annual probability of river flooding, or land having between a 1 in 200 and 1 in 1,000 annual probability of sea flooding.

     Zone 3a has a high probability, with a 1 in 100 or greater annual probability of river flooding, or having a 1 in 200 or greater annual probability of sea flooding.

     Zone 3b is the functional flood plain, being land where water has to flow or be stored in times of flood.

[23]   Flood resilience relates to reducing the impact of water which enters a building; flood resistance concerns preventing or reducing the entry of water into a building in the first place. Further details are available at PPG Section on Flood risk and coastal change, para. 059, which indicates that flood resistance should not be used alone, without also making provision for flood resilience.

[24]   See above for the explanation of this concept in the PPG.

are safe access and escape routes included where appropriate as part of an agreed emergency plan.

11.27   The requirements for certain minor development and changes of use are less intensive. These must still meet the requirement for assessment as set out in Footnote 50 (see above), but do not have to follow the sequential and exception tests. Footnote 51 sets out examples of such types of development (as the list is not closed, there may be eligible development which does not fall within this list):[25]

> "householder development, small non-residential extensions (with a footprint of less than 250 m²) and changes of use; except for changes of use to a caravan, camping or chalet site, or to a mobile home or park home site, where the sequential and exception tests should be applied as appropriate."

11.28   Whether a particular proposal falls within householder development is presumably a function of whether the application constitutes a householder application under Art 2(1) of the Town and Country Planning (Development Management Procedure) (England) Order 2015, which defines a householder application as:

(a)   an application for planning permission for development for an existing dwellinghouse, or development within the curtilage of such a dwellinghouse for any purpose incidental to the enjoyment of the dwellinghouse, or

(b)   an application for any consent, agreement or approval required by or under a planning permission, development order or local development order in relation to such development,

but does not include an application for change of use or an application to change the number of dwellings in a building.

11.29   The PPG nevertheless suggests that minor development may raise flood risk issues in certain situations, where they would have an adverse effect on a watercourse, flood plain or its flood defences, would impede access to flood defence and management facilities, or where the cumulative impact of such developments would have a significant effect on local flood storage capacity or flood flows.[26] An application for planning permission for a material change in use which changes the vulnerability classification of the development may involve an increase in flood risk.[27]

11.30   When considering applications for major development, the default position is that sustainable drainage systems should be provided (NPPF 165). Major development is defined in the Glossary as:

> "For housing, development where 10 or more homes will be provided, or the site has an area of 0.5 hectares or more. For non-residential development it

---

[25]   The PPG does not appear to reflect this, instead offering a definition of "minor development" (See PPG Section on Flood risk and coastal change, para. 046). There was no equivalent of Footnote 51 in the original NPPF, and the NPPF has not yet been amended to reflect this change.

[26]   PPG Section on Flood risk and coastal change, para. 047.

[27]   PPG Section on Flood risk and coastal change, para. 048.

means additional floorspace of 1,000m2 or more, or a site of 1 hectare or more, or as otherwise provided in the Town and Country Planning (Development Management Procedure) (England) Order 2015."

11.31 Sustainable drainage systems need not be provided where there is "clear evidence that this would be inappropriate". However, where they are required, then the systems as designed should take into account advice from the lead local flood authority, have appropriate proposed minimum operational standards, have maintenance arrangements in place to ensure an acceptable standard of operation for the lifetime of the development, and (where possible), provide multifunctional benefits. The PPG explains sustainable drainage systems as systems "designed to control surface water run off close to where it falls and mimic natural drainage as closely as possible".[28] A hierarchy of drainage options for surface run off is set out in the PPG, being in order of preference: discharge into the ground (infiltration), discharge to a surface water body, discharge to a surface water sewer, highway drain, or another drainage system, followed finally by discharge to a combined sewer.[29]

The Sequential Test

11.32 NPPF 158 explains the sequential test. The evidential basis for the sequential test is the strategic flood risk assessment, which will refine the flood zones.[30] The test is to be applied in areas known to be at risk now or in the future from any form of flooding. The reference to "any form of flooding" would presumably include tidal, fluvial, and groundwater flooding, as well as flooding from man-made sources such as sewerage systems. The test states:

> "Development should not be allocated or permitted if there are reasonably available sites appropriate for the proposed development in areas with a lower risk of flooding."

11.33 The PPG puts matters bluntly:[31] "the Sequential Test [within the plan-making process] will help ensure that development can be safely and sustainably delivered and developers do not waste their time promoting proposals which are inappropriate on flood risk grounds."

11.34 The PPG indicates that, where the sequential test is applied in relation to individual applications where the allocation has not been sequentially tested in the development plan, or where the proposed use does not comply with the plan, then the area for the sequential test will be the catchment area for the type of use proposed.[32] However, the fact that land is previously developed is not a reason for the sequential test being unnecessary: *Watermead Parish Council v Aylesbury Vale DC*.[33] The PPG recognises that a pragmatic approach may need to be taken to the application of

---

[28] PPG Section on Flood risk and coastal change, para. 051.

[29] PPG Section on Flood risk and coastal change, para. 080.

[30] PPG Section on Flood risk and coastal change, para. 019.

[31] PPG Section on Flood risk and coastal change, para. 018.

[32] PPG Section on Flood risk and coastal change, para. 033.

[33] [2017] EWCA Civ 152; [2018] PTSR 43.

the sequential test, giving the example of a planning application to extend existing business premises.[34]

The Exception Test

11.35 The exception test may need to be applied if development cannot be located in zones with a lower risk of flooding. Diagram 3 provided with the PPG makes clear that failure of development to meet the exception test does not inevitably mean that the exception test needs to be applied. The need for the exception test depends "on the potential vulnerability of the site and of the development proposed, in line with the Flood Risk Vulnerability Classification set out in national planning guidance" (NPPF 159).

11.36 The flood risk vulnerability classification is set out at Table 2 of the section of the PPG on Flood risk and coastal change, at para. 066. It prioritises essential infrastructure, before listing highly vulnerable sites (including police and ambulance stations, and basement dwellings), more vulnerable sites (including hospitals and buildings in residential use), less vulnerable (including buildings used for shops), and water-compatible development (including navigation facilities and lifeguard and coastguard stations).

11.37 If the exception test is being applied at plan-making stage, then it should be informed by a strategic flood risk assessment. If being applied at application stage, then the flood risk assessment should be site-specific. There are two limbs of the exception test, both of which need to be satisfied. This is clear from the wording (NPPF 160 connects limbs (a) and (b) with the word "and"), but also from NPPF 161 which emphasises that both elements need to be satisfied. The elements are (broadly) (i) wider sustainability benefits, and (ii) acceptability in flooding terms.

11.38 The wider sustainability benefits are benefits to the community. They must outweigh the flood risk. The PPG suggests that such sustainability benefits could be provided through the use of planning conditions, and/or planning obligations.[35] However, decision-makers would need to consider whether any condition satisfies the requirements for conditions as set out in NPPF 55. Likewise, planning obligations would have to meet any legal requirements set out in Regulations 122-123 of the Community Infrastructure Levy Regulations 2010 in order to constitute a reason to grant planning permission. The benefits should be assessed according to the objectives set in the Local Plan's Sustainability Appraisal.[36]

11.39 Acceptability in flooding terms incorporates consideration of the safety of the development for its lifetime (including taking into account the vulnerability of its users). However, the development should not increase flood risk elsewhere, and, where possible, should reduce flood risk overall. The PPG suggests that the lifetime of residential development should be considered for a period of a minimum of 100

---

[34] PPG Section on Flood risk and coastal change, para. 033.

[35] PPG Section on Flood risk and coastal change, para. 024.

[36] PPG Section on Flood risk and coastal change, para. 037.

years, unless there is a specific justification for considering a shorter period.[37] The PPG suggests that a flood risk assessment dealing with the question of safety for the purposes of the second limb of the exception test should cover the following matters:[38]

- the design of any flood defence infrastructure;

- access and egress;

- operation and maintenance;

- design of development to manage and reduce flood risk wherever possible;

- resident awareness;

- flood warning and evacuation procedures...; and

- any funding arrangements necessary for implementing the measures.

---

[37] PPG Section on Flood risk and coastal change, para. 026.
[38] PPG Section on Flood risk and coastal change, para. 038.

Chapter 12

Conserving and Enhancing the Natural Environment

Introduction

12.01 Although national planning policy seeks to promote the delivery of housing, the NPPF does recognise that the countryside itself is worth protecting. Whilst the countryside has intrinsic character and beauty, particular elements of the countryside are given special protection by law and policy. In practice, the most important elements of the NPPF in Chapter 15 concern policy concerning the AONB and national parks, biodiversity, and valued landscapes. There is also policy concerning ground conditions and pollution.

12.02 Changes between the first and second versions of the NPPF are modest, and so the existing case law can be of some assistance in interpreting the new NPPF.

12.03 This chapter will focus on the most potentially controversial aspects of Chapter 15. For instance, there has been detailed consideration of the concept of "valued landscape", now found in NPPF 170. Yet the paragraph features a number of requirements for policy-making and decision-taking, some of which are taken up in more detail in later paragraphs of the Chapter. The topics covered in detail in this chapter are:

(a) The general protection of the countryside provided by the NPPF;

(b) The special protection provided to valued landscapes;

(c) The AONB, National Parks and the Broads;

(d) The Coast;

(e) Habitats and Biodiversity;

(f) Ground conditions and pollution.

General Protection of the Countryside

12.04 NPPF 170(b) makes clear that even countryside which is not designated and has no specific policy protection nevertheless has worth in the planning balance, given that the countryside is said to have intrinsic character and beauty. This policy was previously found as one of the core principles in para. 17 of the old version of the NPPF. Gilbart J deduced from this principle in *Cawrey v SSCLG*[1] at para. 49 that "ordinary countryside" was protected by the NPPF. The fact that the intrinsic character and beauty of the countryside is now mentioned in Chapter 15 itself does not undermine this conclusion.

12.05 How much weight should be given to the protection of an area of countryside, which does not have any designation, will be a matter for the decision-maker. If a local planning authority, or Inspector on appeal, considers that land (although not

---

[1] [2016] EWHC 1198 (Admin).

designated or not reaching the threshold of being a valued landscape) is more attractive, then that would be capable of carrying greater weight in the planning balance.

12.06 In the previous version of the NPPF, there was a specific paragraph concerning best and most versatile agricultural land (para. 112). This required decision-makers to take into account the benefits of such land. It also set out a sequential test that where significant development of agricultural land was shown to be necessary, areas of poorer land were to be used in preference to areas of a higher quality. The policy regarding best and most valuable agricultural land is now split between the general principle recognising the economic and other benefits of such agricultural land in NPPF 170(b), and the sequential test in a footnote to NPPF 171. However, the sequential test now appears to strictly relate only to the plan-making stage; it does not seem to feature as an explicit test in the decision-making role. Whether an amount of land is "significant" for these purposes is entirely a matter of judgment for the decision-maker: *Smyth v SSCLG*.[2] NPPF 171 also provides that plans should "take a strategic approach to maintaining and enhancing… green infrastructure". Green infrastructure is defined in the Glossary as:

> "A network of multi-functional green space, urban and rural, which is capable of delivering a wide range of environmental and quality of life benefits for local communities."

12.07 The PPG indicates that a "strategic approach" involves taking an authority-wide green framework or strategy, which should be evidence-based.[3]

Valued Landscapes

12.08 Valued landscapes should be protected, and enhanced, via planning policies and decisions: NPPF 170(a). In the decision-making context, this boils down to decision-makers taking into account the value to be ascribed to a particular development, and this being a potential reason for refusing planning permission.

12.09 Perhaps unsurprisingly, given the significance of a decision that a landscape is valued, there has been litigation regarding the meaning of the phrase "valued landscape". The matter was considered in detail[4] by Ouseley J in *Stroud DC v SSCLG*.[5] Planning permission had been sought from Stroud DC for around 150 houses, at the foot of the escarpment to the Cotswold Hills. The site was in close proximity to an AONB. Stroud DC refused planning permission, but this decision was overturned by a Planning Inspector on appeal. The local planning authority thereafter sought to challenge the decision in the court.

---

[2] [2013] EWHC 3844 (Admin).

[3] PPG, Section on Natural environment, para. 029. At the time of writing, this Section of the PPG is yet to be updated following the amendment to the NPPF.

[4] Although, as he later recorded in *Ceg Land Promotions II Ltd v SSCLG* [2018] EWHC 1799 (Admin), his judgment in *Stroud DC* was delivered *ex tempore* (i.e. he gave a spoken judgment after oral argument, rather than considering his judgment and giving it later in writing). Furthermore, it was given late on a Friday afternoon.

[5] [2015] EWHC 488 (Admin).

12.10   The Inspector found that the development would not cause significant harm to views out of the AONB. However, given the proportion of Stroud DC's area which is covered by AONB, and given the need for new housing, views from the AONB "were very likely to be affected by new housing development wherever it went".

12.11   The Inspector found that there was no agreed definition of valued landscape, and stated that "I consider that to be valued would require the site to show some demonstrable physical attribute rather than just popularity". He referred to the "absence of any ... designation", and found that the description of valued landscape was not applicable.

12.12   Ouseley J noted that the issue at the inquiry was whether there was an evidential basis on which it could be said that the land could be concluded to have demonstrable physical attributes. There was no basis on which it could be said that the land had any designation. Ouseley J found that landscape being designated is a different matter to it being valued. At para. 13, he stated:

> "The NPPF is clear: that designation is used when designation is meant and valued is used when valued is meant and the two words are not the same."

12.13   Whilst the Inspector could have expressed his wording more clearly, on a proper reading of the decision letter, he had not equated the question of whether the landscape was designated with whether it is valued, and therefore did not err in this respect. Ouseley J considered at para. 15 that the Inspector:

> "...was entitled to conclude on the evidence he had before him that there had been no demonstrated physical attributes to make the land "valued"."

12.14   He went on to state at para. 16:

> "It is not difficult to see that the sort of demonstrable physical attributes which would take this site beyond mere countryside, if I can put it that way, but into something below that which was designated had not been made out in the Inspector's mind."

12.15   The fact that the site was visible in the wider landscape from the AONB did not mean that the site had necessarily to fall within, or constitute a valued landscape.

12.16   Ouseley J therefore referred to whether there were demonstrable physical characteristics, when considering the interpretation of valued landscape. In *Forest of Dean DC v SSCLG*,[6] Hickinbottom J referred at para. 14 to whether there were "physical attributes which took [a site] out of the ordinary". At para. 37, the Judge stated that it would be surprising on the basis of the evidence and submissions put to him, if the Inspector had erred: "whether the Site had physical attributes such as to take its landscape outside the "ordinary" countryside was, quite clearly, an issue that the Inspector was required to consider and determine". The Inspector found that there was nothing to take the site beyond landscape in general.

12.17   Ouseley J returned to the question of valued landscape in *Ceg Land Promotions II*

___

6   [2016] EWHC 2429 (Admin).

Ltd v SSCLG.[7] The application was for residential development in the context of a lack of a five-year supply of housing land, and therefore the Inspector applied the 'tilted balance' in NPPF 11. Despite the application of the tilted balance, the Inspector refused permission, finding that the adverse impacts would significantly and demonstrably outweigh the benefits. The adverse impacts included the "irrevocable loss of part of a valued landscape".

12.18   The developer challenged the Inspector's decision, arguing that the Inspector had not found features of the landscape capable of rendering it a valued landscape for the purposes of NPPF 170(a).

12.19   Ouseley J accepted the developer's argument (para. 33) that the valued landscapes policy in the NPPF was not seeking to bring about a dramatic amendment in national policy, which had previously encouraged the use of criteria-based policies, with rigid local designations applying only where the criteria-based policies were not sufficient.

12.20   Where there is development plan policy protection for valued landscapes, which is (a) as comprehensive as those in the NPPF, (b) consistent with the NPPF and (c) up to date, then NPPF 170(a) does not provide additional development control policy "so as to mean that the harm that breached Local Plan policies could be added to the same harm described as a breach of [NPPF 170(a)]. To do so would be illogical double-counting." National policy would have been met through the terms of the local plan: NPPF 170 seeks to influence not only decision-making on applications but also the formation of planning policies. However, on the decision letter read as a whole, the Inspector had not unlawfully double-counted the harm to the landscape.

12.21   The developer also raised the subtly different point that it would be irrational to give higher weight to an NPPF policy on valued landscape over and above the weight given to development plan policies for the protection of such landscapes, which were designed to meet the NPPF policy. Ouseley J found that the Inspector had not taken such an approach on the facts (para. 51), and so the question of the lawfulness of such an approach did not arise. However, he went on to express his views at para. 53:[8]

> "[O]nce a Local Plan policy and the harm arising is given its due weight because of the fullness to which it reflects the obligation in NPPF 170 of the Framework to produce such policies, then to give the policy, or the harm under it, greater weight because of the Framework policy, is to use the Framework policy twice over: once to give weight to the Local Plan policy because of the Framework and second to give weight to the Framework whose weight has already been reflected in the weight given to the Local Plan policy. That would be as irrational as double-counting harm; it is really just a different

---

[7]   [2018] EWHC 1799 (Admin).

[8]   As this was not necessary for his decision of the case, they are *obiter dicta* and not strictly binding authority. They are likely however to be persuasive authority in future cases which raise the same point.

way of putting the same point and suffers from the same vice."

12.22 This is a potentially surprising conclusion, as the modern trend of decisions regarding the approach to the NPPF is that, notwithstanding the terms of the NPPF, weight is a matter for the decision-maker (*Hopkins Homes Ltd v SSCLG*).[9] However, Ouseley J makes the point:

NPPF 170 requires consideration of valued landscapes in plan-formulation

⇩

New strategic policies fully embody NPPF 170

⇩

Decisions taken in line with the strategic policies will be in line with NPPF 170

⇩

As the strategic policies already encapsulate NPPF 170, giving additional weight, or counting additional harm, because of NPPF 170, would make no sense.

12.23 Ouseley J then turned to his decision in *Stroud DC*. Whilst *Stroud DC* did establish that a landscape did not have to be designated to be valued, it was a decision which otherwise turned on its facts (para. 56). Ouseley J's previous decision in *Stroud DC* did not, he said, seek to hold up "demonstrable physical attributes" as some sort of test which had to be met before a landscape could be treated as valued (para. 58). The precise definition of the site for which planning permission is sought (in terms of the red line boundary) need not be crucial to the question of landscape evaluation (para. 59). Consideration of whether the landscape is valued need not be restricted to that precise question.

12.24 Ouseley J went on to explain (para. 60) that in *Forest of Dean*, Hickinbottom J was applying *Stroud DC* for the point of principle that whether a landscape is valued for the purposes of NPPF 170 is not coterminous with the question of whether it is formally designated. Given the quotation from para. 37 of *Forest of Dean*, set out above, there may be some question as to whether this is correct, but it would be sensible to follow Ouseley J's most recent comments in *Ceg Land Promotions II*.

12.25 What is the role of NPPF 170 if the harm to the valued landscape is only temporary? This was an issue considered by the Court of Appeal in *Preston New Road Action Group v SSCLG*.[10] In the High Court, Dove J had considered that NPPF 170 did not mean that "any harm, including temporary harm other than for a wholly insignificant or *de minimis* period, is a breach of [it]". The development in question in *Preston New Road Action Group* was fracking; the Secretary of State considered

9   [2017] UKSC 37; [2017] 1 WLR 1865.

10 [2018] EWCA Civ 9; [2018] Env LR 18.

that the significant visual effects were temporary only and would be subject to reasonable mitigation. The Court of Appeal held at para. 41:

> "the policy in [NPPF 170(a)] does not compel a decision-maker to find conflict with it when the harmful effects of minerals development on a "valued" landscape would, in the course of the project, be reversed or mitigated. The policy is not framed in terms of preventing any harm at all to such landscape. When applied in the making of a planning decision, it requires from the decision-maker a planning judgment on the question of whether, in the circumstances, the general policy objective of "protecting and enhancing" such landscapes would be offended or not. It is for the decision-maker to consider whether any temporary harm to the landscape would breach the policy. The nature of the damage to the landscape, its duration, the importance of the "valued" landscape, and the degree of formal protection it has been given, if any, are likely to be relevant factors."

12.26   The Inspector had found an adverse impact upon a valued landscape. But, on the facts of the proposal before her, there would be "no conflict in the long-term with the aim of the NPPF to conserve and enhance the natural environment". The Inspector had made a planning judgment which was open to her, and with which the court would not interfere.

12.27   In a change from the previous version of the NPPF, NPPF 170 now states that the protection and enhancement of valued landscapes should be "in a manner commensurate with their... identified quality in the development plan".[11]

The AONB, National Parks, and the Broads

The Significance of Designation

12.28   It is clear from the above that a landscape may be valued without having a particular designation. That said, certain designations do give rise to a high level of protection from national planning policy. In terms of landscape and scenic beauty, NPPF 172 states that National Parks, the Broads and AONBs have the highest status of protection. In *City and District Council of St Albans v Hunston Properties Ltd*,[12] Sir David Keene described these designations as "hostile to development" (para. 6).

12.29   The AONB is provided with statutory protection by section 85(1) of the Countryside and Rights of Way Act 2000, which provides:

> "In exercising or performing any functions in relation to, or so as to affect, land in an area of outstanding natural beauty, a relevant authority shall have regard to the purpose of conserving and enhancing the natural beauty of the area of outstanding natural beauty."

12.30   In *R (Steer) v Shepway DC*,[13] Lang J held that this duty was reflected in the predecessor

---

[11]   I am grateful to Sasha Blackmore for pointing this out.

[12]   [2013] EWCA Civ 1610; [2014] JPL 599.

[13]   [2018] EWHC 238 (Admin); [2018] LLR 368.

of NPPF 172.

12.31   It is worth noting that the protection of National Parks, the Broads, and AONBs is not solely in relation to landscape and scenic beauty. NPPF 172 states that:

> "The conservation and enhancement of wildlife and cultural heritage are also important considerations in these areas, and should be given great weight in National Parks and the Broads"

12.32   Read literally, this suggests that wildlife and cultural heritage are <u>important considerations</u> for all three designations, but policy requires it to be given great weight only for National Parks and the Broads (but not for AONBs). Whilst the protection of wildlife fits easily within Chapter 15 (there are paragraphs specifically about habitats and biodiversity at NPPF 174-177), the protection (and enhancement) of cultural heritage is less obvious. Cultural heritage is not defined in the Glossary to the NPPF. Collins J doubted in *R (Morris) v Wealden DC*[14] whether the sentence quoted above is necessary, given the reference to great weight at the start of the paragraph; however, there is a distinction drawn between landscape and scenic beauty on the one hand, and wildlife and cultural heritage on the other hand.

12.33   The NPPF is clear that plans must recognise a hierarchy of designations, between international, national, and locally designated sites (NPPF 171). This has a dual effect: sites higher up the hierarchy should be adequately protected. But conversely, it may be necessary to give a lower level of protection to those sites which have only a local designation (and local significance). An example of such a phenomenon might be seen in the designation "Area of Great Landscape Value" ("AGLV") in Surrey. Policies have previously attempted to give the AGLV the same level of protection as the AONB, despite the AONB being a national designation. In the process of examination of Waverley BC's new local plan, the Examining Inspector was clear that the AGLV could not be given the same level of policy protection as the AONB.

The Structure of Policies Regarding AONBs, National Parks, and the Broads

12.34   Two paragraphs of the old NPPF (paras 115-116) have been merged into the new NPPF 172. These used to deal separately on the one hand with the issue of great weight to be given in general terms to the protection of National Parks, the Broads, and AONBs, and on the other hand with the question of major development. The merging of the two paragraphs into the single NPPF 172 makes sense. This is because the policy requiring exceptional circumstances for major development in the AONB is an expression of the requirement to give great weight to the protection of the AONB. In *Franks v SSCLG*,[15] the claimant challenged the grant of planning permission on appeal for development in the AONB. The claimant accepted that the Inspector had correctly applied policy requiring exceptional circumstances for major development in the AONB. However, the claimant argued that the Inspector had nevertheless failed to give great weight to the conservation and enhancement of landscape and scenic beauty in the AONB.

---

[14]   [2014] EWHC 4081 (Admin).

[15]   [2015] EWHC 3690 (Admin).

12.35   Ouseley J rejected this argument. The requirement for exceptional circumstances prior to major development being permitted in the AONB was "one way, perhaps not the only way, ordained by the NPPF in which great weight could be given..." (para. 24). Ouseley J went on to state at para. 25 that "...if an Inspector correctly applies his mind to paragraph 116, he will in the normal run of events have properly applied his mind to any harm he has found under paragraph 115."

12.36   NPPF 172 reads as follows (footnotes omitted, underlining added):

> "Great weight should be given to conserving and enhancing landscape and scenic beauty in National Parks, the Broads and Areas of Outstanding Natural Beauty, which have the highest status of protection in relation to these issues. The conservation and enhancement of wildlife and cultural heritage are also important considerations in these areas, and should be given great weight in National Parks and the Broads. The scale and extent of development <u>within these designated areas</u> should be limited. Planning permission should be refused for major development other than in exceptional circumstances, and where it can be demonstrated that the development is in the public interest. Consideration of such applications should include an assessment of:
>
> > (a) the need for the development, including in terms of any national considerations, and the impact of permitting it, or refusing it, upon the local economy;
> >
> > (b) the cost of, and scope for, developing outside the designated area, or meeting the need for it in some other way; and
> >
> > (c) any detrimental effect on the environment, the landscape and recreational opportunities, and the extent to which that could be moderated."

12.37   NPPF 172 could be worded more clearly. The phrase underlined in the quotation of NPPF 172 refers to "these designated areas". The designated areas referred to at the end of the previous sentence are National Parks and the Broads, but not the AONB. One assumes that the underlined phrase is also to be read as including the AONB, but this is not obvious from the wording of the sentence.

12.38   The following sentence ("Planning permission should be refused...") does not refer to in what areas that aspect of policy applies. One assumes that it is the same as the previous sentence. This itself indicates that AONBs must be included in the under-lined phrase, since it is well-established policy from the original NPPF that major development in the AONB should be permitted in only exceptional circumstances.

12.39   The underlined word "within" requires some thought. In para. 116 of the old NPPF, the exceptionality test applied to major development in the designated areas. The question arose in the context of development of a golf course whether the development was in the AONB. Only one fairway and one tee of the golf course was going to be within the AONB. In the High Court in *R (Cherkley Campaign Ltd) v Mole Valley DC*, Haddon-Cave J held[16] that it would be "artificial, and frankly myopic, to focus simply on the one tee and hole physically within the curtilage of the AONB and ignore the other 17 tees and holes course along the border of the NPPF" (para. 147). The Court of Appeal disagreed (para. 44),[17] finding that the focus is on the wording of the NPPF itself. It appears that the implication of the Court of Appeal's decision is that, if only part of a development is in the AONB, then that part would need to be major. If major development was proposed outside the AONB, then that could be taken into account when considering the great weight to be given to preservation, but the exceptionality test would not apply. Although the new version of the NPPF uses the word "within" rather than "in", there is no indication that this would make a difference to the meaning.

12.40   Aside from the question of to which areas it applies, the reference to limiting the scale and extent of development is of interest because it was introduced to the NPPF only in the second version. It is not clear in what way the extent of development is a different concept to the scale of development; it may be that the two words are used for emphasis.

Great Weight

12.41   Whilst NPPF 172 refers to the need to give great weight to conservation and enhancement of landscape and scenic beauty,[18] the Court of Appeal in *Bayliss v SSCLG*[19] held that a decision does not necessarily need to use that exact phrase as "some form of incantation". Sir David Keene, giving the sole judgment of the Court of Appeal, noted that "the effect of a proposal on an AONB will itself vary". Different weights can be given, he said, dependent upon the degree of harm; finding that it would be irrational for a decision-maker to do otherwise (para. 18). Collins J considered Sir David Keene's decision in *Morris*, and considered that the effect of his decision was that, when considering the meaning of "great", it would have to be considered in relation to the harm which would be brought about by a particular proposal. He gave an example of where harm was trivial only. In those circumstances, "the great weight to be attached could more easily be outweighed by an advantages that accrued from the development in question" (para. 54). That said, the AONB is a "special category of material consideration": *R (Mevagissey Parish Council) v Cornwall Council*,[20] para. 51.

12.42   In *Stroud DC*, Ouseley J considered para. 115 of the old NPPF. As stated above, paragraphs of the old NPPF have been merged into the new NPPF 172, but Ouseley J was considering policy which states that great weight should be given to conserving landscape and scenic beauty in National Parks, the Broads and AONBs. He

---

[16] [2013] EWHC 2582 (Admin); [2014] 1 P&CR 12.

[17] [2014] EWCA Civ 567.

[18] The PPG makes clear that the requirement to give great weight applies regardless of whether the proposed development constitutes major development (considered further below): PPG, Section on Natural Environment, para. 005. This was also considered by Ouseley J in *Franks* (above).

[19] [2014] EWCA Civ 347.

[20] [2013] EWHC 3684 (Admin).

stated at para. 26 of his decision:

> "So the question is whether on the proper interpretation of paragraph 115 views of the AONB from outside the AONB fall within its scope. It is my judgment that that is not what policy 115 is intended to cover. It certainly covers the impact on the scenic beauty of the land actually within the AONB. It seems to me that it would be unduly restrictive to say that it could not cover the impact of land viewed in conjunction with the AONB from the AONB. But to go so far as to say that it must also cover land from which the AONB can be seen and great weight must be given to the conservation of beauty in the AONB by reference to that impact reads too much into paragraph 115. The effect of [Counsel for the Claimant's] approach would be to give very widespread protection to land outside the AONB and not significant in views from the AONB. The Inspector noted that almost everywhere in Stroud District would fall into that category. That could not be, in my judgment, the correct interpretation of paragraph 115, and the word "in"."

Major Development in AONBs, National Parks and the Broads

12.43 The question of whether development is "in" these designated areas is considered above. Two questions remain regarding the exceptional circumstances test: what constitutes major development, and is there any guidance regarding what will constitute an exceptional circumstance in this context?

12.44 "Major development" is defined in the Glossary to the NPPF. However, this definition does <u>not</u> apply to NPPF 172-173. Footnote 55 to the NPPF makes clear that, for the purposes of those paragraphs, "whether a proposal is 'major development' is a matter for the decision maker, taking into account its nature, scale and setting, and whether it could have a significant adverse impact on the purpose for which the area has been designated or defined". This was a change to the revised NPPF added after consultation; in the consultation version of the amended NPPF, the general Glossary definition of "major development", which is prescriptive in form, would have applied to development in AONBs, National Parks and the Broads.

12.45 A decision-maker has to decide whether or not proposed development is a major development. This is a matter of sufficient significance that a decision-maker cannot sit on the fence on the issue: *R (Steer) v Shepway DC*,[21] para. 27.

12.46 The general principle that the question of whether development is major reflects case law on the original NPPF. In *Aston v SSCLG*,[22] the claimants challenged the grant of planning permission on appeal for fourteen dwellings on a site within the Surrey Hills AONB. The Inspector expressed in trenchant terms his conclusion that the development was not major development: he found that it could not properly be described as major "by any published or even commonsense criterion". The claimants argued that this was an error: as a matter of law, the phrase "major development" should have a homogenous meaning across planning law and policy.

---

[21] [2018] EWHC 238 (Admin); [2018] LLR 368.

[22] [2013] EWHC 1936 (Admin); [2014] 2 P&CR 10.

The ten-unit threshold for major development, set out in the Town and Country Planning (Development Management Procedure) Order 2010 should therefore apply. According to that definition, the proposed development would be major development, and the Inspector should have applied the exceptionality test.

12.47   Wyn Williams J rejected this argument. He noted that, in the original version of the NPPF, unlike Footnote 55 of the amended NPPF, there was no definition or illustration of the meaning of "major developments". There was no reason for the phrase to have a uniform meaning in all policy documents, procedural rules or Government guidance.[23] Wyn Williams J considered that "the term should be construed in the context of the document in which it appears". The context of the material paragraphs of the NPPF militated against a precise definition. The definition in the Development Management Procedure Order would be artificial; the context of the Order was procedural (unlike the NPPF, which constitutes a detailed policy framework). On the facts of the case, the Inspector's conclusion was open to him.

12.48   Lindblom J followed *Aston* on this point in *R (The Forge Field Society) v Sevenoaks DC*.[24] In *Forge Field*, the local planning authority had granted planning permission for affordable housing. The claimants challenged this grant of planning permission, including on grounds that the Council should have treated a development of six affordable houses as "major development". Having agreed with Wyn Williams J, Lindblom J went on to say at para. 67:

> "In this context I think "major developments" would normally be projects much larger than six dwellings on a site the size of Forge Field, but in any event it was clearly open to the Council to conclude that the proposed development in this case was not a major development to which the policy in para.116 applied. This too was an entirely reasonable exercise of planning judgment, and the court should not interfere with it."

12.49   Further consideration of the phrase "major development" was provided by Lang J in *Steer*. She held at para. 40:

> "… In my view, the question as to whether or not this particular proposal was a "major development" could have been decided either way, on the evidence. On the one hand, there would only be twelve lodges, but on the other hand, this was a sizeable holiday park, with construction of a reception building, a store, a fishing lake, a car park, tennis courts, a children's play area and a putting green, on what was agricultural land, located next to a wood classified as Ancient Woodland. In the light of the OR, and the numerous objections, it needed express consideration by the Committee."

12.50   Stuart-Smith J considered the meaning of "major development" in *R (JH and FW*

---

[23]   One might contrast the approach to the Green Belt, where the meaning of the word "development" is to be taken as that found in section 55 TCPA: *Fordent Holdings Ltd v SSCLG* [2013] EWHC 2844 (Admin); [2014] 2 P&CR 12, *Europa Oil and Gas Ltd v SSCLG* [2013] EWHC 2643 (Admin); [2013] 1 P&CR 3, para. 53 [see Chapter 3: The Interpretation of Policy].

[24]   [2014] EWHC 1895 (Admin); [2015] JPL 22.

Green Ltd) v South Downs National Park Authority.[25] The Judge noted at para. 27 that, subject to a "limited dispute about the word 'potential'"[26], the parties agreed that reasonable working guidance for the meaning of "major development" is:

"any development which, by reason of its scale character or nature, has the potential to have a serious adverse impact on the natural beauty, recreational opportunities, wildlife or cultural heritage provided by a National Park. Obviously, the assessment of whether the proposal is major is therefore a matter of judgment based on all the circumstances, including the local context."

12.51   Stuart-Smith J rejected the proposition (at para. 33) that the definition of "major development" in the DMPO would be a relevant consideration when determining whether a proposal was for major development for the purposes of natural environment policy in the NPPF. He accepted that the DMPO definition may, in theory, be relevant and material in some cases (para. 35). However, the only reason why the DMPO requirement would be met in the present case was because of the size of the application site, which indicates nothing about the actual changes which would be brought about by the proposed development.

12.52   Turning to the definition in Footnote 55, the question as to whether proposed development constitutes major development is a matter which includes not only consideration of the development itself, but also "whether it could have a significant adverse impact on the purpose for which the area has been designated or defined". One might think that this is a question which goes to whether the development should be permitted, rather than whether it constitutes major development, but it nevertheless represents part of the definition to be found in national policy. The decision in *JH and FW Green* suggests that this may have been an element of policy in the original NPPF in any event.

12.53   The meaning of "exceptional circumstances" was considered by Hickinbottom J in *R (Mevagissey Parish Council) v Cornwall Council.*[27] Planning permission was granted for 31 dwellings, of which 21 were affordable homes, with associated development. The case is useful for its consideration of when the exceptional circumstances test will be viewed as satisfied. At para. 7, Hickinbottom J stated that exceptional connotes rarity. He considered that the provision of affordable housing may "be a significant factor of whether the circumstances are exceptional", but found that: (a) there was no evidence (beyond assertion) of particular need in the area being exceptional in the sense of unusual or rare; (b) the assessment of exceptionality must be done in respect of a specific proposed development; (c) the Council did not say that the need for affordable housing constituted "exceptional circumstances" for the purpose of AONB policy in the NPPF. Even an exceptional need for affordable housing

---

[25]   [2018] EWHC 604 (Admin).

[26]   At para. 55, Stuart-Smith J held that he found any distinction between "potential" for harm and "likelihood" of harm, in the context of the officer report as a whole, "sterile and unimportant". He rejected a proposition that "the existence of any possibility at all of serious harm would require any development to be categorised as a "major development" within [the policy]".

[27]   [2013] EWHC 3684 (Admin).

would not necessary mean that the exceptionality test was satisfied in relation to a particular development, as there could be alternative sites which would cause less harm to the AONB. On the facts of the case, the decision was unlawful since the planning committee seemed to have carried out a simple balancing exercise, which was not a legitimate approach (para. 58).

12.54　The Court of Appeal considered alternative sites for housing development in the AONB in *SSCLG v Wealden DC*.[28] In the High Court, Lang J had found that the Inspector had erred in the assessment of alternatives. The Court of Appeal disagreed. Lindblom LJ stressed at para. 63 that the exceptional circumstances test remains an exercise of planning judgment:

> "The policy requires the exercise of planning judgment. The decision-maker must consider whether there are "exceptional circumstances" justifying the granting of planning permission for the development in question, and whether granting permission would be "in the public interest". The three bullet points[29] do not exclude other considerations relevant to those questions. The first requires the decision-maker to consider the "need for the development", including "any national considerations"- for example, the considerations of national policy for housing need and supply. The second bullet point does not refer specifically to alternative sites. It refers to the "cost" and "scope" for development "elsewhere outside the designated area", and to the possibility of meeting of the need for the development "in some other way". In many cases, this will involve the consideration of alternative sites. But the policy does not prescribe for the decision-maker how alternative sites are to be assessed in any particular case. It does not say that this exercise must relate to the whole of a local planning authority's administrative area, or to an area larger or smaller than that. This will always depend on the circumstances of the case in hand. The third bullet point requires the decision-maker to consider potential harm in the three respects referred to - again, always a matter of planning judgment."

12.55　The terms of national policy did not require an Inspector to deal "with every potential site for housing in the district, one by one" (para. 68).

12.56　NPPF 172(c) refers to the consideration of the "extent to which [detrimental effect] could be moderated". The meaning of this is not clear: it might refer to whether the detrimental effect can be moderated through the decision-making process (such as by condition or obligation under section 106 TCPA), or it may mean whether the detrimental effect could be moderated only by refusing the consent and granting permission for an alternative proposal.

The Coast

12.57　The character of the undeveloped coast is identified as a matter to be contributed to and enhanced, whilst improving public access as is appropriate (NPPF 170(c)).

---

[28]　[2017] EWCA Civ 39; [2018] Env LR 5.

[29]　In the new NPPF, these are marked (a), (b) and (c).

12.58　The status of the Heritage Coast is raised in the new NPPF. The Heritage Coast is defined in the Glossary as:

> "Areas of undeveloped coastline which are managed to conserve their natural beauty and, where appropriate, to improve accessibility for visitors."

12.59　NPPF 173 states that planning policies and decisions should be "consistent with the special character of the area and the importance of its conservation". Major development[30] is considered unlikely to be appropriate in the heritage coast, unless compatible with its special character.

Habitats and Biodiversity

12.60　NPPF 174 sets out requirements for plans as respects biodiversity and geodiversity. This includes aims of both safeguarding habitats and ecological networks, but also promoting conservation, restoration and enhancement. Unlike in the previous NPPF, there is no express reference to a requirement to plan for biodiversity at a landscape-scale across local authority boundaries. Neither is there a reference to the Nature Improvement Areas programme. There is a reference to "local wildlife-rich habitats" in NPPF 174: local wildlife issues was an important matter raised in the consultation on the draft amended NPPF. However, it is now said that plans should "identify and pursue opportunities for securing measurable net gains for biodiversity". Plans should not only identify sites, but also "wildlife corridors and stepping stones that connect them". A wildlife corridor is defined in the Glossary as "[a]reas of habitat connecting wildlife populations". Stepping stones are defined in the Glossary as "[p]ockets of habitat that, while not necessarily connected, facilitate the movement of species across otherwise inhospitable landscapes".

12.61　NPPF 175 relates to determining planning applications, and sets out principles to apply (rather than merely matters to take into account).

12.62　NPPF 175(a) sets out a situation in which planning permission should be refused, if significant harm to biodiversity cannot be avoided, mitigated, or compensated for. Compensation is a last resort, but nevertheless adequate compensation would mean that planning permission could nevertheless be granted.

12.63　In terms of assessment of significant harm, Lindblom J considered in *R (Prideaux) v Buckinghamshire County Council*[31] that mitigation measures could be taken into account in considering whether significant harm would be caused by the development. *Prideaux* relies on the decision of the High Court in *R (Hart DC) v SSCLG*,[32] in the context of the Habitats Directive. *Hart DC* is no longer good law, in the context of the Habitats Directive, after the decision of the CJEU in Case C-323/17 *People Over Wind v Coillte Teoranta*.[33] However, the CJEU's decision related to the Habitats

---

[30]　Applying the same meaning of "major development" as considered above, not the definition in the Glossary.

[31]　[2013] EWHC 1054 (Admin); [2013] Env LR 32.

[32]　[2008] EWHC 1204 (Admin); [2008] 2 P&CR 16.

[33]　[2018] PTSR 1668.

Directive and the protection of Special Areas of Conservation under European Union law. It is unlikely that the domestic courts would find that *Prideaux* could no longer be followed on this point in relation to sites which do not have European level protection.

12.64   NPPF 175(b) concerns development on land within or outside a SSSI. It is said that development which is likely to have an adverse effect on the SSSI should not be permitted. Whilst this would appear to give a wide scope of discretion to the decision-maker, the paragraph should be read as a whole: it is later specified that there is only one exception, namely where the benefits of the proposal clearly outweigh the likely impact on the features of the SSSI which make it of special scientific interest, and any broader impacts on the national network of SSSIs. This is therefore a lower level of protection than is given to European sites under Article 6 of the Habitats Directive, which permits development that would have an adverse effect on the integrity of a European site only where there are imperative reasons of overriding public interest (Article 6(4)), and where compensation habitat is provided.

12.65   NPPF 175(c) concerns irreplaceable habitats. Examples given of irreplaceable habitats are given as ancient woodland and ancient or veteran trees. Ancient woodland is defined in the Glossary as "[a]n area that has been wooded continuously since at least 1600 AD, and includes ancient semi-natural woodland and plantations on ancient woodland sites". Ancient or veteran trees are also defined in the Glossary. An ancient or veteran tree is a tree which, because of its age, size and condition, is of exceptional biodiversity, cultural or heritage value. It is said that all ancient trees are veteran trees. However not all veteran trees are ancient. Veteran trees have to be old relative to other trees of the same species. The definition states that "Very few trees of any species reach the ancient life-stage".

12.66   It is worth noting that to be ancient or veteran, any one of the three values (biodiversity, cultural, or heritage) can be satisfied. However, in order to satisfy one of the three values, all three of the criteria age, size and condition must be taken into account. Presumably there is some flexibility in relation to this, otherwise it might be suggested that a very small tree which was nevertheless extremely old and in a good condition might not meet the criteria.

12.67   Irreplaceable habitats are provided with a high degree of protection, and this level of protection has been increased from the previous version of the NPPF. Indeed, the justification for the loss (or even deterioration) of irreplaceable habitat are wholly exceptional reasons, and where there is a suitable compensation strategy. The test of wholly exceptional reasons is a higher threshold than for major development in the AONB. A footnote gives examples of such reasons being "infrastructure projects (including nationally significant infrastructure projects, orders under the Transport and Works Act and hybrid bills), where the public benefit would clearly outweigh the loss or deterioration of habitat."

12.68   Habitats site is defined in the Glossary as:

> "Any site which would be included within the definition at regulation 8 of the Conservation of Habitats and Species Regulations 2017 for the purpose

of those regulations, including candidate Special Areas of Conservation, Sites of Community Importance, Special Areas of Conservation, Special Protection Areas and any relevant Marine Sites."

12.69   Potential SPAs, possible SACs and proposed Ramsar sites are to be given the same protection as habitats sites (NPPF 176). These are explained further in Footnote 59:

"Potential Special Protection Areas, possible Special Areas of Conservation and proposed Ramsar sites are sites on which Government has initiated public consultation on the scientific case for designation as a Special Protection Area, candidate Special Area or Conservation or Ramsar site."

12.70   In *Savage v Mansfield DC*,[34] Lewison LJ held that the NPPF does not provide protection for a site unless and until the Government has started public consultation. Where a site is not even a potential SPA, there is no obligation for a local planning authority to carry out an equivalent to an appropriate assessment under the Habitats Directive: the obligation does not arise as the proposed development is not within the scope of that protection.

12.71   The NPPF gives protection (NPPF 176(c)) to sites which are identified as, or required as, compensatory measures for adverse effects on protected sites (whether a Habitats Site or a potential, possible or proposed site).

12.72   It is worth noting that the requirement in the old NPPF for planning policies to aim to prevent harm to geological conservation interests is no longer expressly found in the new NPPF.

12.73   NPPF 177 disapplies the presumption in favour of sustainable development where an appropriate assessment is required under the Habitats Directive. The implication of the decision of the CJEU in *People Over Wind* for NPPF 177 is considered above. Whilst it may be that the courts attempt to restrict the effect of the CJEU's decision, it is likely that *People Over Wind* will mean that the effect of the presumption is lost in a number of cases where previously it would have been available.

Ground Conditions and Pollution

12.74   This section of Chapter 15 has some changes from the previous version of the NPPF. Many of the changes are cosmetic (re-ordering of the paragraphs and changing presentation), but there are a number of alterations to the substance.

12.75   NPPF 178 and 180 set out a number of aims for both policies and decisions. NPPF 178 concerns ground conditions, seeking to ensure that sites are suitable, that any remediation is of an appropriate standard (defined by reference to the threshold of 'contaminated land' under Part IIA of the Environmental Protection Act 1990). Site investigation information must be available, having been prepared by a competent

---

[34]   [2015] EWCA Civ 4.

person.[35] Land suitability also must be taken into account in assessing suitability,[36] not only in decision-taking, but also in making plans.[37]

12.76 NPPF 179 was formerly part of the equivalent of NPPF 178 in the old NPPF. It states that if there are contamination or land stability issues, then responsibility for securing a safe development lies with the developer and/or landowner. By making it a separate paragraph, it is not clear how this aim is to be secured. Presumably that this would be best achieved through decision-making, including by the imposition of suitable conditions.

12.77 NPPF 180 relates to development being appropriate for its location, but refers specifically to the impacts from noise, and light pollution. The guidance concerning noise is a more compact version of previous policy found in para. 123 of the previous NPPF. This policy was considered in *May v Rother DC*.[38] The court had to consider whether development plan policy was materially different to the NPPF. Ian Dove QC, sitting as a Deputy High Court Judge, found the discussion "unnecessarily and unhelpfully philosophical". He found that both texts "are policies which have to be read purposely with an object in mind of ensuring that noise pollution does not imperil a reasonable and appropriate standard of residential amenity for people's homes. They have to be applied in a practical context" (para. 46). He found that there is no practical difference between considering whether adverse impact is kept to a minimum, or whether noise would have an unreasonable impact upon amenity, these being "two formulations of essentially the same practical question" (para. 48). However, there may be an impact upon noise which may not reach the threshold of a noise nuisance (para. 49).

12.78 NPPF 181 concerns air quality and air pollution. This is a slight expansion on the text found in the original NPPF. However, it is notable that there is no longer a reference to EU limit values: the removal of a reference to the EU from this paragraph of the new NPPF may be an attempt to ensure that it remains appropriate even after the UK leaves the European Union. The new version of the policy also includes a requirement to identify opportunities to improve air quality or mitigate

---

[35] The PPG indicates that the information sought from an applicant for outline planning permission should be proportionate to the decision at outline stage, but the local planning authority will need to be satisfied, prior to granting permission, that "it understands the contaminated condition of the site; the proposed development is appropriate as a means of remediating it; and it has sufficient information to be confident that it will be able to grant permission in full at a later stage bearing in mind the need for the necessary remediation to be viable and practicable" (PPG, Section on Land affected by contamination, para. 008). At the time of writing, this Section of the PPG is yet to be amended following the new NPPF.

[36] PPG, Section on Land stability, para. 001, states that the planning system has an important role in considering land stability by "minimising the risk and effects of land stability on property, infrastructure and the public; helping ensure that various types of development should not be placed in unstable locations without various precautions; and to bring unstable land, wherever possible, back into productive use". However, the PPG also notes, Section on Land stability, para. 002, that land stability is not solely a planning issue.

[37] PPG, Section on land stability, para. 003. At the time of writing, this Section of the PPG is yet to be amended following the new NPPF.

[38] [2014] EWHC 456; [2014] LLR 535.

impacts. It is also proposed that air quality issues should, as far as possible, be considered at the plan-making stage. If done, this may limit the need for issues to be reconsidered at the decision-making stage.[39]

12.79 NPPF 182, on the effective integration of new development with existing businesses and facilities, is also an expansion of the previous version of the NPPF. The expansion appears to emphasise the weight that should be given to existing businesses and community uses when deciding whether to grant planning permission: they should not be subject to unreasonable restrictions as a result of development permitted after they were established. The new version has inserted a requirement for a developer to provide suitable mitigation before completion of the mitigation where the operation of an existing business/community facility could have a significant adverse effect on new development. It is not expressly stated what approach should be taken if it is not possible to provide suitable mitigation, or the mitigation would not reduce the adverse effect to an acceptable level. Reading the paragraph as a whole, the approach would appear to be that planning permission should be refused in those circumstances.

12.80 NPPF 183 replicates previous policy regarding separate processes under the pollution control regimes. Each regime should assume that the other operates effectively. Planning permission is about land use, and should not focus on the control of processes or emissions. Likewise, the permitting regimes operating in relation to pollution should not seek to reopen planning issues. As the Court of Appeal held in *Preston New Road Action Group v SSCLG*,[40] the policy in NPPF 183 is "not easy to reconcile"[41] with an argument that a decision-maker has acted unreasonably in relying upon other regulatory regimes operating as they should. However, as has been made clear in *Gladman Developments v SSCLG*,[42] the policy applies only where there is in fact a parallel system of control. Where a decision had to consider the Air Quality Directive, NPPF 183 did not apply, since there was no separate licensing or permitting decision that would address the air quality impacts of the proposed development.

---

[39] This is consistent with the approach of the new version of the NPPF to viability: that issues should as much as possible be resolved at plan-making stage, to reduce the complexity of decisions on individual applications.

[40] [2018] EWCA Civ 9; [2018] Env LR 18.

[41] It may be that the Court of Appeal expressed itself somewhat mildly.

[42] [2017] EWHC 2768 (Admin); [2018] PTSR 616.

Chapter 13

Conserving and Enhancing the Historic Environment

Introduction

13.01   The Section of the first version of the NPPF concerning the historic environment
has been the subject of a large amount of litigation. This is in part due to the fact
that the historic environment is protected not only by policy, but also by a particular legislative regime (in the Planning (Listed Buildings and Conservation Areas)
Act 1990).[1] There has been a large amount of consideration of the interrelation
between national planning policy, and the legal duties imposed upon decision-
makers by statute.

13.02   Another reason for the large amount of litigation is that national planning policy is
restrictive of development. Rather than merely giving the decision-maker matters to
take into account, in places it imposes a policy framework which is heavily restrictive
of development having certain effects. However, the Government is keen to stress
that heritage assets are not simply a burden; the PPG states that effective conservation "delivers wider social, cultural, economic and environmental benefits".[2]

13.03   There have not been fundamental changes to heritage policy brought about by
the new NPPF. The NPPF states that the policies in Chapter 16 apply not only
to plan-making and decision-taking under the TCPA, but also to heritage-related
consent regimes for which local planning authorities are responsible under the Listed
Buildings Act. NPPF 186 sets out a consideration which local authorities must take
into account when deciding whether to designate conservation areas (see below).

The Scheme of National Policy

13.04   National planning policy recognises the range of different heritage assets (NPPF
184). A major distinction which it draws is between *designated* and *non-designated*
heritage assets. Both, however, constitute heritage assets.

13.05   Heritage assets are defined in the Glossary as:

> "A building, monument, site, place, area or landscape identified as having a
> degree of significance meriting consideration in planning decisions, because
> of its heritage interest. It includes designated heritage assets and assets identi-
> fied by the local planning authority (including local listing)."

13.06   Designated heritage assets are defined in the Glossary as:

> "A World Heritage Site, Scheduled Monument, Listed Building, Protected
> Wreck Site, Registered Park and Garden, Registered Battlefield or Conservation
> Area designated under the relevant legislation."

---

[1]   Referred to in this chapter as the Listed Buildings Act, although it also contains important provisions
regarding conservation areas.

[2]   PPG, Section on Conserving and enhancing the historic environment, para. 003. NB, at the time of
writing, this section of the PPG is yet to be reviewed following the new NPPF.

13.07   "Significance (for heritage policy)" is defined in the Glossary as:

> "The value of a heritage asset to this and future generations because of its heritage interest. The interest may be archaeological, architectural, artistic or historic. Significance derives not only from a heritage asset's physical presence, but also from its setting. For World Heritage Sites, the cultural value described within each site's Statement of Outstanding Universal Value forms part of its significance."

13.08   "Setting of a heritage asset" is defined in the Glossary as:

> "The surroundings in which a heritage asset is experienced. Its extent is not fixed and may change as the asset and its surroundings evolve. Elements of a setting may make a positive or negative contribution to the significance of an asset, may affect the ability to appreciate that significance or may be neutral."

13.09   The level of protection which is provided is greater to designated heritage assets than to non-designated heritage assets (compare NPPF 194-196 with NPPF 197).

13.10   Another key distinction drawn in Chapter 16 is between harm which is substantial, and less than substantial harm. Simply put, this affects the level of planning benefit which the proposal would need to demonstrate in order to be supported by the NPPF. Unsurprisingly, the threshold for justifying substantial harm to a heritage asset is higher than the threshold for justifying less than substantial harm.

13.11   Chapter 16 not only imposes requirements on local planning authorities when determining a planning application or drafting a development plan document, but also imposes a requirement for them to "maintain or have access to a historic environment record" (NPPF 187). This should be kept up to date, and is to be used to assess the significance of heritage assets and the contribution they make to their environment, and to predict the likelihood of the discovery of currently unidentified heritage assets.

13.12   There is also a requirement for local planning authorities to make information about the historic environment, which is gathered as part of their planning functions, available to the public (NPPF 188).

13.13   Whilst the primary impact of the policies in Chapter 16 is restrictive, there is a duty for local authorities to "look for opportunities for new development" which would enhance or better reveal the significance of Conservation Areas, World Heritage Sites, or heritage assets (NPPF 200).

The Statutory Regime

13.14   Section 66(1) of the Listed Buildings Act provides:

> "In considering whether to grant planning permission or permission in principle or development which affects a listed building or its setting, the local planning authority or, as the case may be, the Secretary of State shall have special regard to the desirability of preserving the building or its setting or any features of special architectural or historic interest which it possesses."

13.15   Section 72(1) concerns conservation areas, and provides:

> "In the exercise, with respect to any buildings or other land in a conservation
> area, of any functions under or by virtue of any of the provisions mentioned
> in subsection (2), special attention shall be paid to the desirability of preserv-
> ing or enhancing the character or appearance of that area."

13.16   In the context of this legislation, "preserving" means doing no harm (*South Lakeland
        DC v Secretary of State for the Environment*).[3]

13.17   The courts have found that there is "no conflict" between the duty in section 66(1)
        of the Listed Buildings Act, and national policy regarding listed buildings in the
        NPPF: *Forest of Dean DC v SSCLG*.[4] In *North Norfolk DC v SSCLG*,[5] a Deputy High
        Court Judge agreed with this, but gave decision-makers a warning about the weight
        to be given to heritage harm. Hickinbottom J, in *R (Austin) v Wiltshire Council*,[6] held
        that section 66(1) is reflected in the requirement in NPPF 193 to give great weight
        to conservation; in *R (Hughes) v South Lakeland DC*,[7] HHJ Waksman QC, sitting as
        a Judge of the High Court, held at para. 52 that the same applies to section 72(1)
        in the context of conservation areas.

13.18   The requirement to have "special regard" or "special attention"[8] to the importance
        of preservation is not merely a procedural matter. It cannot be satisfied merely by
        a decision-maker expressing that they have thought carefully about the benefits of
        preservation of the heritage asset. The requirements in these provisions (unusually)[9]
        prescribe the weight which the decision-maker must give to the protection of the
        historic environment. In *East Northamptonshire DC v Secretary of State for Communities
        and Local Government*,[10] the Court of Appeal held that the degree of harm to the
        setting of a listed building was a matter of planning judgment. However, unusu-
        ally in the context of planning decisions, it is not open to a decision-maker to give
        such weight to that harm as she wishes when carrying out a balancing exercise: a
        finding of harm to a heritage asset is a matter which <u>must</u> be given "considerable
        importance and weight" (para. 22). Furthermore, there is a "strong presumption"
        against the granting planning permission for development which would harm the
        character or appearance of a conservation area (para. 23).

13.19   The duties in sections 66(1) and 72(1) do not permit the decision-maker to simply

---

[3]   [1992] 2 AC 141.

[4]   [2013] EWHC 4052 (Admin).

[5]   [2014] EWHC 279 (Admin).

[6]   [2017] EWHC 38 (Admin).

[7]   [2014] EWHC 3979 (Admin).

[8]   There appears to be no difference between these two phrases: *Heatherington (UK) Ltd v Secretary of State
      for the Environment* (1995) 69 P&CR 374, 379-380.

[9]   In a passage much loved by barristers defending against claims brought in the Planning Court, in *Tesco
      Stores Ltd v Secretary of State for the Environment* [1995] 1 WLR 759, Lord Hoffmann said at p.780 "If
      there is one principle of planning law more firmly settled than any other, it is that matters of planning
      judgment are within the exclusive province of the local planning authority or the Secretary of State".

[10] [2014] EWCA Civ 137; [2015] 1 WLR 45. This case is commonly known as "Barnwell Manor".

treat the desirability of preservation merely as another material consideration: *R (The Forge Field Society) v Sevenoaks DC*,[11] para. 46.

13.20   The requirement that the decision-maker give considerable importance and weight to heritage matters is legally less problematic following the decision of the Court of Appeal in *Jones v Mordue*.[12] A Planning Inspector had found that a proposal for a single wind turbine would cause less than substantial harm to the setting of a Grade II listed building. In the High Court, the decision of the Inspector was quashed on the basis that there was no indication either way that the Inspector had given considerable importance and weight to preserving the setting of a listed building.

13.21   On appeal, the Court of Appeal reversed the High Court's decision and reinstated the decision of the Inspector. Where a person aggrieved by the decision of an Inspector wishes to challenge that decision on the basis of a failure by the Inspector to give considerable importance and weight to preserving the heritage asset, the challenger must be able to provide some positive indication that the Inspector failed to do so. There was no indication one way or the other in the case before the Court of Appeal whether the Inspector had given considerable importance and weight to the setting of the listed church, or whether he had carried out a simple balancing exercise.

13.22   The implication of the Court of Appeal's decision is that a court should be slow to find that an expert Planning Inspector had failed to apply section 66(1).[13] Where an Inspector refers to the relevant passages of the NPPF, this implies that he will have taken into account the statutory duty (para. 28):

> "[NPPF 196] appears as part of a fasciculus of paragraphs, set out above, which lay down an approach which corresponds with the duty in section 66(1). Generally, a decision-maker who works through those paragraphs in accordance with their terms will have complied with the section 66(1) duty. When an expert planning inspector refers to a paragraph within that grouping of provisions (as the Inspector referred to [NPPF 196] in the decision letter in this case) then - absent some positive contrary indication in other parts of the text of his reasons - the appropriate inference is that he has taken properly into account all those provisions, not that he has forgotten about all the other paragraphs apart from the specific one he has mentioned. Working through these paragraphs, a decision-maker who had properly directed himself by reference to them would indeed have arrived at the conclusion that the case fell within [NPPF 196], as the Inspector did."

13.23   In practice, it is safer for those making decisions to make clear that they are giving considerable importance and weight to the preservation of heritage assets. Whilst

---

[11]   [2014] EWHC 1895 (Admin); [2015] JPL 22.

[12]   [2015] EWCA Civ 1243; [2016] 1 WLR 2682.

[13]   This is part of a trend in English public law of giving weight to the expert views of decision-makers: *AH (Sudan) v Secretary of State for the Home Department* [2007] UKHL 49; [2008] 1 AC 678. *AH (Sudan)* was cited in the planning context by Lord Carnwath JSC in *Hopkins Homes Ltd v SSCLG* [2017] UKSC 37; [2017] 1 WLR 1865, when he said that the courts should start from the presumption that specialist Planning Inspectors have understood the policy framework correctly (para. 25).

what matters is substance and not form, and the courts will not be impressed by the invocation of a phrase without applying it in substance (or merely going through a "box-ticking" exercise), referring to the duty to give considerable importance and weight will help defend a decision.

13.24 Conversely, for those considering a challenge on the basis of a failure to comply with section 66(1) or section 72(1), it will be necessary to provide some positive indication that something has gone wrong with the decision-maker. If there is a reference in a decision to carrying out a balance or weighing exercise without any reference to heritage factors weighing especially heavily in that balance, this will assist in the bringing of such a challenge.

Plan-making

13.25 When devising plans, local planning authorities should "set out a positive strategy for the conservation and enjoyment of the historic environment" (NPPF 185). NPPF 185 stresses the positive contributions which the historic environment can play in an area. Heritage assets should not merely be seen as a burden, holding back development. The PPG suggests that it may be helpful to include provision for non-designated heritage assets when a plan is being prepared, both in terms of the criteria for identifying such assets, and information about the location of existing assets.[14] This version of the PPG related to the original NPPF. It may be that the criteria for the identification of non-designated heritage assets are, under the language of the new NPPF, a matter for strategic policies, and the identification of existing assets is a matter for non-strategic policies or neighbourhood plans.

Making Applications

13.26 Applicants for planning permission which may affect heritage assets must describe the significance of the heritage assets, including contribution made by their setting (NPPF 189). This is not an open or empty requirement: a court has quashed a grant of planning permission where there has been a failure on the part of the decision-maker to do so. In *Obar Camden Ltd v Camden LBC*,[15] the local planning authority had granted (by its planning committee) permission for change of use of a pub to mixed use including retail/estate agent's officers and residential development. The claimant's premises were in a Grade II listed building next to the application site.[16] They sought to quash the grant of planning permission by judicial review.

13.27 There was no assessment of the significance of heritage assets in the Officer Report. Neither were Councillors informed that NPPF 189 required the applicant to describe the significance of heritage assets affected. Stewart J was unimpressed with the Council's argument that this process had been "truncated", that officers had decided that there was no harm, and reliance upon the experience of the committee. There

---

[14] PPG, Section on Conserving and enhancing the historic environment, para. 006.

[15] [2015] EWHC 2475 (Admin); [2016] JPL 241.

[16] The Commentary in the Journal of Planning and Environmental Law by Martin Edwards also makes clear the listed building's significance as a music venue: amongst other things, Coldplay launched their album X&Y from there.

were other significant failings on the part of the Council; the Council's argument that the permission should stand despite the errors was unsuccessful. NPPF 199 provides that developers must "record and advance understanding of the significance of any heritage assets to be lost (wholly or in part) in a manner proportionate to their importance and the impact". This research must be made publicly available. NPPF 199 restates that "the ability to record evidence of our past should not be a factor in deciding whether such loss should be permitted". In *R (Hayes) v York CC*,[17] Kerr J held at para. 81 that this sentence should be read as meaning that the ability to record evidence "should not be a *decisive* factor".

General Considerations in Determining Planning Applications

13.28　In *Lyndon-Stanford QC v Mid Suffolk District Council*,[18] John Howell QC, sitting as a Deputy High Court Judge, considered the lawfulness of a decision to grant planning permission and listed building consent for works to provide three dwellings and demolish four modern buildings. The Deputy Judge considered (para. 71) that the reference now in NPPF 185(a) and 192(a), to "the desirability of sustaining and enhancing the significance of heritage assets, and putting them to viable uses consistent with their conservation", reflects the obligation in section 66(1) of the Listed Buildings Act.

13.29　Regardless of whether the harm is substantial or less than substantial, or indeed the development proposed would result in total loss of the asset,[19] where there may be an impact upon a designated heritage asset, "great weight should be given to the asset's conservation" (NPPF 193). Greater weight should be given to the conservation of more important assets. In *Bedford BC v SSCLG*,[20] Jay J expressed this by saying that "the test for the grant of planning harm varies according to the quantum of harm to significance".

13.30　Chapter 16 of the NPPF must be read as a whole. NPPF 193 does refer to "great weight", but in making a decision in the context of heritage harm, the decision-maker must apply the test in the relevant paragraph of the NPPF. If, therefore, less than substantial harm is caused, then the relevant policy test is found in NPPF 196 (bearing in mind the legal duties which apply by virtue of section 66(1) and section 72(1)). In *Pugh v SSCLG*,[21] Gilbart J considered a challenge to the grant of permission on appeal for a single wind turbine. The claimant argued that the Inspector, after finding less than substantial harm to the significance of the heritage asset, could not simply apply the test in NPPF 196. This was because of what NPPF 193 says about weight. Gilbart J rejected that argument: the NPPF takes a sequential approach. The assessment of the level of harm will involve assessment of value and significance (see below). However, once the decision-maker has lawfully decided that the level of harm is less than substantial, then the test to be applied is that

---

[17]　[2017] EWHC 1374 (Admin); [2017] PTSR 1587.

[18]　[2016] EWHC 3284 (Admin).

[19]　This clarification is new to the amended NPPF: see Historic England's Briefing on the new NPPF, p. 6.

[20]　[2013] EWHC 2847 (Admin).

[21]　[2015] EWHC 3 (Admin).

in NPPF 196 (para. 50). The decision-maker had taken the sequential approach required by the NPPF, and the decision was therefore lawful.

13.31 Harm to, or loss of, significance, must be given clear and convincing justification (NPPF 194). However, in *Bedford BC*, Jay J found that the reference to "clear and convincing justification" does not impose a freestanding test (para. 29). This phrase was considered by Gilbart J in *Pugh v SSCLG*, who said at para. 53:

> "It might be thought difficult to be convincing without being clear, but it seems to me that the author of NPPF is saying no more than that if harm would be caused, then the case must be made for permitting the development in question, and that the sequential test in paragraphs 132-4 sets out how that is to be done."

13.32 Harm and loss are different concepts: *R (East Meon Forge and Cricket Ground Protection Association (acting by its Chairman George Bartlett) v East Hampshire DC.*[22]

13.33 NPPF 190 requires decision-makers to avoid or minimise the impact of proposed development on the conservation of a heritage asset. This may be achieved by conditions which screen the development so as to minimise the impact on the setting of the listed building, or possibly a construction management plan in a section 106 obligation so as to reduce disruption during the construction phase of development.

13.34 The High Court has stressed how the scheme of policy in the NPPF includes elements of balance. It does not merely prevent development which may have a negative impact upon heritage assets. It provides a framework for considering whether permission should nevertheless be granted. In *Colman v SSCLG*,[23] an objector sought to quash the grant of planning permission on appeal for a number of wind turbines. Policies in the local plan were in very restrictive terms (the Judge finding that any development which would not preserve the status quo would breach the policies). Kenneth Parker J found this to be in contrast with the policies in the NPPF, which were balanced, emphasising that conservation should be in a manner appropriate to significance, and applying a threshold of substantial harm. The NPPF can provide policy support even for substantial harm to significance.[24]

13.35 Nevertheless, in *R (Lady Hart of Chilton) v Babergh DC*,[25] Sales J considered that the NPPF "creates a strong presumption against the grant of planning permission for development which will harm heritage assets, requiring particularly strong countervailing factors to be identified before it can be treated as overridden" (para. 14).

13.36 The desirability of sustaining and enhancing the significance of heritage assets, and putting them to viable uses consistent with their conservation (NPPF 185(a)), reflects section 66(1) of the Listed Buildings Act: *Lyndon-Stanford QC v Mid Suffolk*

---

[22] [2014] EWHC 3543 (Admin).

[23] [2013] EWHC 1138 (Admin).

[24] A recent decision, made in the era of the NPPF, where a lawful decision for development would cause less than substantial harm can be found in *R (Historic England) v Milton Keynes Council* [2018] EWHC 2007 (Admin).

[25] [2014] EWHC 3261 (Admin); [2015] JPL 491.

District Council.[26]

13.37   Permission for the loss of harm to a heritage asset should not be permitted without a local planning authority taking all reasonable steps to ensure that the development will proceed after the loss (NPPF 198). In *Bohm v SSCLG*,[27] the claimant argued that this required the imposition of a condition which would have this effect. Historic England suggests that type of condition as one of the common types of conditions. However, Nathalie Lieven QC, sitting as a Deputy High Court Judge, was satisfied that the decision was lawful, notwithstanding the lack of such a condition. On the facts, there was no doubt that the development would proceed. Furthermore, NPPF 198 requires the taking of reasonable steps; it does not say on its face that a condition is required. The judgment of what is reasonable is a matter for the local planning authority (or, on appeal, the Inspector).

13.38   There is no generally applicable legal obligation upon the owners of heritage assets to keep them in good repair.[28] However, NPPF 191 states that, where there is evidence of deliberate neglect of a heritage asset, or deliberate damage to it, then the fact that the heritage asset is in a deteriorated state should not be taken into account in any decision. This was expressed crisply by the Deputy Judge in *Bohm*. *Bohm* concerned the planning permission, granted on appeal, for the demolition and replacement of an existing building in a conservation area, and its effect on a non-designated heritage asset. The Deputy Judge explained the policy at para. 46:

> "[NPPF 191] arises where a developer argues that s/he should be granted permission to remove a building, or permission for enabling development, because of the poor state of repair of that building. The point of [NPPF 191] is to prevent a developer in those circumstances relying on his/her own default. But that situation does not arise here, because the Inspector placed no reliance on the poor state of repair of the existing building."

Substantial Harm

13.39   Whether a proposal will cause substantial harm is a matter of planning judgment for the decision-maker. Indeed, the scheme of NPPF 193-196 does not purport to explain the meaning of "substantial": *Bedford BC v SSCLG*,[29] para. 19. However, the Inspector did not err in using the word "serious" as synonymous to "substantial" (para. 21). In *Pugh*, Gilbart J held that, when deciding whether harm is substantial or not, the decision-maker must address "all the relevant considerations about value, significance and the nature of the harm" (para. 50).

13.40   NPPF 194 sets out that substantial harm to, or loss of, grade II listed buildings, or grade II registered parks or gardens, should be exceptional. Substantial harm to, or loss of, scheduled monuments, protected wreck sites, registered battlefields,

---

[26]   [2016] EWHC 3284 (Admin).

[27]   [2017] EWHC 3217 (Admin).

[28]   For detail regarding the legal obligations on owners of heritage assets, see *Listed Buildings and Other Heritage Assets* - Mynors and Hewitson, Sweet & Maxwell, 2017.

[29]   [2013] EWHC 2847 (Admin).

grade I and II* listed buildings, grade I and II* registered parks and gardens, and World Heritage Sites, should be wholly exceptional.

13.41   In *Lady Hart of Chilton*, the local planning authority had granted planning permission for warehouses, office accommodation, service yards and car parking in close proximity to several listed heritage assets (including a Grade I listed medieval church), even though the Council accepted that the development would cause substantial harm to the church. The claimant argued that it was not lawfully open to the Council to decide that the benefits of the application were such as to make it "wholly exceptional". Sales J rejected this argument at para. 73, saying that the Council was "plainly entitled" to come to this view.

13.42   In *Lady Hart of Chilton*, the Council had decided that the proposed development was justified on the basis of bringing about substantial public benefits. The claimant argued that the Council failed to consider whether the harm was necessary, and whether the benefits of the development could be achieved in some other way which would cause less harm. Sales J rejected this argument, the Council having had regard to the fact that the applicant had unsuccessfully attempted to find other suitable sites in the area for development of this scale (para. 81).

13.43   The claimant alleged that the public benefits on which the Council relied were not sufficiently legally secured. This argument was also rejected: there had been negotiation between the Council and the developer regarding the terms, but the developer was for commercial reasons not willing to enter into more stringent terms. The Council was therefore entitled to conclude that the terms which it was able to agree with the developer represented the best achievable. The developer did intend to develop the site, even though it could not accept tighter contractual terms. The Council could rationally make the decision that there was a sufficient prospect of the benefits coming forward to justify granting permission in line with NPPF 194.

Less Than Substantial Harm

13.44   NPPF 196 sets out the test for a decision-maker to apply in cases of less than substantial harm to the significance of the heritage asset. The harm is to be "weighed against the public benefits of the proposal including, where appropriate, securing its optimum viable use".

13.45   The potential risk with this wording is that it suggests that there is a simple balance between heritage harm and benefits of the proposal. Taking this approach would not necessarily give "considerable importance and weight" to preserving the heritage asset (as required by section 66(1) of the Listed Buildings Act, see above). The answer is that NPPF 196 has to be read in the light of the statutory context, and also the preceding policy in the NPPF, including the requirement to give great weight to conservation.

13.46   This point was considered by HHJ Waksman QC, sitting as a Judge of the High Court, in *R (Hughes) v South Lakeland DC*.[30] Planning permission was granted for the

---

[30]   [2014] EWHC 3979 (Admin).

demolition of a number of buildings and the construction of a new supermarket, car park, and retail/office building. This was all within a conservation area. The Judge held at para. 53:

> "in a [NPPF 196] case, the fact of harm to a heritage asset is still to be given more weight than if it were simply a factor to be taken into account along with all other material considerations, and paragraph [196] needs to be read in that way. By way of contrast, where non-designated heritage assets are being considered, the potential harm should simply be "taken into account" in a "balanced judgment" - see paragraph [197]. It follows that paragraph [196] is something of a trap for the unwary if read - and applied - in isolation."

13.47 How the Judge dealt with this argument on the facts (finding that it was not clear that the Council had applied the presumption against grant of planning permission which causes heritage harm) may now be different after the decision of the Court of Appeal in *Jones v Mordue* (see above). However, that is a point about <u>scrutiny</u> of decisions. The Judge's point regarding the substance of how a decision-maker should approach a decision remains valid.

13.48 In *Pugh v SSCLG*,[31] Gilbart J agreed with HHJ Waksman QC's views on this point.

13.49 The approach to weight to be given to various factors in the context of NPPF 196 was considered by Holgate J in *R (Leckhampton Green Land Action Group Ltd) v Tewkesbury BC*.[32] Having reviewed *East Northamptonshire* and *Jones v Mordue*, Holgate J stated at para. 49:

> "[The cases] make it plain that the balancing exercise required by [NPPF 196] is to give effect to the presumption *against* granting permission for development which harms the setting of a listed building. Under [NPPF 196] there is a tilt in favour of the preservation of that setting. How much weight to give to the harm to the setting of a listed building and to that tilt is, of course, a matter for the decision-maker. But where a proposal would result in harm to the setting of a listed building, the "Barnwell Manor" tilt in s.66(1) (and in the NPPF - see for example [NPPF 196]), leans in the opposite direction to the presumption in [NPPF 11] in favour of the grant of planning permission."

13.50 At para. 49, Gilbart J in *Pugh* also indicated that the significance of the asset is a matter which carries weight at the balancing exercise in NPPF 196. The Judge hinted that may not be consistent with suggestions made in *Bedford BC* and *Colman*. However, *Bedford BC* and *Colman* do not forcefully make the point. In any event, Gilbart J's view is persuasive. Whilst not in NPPF 196 itself, NPPF 193 states "great weight should be given to the asset's conservation (and the more important the asset, the greater the weight should be)". It might be said that this is reflected in the distinction between designated and non-designated heritage assets. It may also be said that the weight is a matter to be taken into account <u>solely</u> when determining whether harm is substantial or less than substantial. However, the force in Gilbart

---

[31] [2015] EWHC 3 (Admin).

[32] [2017] EWHC 198 (Admin); [2017] Env LR 28 (emphasis in original).

J's position is that it does not restrict the consideration carried out by the decision-maker. Perhaps unsurprisingly, Gilbert J followed his own decision in *Pugh* when deciding *R (Irving) v Mid-Sussex DC*.[33]

13.51 In *Austin*, the claimant challenged the grant of planning permission for holiday lodges, touring units and camping pods. The Officer Report found an impact on a Grade II listed church. The Officer Report stated that the Council's Conservation Officer's views were that the proposal would not cause substantial harm to heritage assets or setting, and "[t]he proposal is therefore considered to comply with [local policy] and section 66 of the [Listed Buildings] Act 1990". The claimant argued that this showed the wrong approach: under NPPF 196, a finding that there is less than substantial harm to the significance of the heritage asset does not mean that the harm can be ignored. Indeed, section 66(1) still applied. However, Hickinbottom J found that the Officer Report was good enough so as not to give rise to a legal error. The proper reading of the Officer Report was that there would be no harm to the significance of the heritage asset (para. 54).

13.52 Is it relevant to the making of a decision under NPPF 196 that there would be alternative proposals which would secure the benefits, without causing the same level of heritage harm? This question was raised, but not decided, in *R (Nicholson) v Allerdale BC*.[34] The applicant applied for planning permission for a car manufacturing and evaluation centre, and a testing and evaluation facility, with parking and other ancillary development. The claimant argued that the Council had failed to consider the possibility of benefits to be delivered being achieved in a manner which did not cause harm to the setting of the listed building, or by causing a lesser amount of harm. Holgate J stated that he would "assume in the claimant's favour, without deciding, that that is a correct understanding of [NPPF 196]", but found that this was not necessary to determine the point. The matter was addressed in the Officer Report.

13.53 The question of alternatives received more consideration in the decision of Stuart-Smith J in *R (JH and FW Green Ltd) v South Downs National Park Authority*.[35] What is the implication of the NPPF's reference to a "sole viable use"? A sole viable use will be the optimum viable use. Stuart-Smith J however noted that the position was more complex in relation to a situation in which there are more than one viable uses. He held at para. 62, in considering situations where there are two viable uses:

> "If the proposal is the one likely to cause the least harm to the significance of the asset, then it will be the optimum viable use, which [NPPF 196] states should be included in the public benefits that are brought into the balance. Even so, the terms of [NPPF 196] do not require that any and all other viable uses should be excluded from consideration. Furthermore, if the proposal were not to be the optimum viable use because (as explained in the guidance) there is another viable use which is likely to cause less harm than

---

[33] [2016] EWHC 1529 (Admin); [2016] PTSR 1365.

[34] [2015] EWHC 2510 (Admin); [2016] LLR 214.

[35] [2018] EWHC 604 (Admin).

the proposal, the terms of [NPPF 196] do not require automatic refusal of permission for that reason."

13.54   Stuart-Smith J considered the decisions of the High Court in *R (Gibson) v Waverley BC (No. 1)*[36] and *R (Gibson) v Waverley BC (No. 2)*.[37] In *Gibson 1*, Cranston J held that the existence of a convincing alternative which constituted the optimum viable use was a "highly material planning consideration", and provided a "compelling basis for refusing permission". However, by the stage of *Gibson 2*, the likelihood of the alternative proposal coming forward had diminished. Foskett J found that the National Park Authority's decision was not rendered unlawful by virtue of it not identifying the proposed alternative as a viable option.

13.55   Stuart-Smith J made this comment on the *Gibson* cases at para. 4 of *JH and FW Green Ltd* at para. 66:

> "With one minor gloss, I respectfully agree with and adopt the approach of Cranston J and Foskett J in the two *Gibson* cases. To my mind, they emphasise the need for alternative proposals to be demonstrably substantial rather than speculative before they can realistically be considered as candidates to be the optimum viable use. A proposal which is merely speculative is not viable, whether or not it might otherwise be optimal. This is, to my mind, clear both from the current guidance and from the *Gibson* cases. The gloss is that I can envisage circumstances where the difference in the level of harm inflicted by two proposals was limited so that, although one would be regarded as the optimum viable use, it would not be right to regard that as a compelling basis for refusing permission to the other if the overall balance between harm and public benefits favoured the other. This serves to reinforce that the planning authority's task is to weigh any harm to the significance of a designated heritage asset against the public benefits of the proposal and that securing optimum viable use is only one part of that balancing exercise."

13.56   The requirement to assess alternatives is potentially burdensome. The courts are generally slow to impose a requirement to consider alternatives.[38] In *R (Smech Properties Ltd) v Runnymede DC*,[39] Patterson J held that there was nothing in Green Belt policy (expressly or impliedly) requiring a decision-maker to consider alternatives.[40] Given the high level of protection which is conferred upon the Green Belt [see Chapter 10: The Green Belt], this contrast is striking.

13.57   The PPG indicates that the optimum viable use "may not necessarily be the most

---

[36]   [2012] EWHC 1472 (Admin).

[37]   [2015] EWHC 3784 (Admin).

[38]   This is potentially different to NPPF 195 regarding substantial harm. There, the harm can be justified if <u>necessary</u> to achieve substantial public benefits. An argument of failure to consider alternatives was rejected, but on its facts, in *Lady Hart of Chilton* (see above).

[39]   [2015] EWHC 823 (Admin).

[40]   However, it may be that Patterson J's decision was in fact made on the basis that there were no true alternatives to the site on which development was proposed in that case: para. 64.

profitable one".[41]

Non-Designated Heritage Assets

13.58 When considering whether an asset should be treated as a non-designated heritage asset or not, the decision of the local planning authority is conclusive. In *Holland v SSCLG*,[42] Lang J considered an appeal against refusal of planning permission and conservation area consent for the demolition of a dwelling house and the construction of a new house within a conservation area. An action group had applied for the original building (which was designed by a named architect in a modernist style) to be listed, but Historic England refused. A Planning Inspector granted planning permission and listed building consent on appeal. The lead member of the action group sought to challenge this decision. The Inspector noted that the local planning authority had identified the original building as a non-designated heritage asset when deciding to refuse planning permission. Lang J noted that the definition of heritage asset in the Glossary to the NPPF which states:[43]

> "It includes designated heritage assets and assets identified by the local planning authority (including local listing)."

13.59 At para. 24, Lang J held that the Inspector had been required to treat the house as a non-designated heritage asset, as the Council had identified it as such. There was no error of law in the Inspector's decision, and so the challenge to the decision failed.

13.60 In *Bohm*, the High Court stated that the existing building makes a positive contribution to the conservation area, and has some architectural interest. It was therefore no issue that the building was a non-designated heritage asset. It is not clear from the report that the local planning authority had identified the building as such an asset (applying the reasoning in *Holland*), but the status of the building does not appear to have been in dispute between the parties, and therefore the High Court may not have seen it as necessary to go into detail on this point.

13.61 NPPF 197 merely requires that the significance of a non-designated heritage asset is "taken into account" in deciding an application. This was made clear by the decision of HHJ Jarman QC, sitting as a High Court Judge, in *Travis Perkins (Properties) Ltd v Westminster CC*.[44] The case concerned the redevelopment of a timber yard for mixed residential and retail use. The site fell within a conservation area. Having considered NPPF 197, the Judge held at para. 46 that the "effect of the application on the significance of the yard should be taken into account, nothing more, and nothing less". The decision-maker must make a "balanced judgment", taking into account the scale of any harm or loss, and the asset's significance.

13.62 The Claimant in *Bohm* argued that the Inspector had erred in the approach to

---

[41] PPG, Section on Conserving and enhancing the historic environment, para. 015.

[42] [2014] EWHC 3979 (Admin).

[43] This is the wording of the new NPPF. This constitutes a minor change from the original NPPF, which had previously stated "Heritage asset includes designated heritage assets…". The change in the wording makes no difference, apart from to make it more elegant.

[44] [2017] EWHC 2738 (Admin).

determining the application for demolition and rebuilding of a non-designated heritage asset which made a positive contribution to the conservation area. The claim was rejected. The Judge held at para. 34 that:

> "[NPPF 197] calls for weighing "applications" that affect an NDHA,[45] in other words the consideration under that paragraph must be of the application as a whole, not merely the demolition but also the construction of the new building. It then requires a balanced judgement to be made by the decision maker. The NPPF does not seek to prescribe how that balance should be undertaken, or what weight should be given to any particular matter."

13.63   The Inspector had found that the non-designated asset had some limited local heritage, but this did not carry significant weight in favour of retention. She found that there would not be an adverse impact from the loss. The Inspector then considered the impact upon the conservation area, and found that the net effect would at worst would be neutral. This was a lawful approach, the Deputy Judge finding that there is no requirement for a two-stage approach of considering demolition separately from proposed new development.

Conservation Areas

13.64   National planning policy is clear that, if too many conservation areas are designated, then this risks diminishing the value of the designation. NPPF 186 requires local authorities, when considering the designation, to "ensure that an area justifies such status because of its special architectural or historic interest".

13.65   NPPF 201 indicates that it is necessary to consider the actual impact of proposed development upon the significance of a conservation area, as not every element of a conservation area necessarily contributes to its significance. In *Bohm*, the possibility was considered that the loss of a non-designated heritage asset which makes a positive contribution to the significance of a conservation area must be treated in the same way as the impact upon a designated heritage asset. Instead, the correct approach is to weigh any harm to the conservation area against the public benefits of the proposal. The loss of the non-designated heritage asset should not be treated as the same way as a designated heritage asset (para. 40).

13.66   NPPF 201 states that, where proposed development would cause <u>loss</u> of a building (or other element) which makes a positive contribution to the significance of a conservation area or World Heritage Site, then that loss should be treated as substantial harm under NPPF 195, or less than substantial harm under NPPF 196. Lang J made an interesting observation about the version of this paragraph in the original NPPF, and its reference to loss, in *R (East Meon Forge and Cricket Ground Protection Association (acting by its Chairman George Bartlett) v East Hampshire DC*,[46] at para. 50:

> "It seems to me that [Leading Counsel for the local planning authority] is correct in submitting that [NPPF 201] only applies where there is a loss of a

---

[45]   The abbreviation used in the judgment for "non-designated heritage asset".

[46]   [2014] EWHC 3543 (Admin).

building or other element. Throughout [Chapter 16], it is clear that 'harm' and 'loss' are different concepts. Although the development may harm the character and appearance of The Forge, there is no suggestion that it will be lost. However, I am unclear why the principle expressed in [NPPF 201] should be confined to cases of loss, and so I am uncertain about the intended scope of this paragraph."

13.67   In the new version of the NPPF, there has been no explanation of the restriction of the effect of NPPF 201 to loss only (rather than including harm). However, neither has there been any amendment to NPPF 201 to also include harm, despite the terms of Lang J's judgment. The Secretary of State must be assumed to be aware of the decision in *East Meon Forge*, and so it can only be assumed that the reference to loss, and the exclusion of harm, is intentional.

13.68   The protection of conservation areas was considered in some detail by Gilbart J in *R (Irving) v Mid-Sussex DC*.[47] The Council had granted planning permission for the construction of a dwelling in a conservation area. The Officer Report found that, whilst there would be harm to the character of the conservation area, the overall character and appearance of the conservation area would nevertheless be preserved. Gilbart J found that this approach was unacceptable, holding at para. 58:

> "If there is harm to the character and appearance of one part of the conservation area, the fact that the whole will still have a special character does not overcome the fact of that harm. It follows that the character and appearance will be harmed. While I accept that the question of the extent of the harm is relevant to consideration of its effects, it cannot be right that harm to one part of a conservation area does not amount to harm for the purposes of considering the duty under section 72 of the [Listed Buildings Act 1990]."

World Heritage Sites

13.69   World Heritage Sites benefit from a high level of protection in Chapter 16 of the NPPF.[48] There has been little litigation concerning them (perhaps due to the relatively small number of such Sites,[49] or perhaps due to the various players in the planning process being generally agreed that such Sites should be granted a high level of protection).

13.70   The Liverpool-Maritime Mercantile City World Heritage Site was considered in *R (Save Britain's Heritage) v Liverpool CC*.[50] However, *Save Britain's Heritage* concerns not the NPPF, but a request in the PPG for local planning authorities to inform the Department for Culture, Media and Sport of proposed development.

---

[47]   [2016] EWHC 1529 (Admin); [2016] PTSR 1365.

[48]   Historic England's Briefing on the new NPPF (p.6) notes that there is greater reference to World Heritage Sites in the new NPPF than there were in the previous version.

[49]   There are only 29 World Heritage Sites in the whole of the UK.

[50]   [2016] EWCA Civ 806; [2017] JPL 39.

13.71   Stocker LJ indicated in *The Bath Society v Secretary of State for the Environment*[51] that the obligation (now found in section 72 of the Listed Buildings Act 1990) "is of particular importance" in the case of World Heritage Sites.

---

[51]   [1991] 1 WLR 1303.

Chapter 14

Minerals

Introduction

14.01   The NPPF provides policy support for the production of minerals.[1] Minerals are significant to facilitating many other desirable aims, including strengthening the economy, delivering housing, supplying infrastructure, and contributing to the power supply. However, as the NPPF itself observes, minerals can be worked only where they are found, and are a finite resource. The planning regime affects minerals in a number of ways: granting planning permission for exploration for minerals, granting planning permission for the excavation of minerals, granting planning permission for facilities to process minerals, refusing planning permission for non-minerals development which may restrict the ability to access minerals, and landbanking to maintain a supply. The NPPF provides limited support for the extraction of coal, and does not support the extraction of peat.

14.02   This chapter will not seek to summarise every aspect of Chapter 17 of the NPPF concerning minerals, instead referring to some of the key elements.

Policy-making

14.03   NPPF 204 sets out some guidance in relation to plan-making. Plans are to generally support the extraction of minerals resources of local and national importance. The Glossary defines "Minerals resources of local and national importance as":[2]

> "Minerals which are necessary to meet society's needs, including aggregates, brickclay (especially Etruria Marl and fireclay), silica sand (including high grade silica sands), cement raw materials, gypsum, salt, fluorspar, shallow and deep-mined coal, oil and gas (including convention and unconventional hydrocarbons), tungsten, kaolin, ball clay, potash, polyhalite and local minerals of importance to heritage assets and local distinctiveness."

14.04   However, this support in plans should not extend to new sites for the extraction of peat (or even for the extension of existing peat extraction sites): NPPF 204(a). Local planning authorities are to plan for the contribution from the alternatives to the extraction of primary materials, being the use of substitute or secondary or recycled materials, and minerals waste (NPPF 204(b)). However, local planning authorities should still aim to source minerals supplies indigenously.

---

[1]   The PPG describes mineral resources as "natural concentrations of minerals, or in the case of aggregates, bodies of rock that are, or may become, of potential economic interest due to their inherent properties": PPG, Section on Minerals, para. 001. At time of writing, this Section of the PPG has not been updated since the introduction of the new NPPF.

[2]   The PPG, Section on Minerals, para. 091, defines conventional hydrocarbons as "oil and gas where the reservoir is sandstone or limestone"; unconventional hydrocarbons are "oil and gas which comes from sources such as shale or coal seams which act as the reservoirs". At para. 221, it defines aggregate minerals as "minerals which are used primarily to support the construction industry including soft sand, sand and gravel, and crushed rock".

14.05   NPPF 204(c) indicates that local planning authorities should set Mineral Safeguarding Areas. A Mineral Safeguarding Area is defined in the Glossary as:

> "An area designated by minerals planning authorities which covers known deposits of minerals which are desired to be kept safeguarded from unnecessary sterilisation by non-mineral development."

14.06   However, the creation of a Minerals Safeguarding Area does not create a presumption that the resources defined will be worked.

14.07   If possible and acceptable in planning terms to do so, policies should encourage prior extraction of minerals, if necessary for non-mineral development to take place (NPPF 204(d)). Local plans should also set requirements to ensure that minerals development is not otherwise unacceptable in planning terms (NPPF 204(f)-(h)). The NPPF supports policies for necessary parts of the minerals supply chain other than the extraction itself: bulk transport, handling and process of minerals, concrete processes, and processes concerning substitute, recycled and secondary aggregate material (NPPF 204(e)).

14.08   There is extensive guidance - which expresses policy - in the PPG.[3] It is not clear to what extent this policy will be retained after the amendment to the NPPF. The PPG suggest a hierarchy between designating specific sites for mineral extraction, designating preferred areas, and designating areas of search, and limitations on designation in the National Parks and the AONB.

Planning Applications

14.09   The NPPF says that, in determining applications, local planning authorities should give "great weight" to the benefits of mineral extraction, including to the economy (NPPF 205). The extraction of coal is not included in this general policy, being dealt with separately. Notwithstanding the general support provided, the NPPF requires decision-makers to avoid development which would have an unacceptable planning impact, including taking into account cumulative impacts.[4] Aftercare of minerals extraction sites should be carried out to high standards, and as soon as possible.[5] This is to be secured by condition, but "[b]onds or other financial guarantees to underpin planning conditions should only be sought in exceptional circumstances"

---

[3]   PPG, Section on Minerals, see paras. 007ff.

[4]   The PPG indicates that, where there are significant environmental impacts, there should be an environmental statement: PPG, Section on Minerals, para. 011. Paragraph 013 provides a list of potential impacts from minerals development which should be considered. Paragraph 019 indicates that the assessment of noise should take into account of the prevailing acoustic environment, as well as estimating the likely future noise. Considerable detail is provided regarding the assessment of dust impact: paras 023-031.

[5]   Guidance on restoration and aftercare is set out in the PPG, Section on Minerals, paras 36-59. The guidance for hydrocarbons extraction is at para. 127. Aftercare is defined at para. 221 as "operations necessary to maintain restored land in a condition necessary for an agreed afteruse to continue". Afteruse is defined as "the use that land, used for minerals working, is put to after restoration".

(NPPF 205(e)).[6] Planning permission for new or extended peat extraction should be refused (NPPF 205(d)). Particular support is given to the small scale extraction of building stone at or near relic quarries needed to repair heritage assets (NPPF 205(f)). Particular provision is given for building and roofing stone quarries (NPPF 205(g)). The PPG explains in relation to building stone quarries:[7]

> "Mineral planning authorities should recognise that, compared to other types of mineral extraction, most building stone quarries are small-scale and have a far lower rate of extraction when compared to other quarries. This means that their local environmental impacts may be significantly less. Such quarries often continue in operation for a very long period, and may be worked intermittently but intensively ("campaign working"), involving stockpiling of stone."

14.10   In line with the purpose of Mineral Safeguarding Areas, NPPF 206 provides that development proposals which may prejudice the use of such areas for minerals working[8] should not normally be permitted.

Maintaining Supply

14.11   NPPF 207 sets out detailed provision to ensure a "steady and adequate supply of aggregates". NPPF 208 makes provision for such a supply for industrial minerals.

14.12   Concerning aggregates, minerals planning authorities must prepare an annual Local Aggregate Assessment, to forecast demand and consider supply options. Local minerals authorities may do this either individually or jointly. Minerals planning authorities must participate in the operation of an Aggregate Working Party,[9] and take into account the advice of that working party when preparing the Assessment. Minerals planning authorities should make provision for landbanking of minerals, but ensure that large landbanks in only a very few sites is not harmful to competition. Where aggregate materials of a specific type or quality have a distinct or separate market, then the minerals planning authority should calculate and maintain separate

---

[6]   The PPG, Section on Minerals, para. 048, gives an example of such cases: "very long-term new projects where progressive reclamation is not practicable, such as an extremely large limestone quarry; where a novel approach or technique is to be used, but the minerals planning authority considers it is justifiable to give permission for the development; where there is reliable evidence of the likelihood of either financial or technical failure, but these concerns are not such as to justify refusal of permission". However, the PPG also suggests that where an operator is contributing to an established mutual funding scheme, then a guarantee against financial failure should not be necessary.

[7]   PPG, Section on Minerals, para. 016.

[8]   In an old decision, the Court of Appeal considered in *English Clays Lovering Pochin Ltd v Plymouth Corporation* [1974] 1 WLR 742, p. 746 that "to 'win' a mineral is to make it available or accessible to be removed from the land, and to 'work' a mineral is (at least initially) to remove it from its position in the land". This approach was followed by the Court of Appeal in *SSCLG v Bleaklow Industries Ltd* [2009] EWCA Civ 206; [2009] 2 P&CR 21. The Court of Appeal's decision in *Europa Oil and Gas Ltd v SSCLG* [2014] EWCA Civ 825; [2014] PTSR 1471 (a decision on the previous NPPF) refers to *Bleaklow*.

[9]   The role of the Aggregate Working Party is set out in the PPG, Section on Minerals, para. 073. It includes assessment of overall demand and supply in the Working Party's area, and providing data on minerals activity in the area.

landbanks. Landbanks are a means of monitoring the supply of minerals.[10]

14.13   NPPF 208 concerns the steps minerals planning authorities should take to plan for the supply of industrial minerals.[11] National policy requires co-operation not only with neighbouring authorities but also those which are more distant, to ensure that there is an adequate provision of industrial minerals. Safeguarding and stockpiling is to be encouraged, to ensure availability. A stock of permitted reserves should be permitted (with the different levels of reserves required set out in Footnote 68). NPPF 208(d) observes that brick clay from different sources may be needed in order to enable appropriate blends to be made; minerals planning authorities should take this into account.

Exploration and Extraction of Oil, Gas and Coal

14.14   NPPF 209-211 concerns the exploration for and extraction of oil, gas and coal. The policy support for oil and gas extraction is more positive than that for coal. The benefits of on-shore oil and gas development are to be recognised, given their implications for the security of energy supply and supporting the transition to a low-carbon economy, and minerals planning authorities should put in place policies to facilitate their exploration and extraction (NPPF 209(a)). Minerals planning authorities should plan positively not only for the production of oil and gas, but also exploration and appraisal (NPPF 209(b)). In relation to this aspect of the previous version of the NPPF, Ouseley J stated in *Europa Oil and Gas Ltd v SSCLG* at para. 44:[12]

> "The three phrases are treated as components of the one process, the one process they naturally make up is the overall process of extraction. The need to distinguish them derives from the need to address constraints on production in licenced areas, not to increase constraints on necessary parts of the process."

14.15   The second sentence of that quotation, however, referred to an aspect of the previous version of the NPPF which no longer exists in the current version, requiring minerals planning authorities to "address constraints on production and processing within areas that are licensed for oil and gas exploration or production". However, Ouseley J's point that exploration, appraisal and production of oil and gas all make up part of the process of extraction likely still holds good. The context of Ouseley J's consideration of the minerals policies related to a challenge to the decision of a Planning Inspector concerning the Green Belt [see Chapter 10: The Green Belt]. In the Court of Appeal,[13] Richards LJ stated that he found Ouseley J's reasoning "cogent" (para. 21).

---

[10]   See PPG, Section on Minerals, para. 080.

[11]   Industrial minerals are defined in the PPG, Section on Minerals, para. 221, as "minerals which are necessary to support industrial and manufacturing processes and other non-aggregate uses. These include minerals of recognised national importance including: brickclay (especially Etruria Marl and fireclay), silica sand (including high grade silica sands), industrial grade limestone, cement raw materials, gypsum, salt fluorspar, tungsten, kaolin, ball clay and potash.

[12]   [2013] EWHC 2643 (Admin); [2014] 1 P&CR 3.

[13]   [2014] EWCA Civ 825; [2014] PTSR 1471.

14.16   If local geological circumstances indicate it to be feasible, minerals planning authorities should encourage underground gas and carbon storage, and associated infrastructure (NPPF 209(c)). However, when determining planning applications, the integrity and safety of underground storage must be appropriate (NPPF 210).

14.17   The starting point for the extraction of coal, set out in NPPF 211, is that planning permission should not be granted. However, permission may be granted if the process is environmentally acceptable (or can be made so by conditions or obligations), or if not acceptable, then the benefits (national, local or community) clearly outweigh likely impacts, including residual environmental impacts. Minerals planning authorities should indicate acceptable areas for the extraction of coal and the disposal of colliery spoil (NPPF 209(d)). They should also encourage the capture and use of methane from coal mines, both in active and abandoned coalfield areas (NPPF 209(e)). Provision should be made for coal producers to extract fireclay separately, so that it can be available for use, and stockpile it if necessary (NPPF 209(f)).

Chapter 15

Challenging Decisions Interpreting the NPPF

Introduction

15.01 If a decision is made in which a decision-maker refers to the NPPF, what should you do if you consider that the decision-maker has misinterpreted national planning policy? This question deals with the following questions:

(a) In what forum can a challenge be brought?

(b) What is the time limit for bringing a court claim?

(c) Who can bring a court claim?

(d) What are the hallmarks of a successful claim?

(e) What procedure will a claim follow?

(f) Who will bear the costs of a claim?

15.02 This chapter sets out the procedure for challenging decisions on planning applications, but provides only the barest outline. In relation to the principles of court challenges to the decisions of public authority, the reader is directed to the full length works on administrative law and judicial review.[1]

Forum for Challenging a Planning Decision

Challenges by Developers

15.03 If an applicant is refused planning permission for a proposal, then he has the right of appeal to the Secretary of State under section 78 TCPA. In practice, such an appeal is usually determined by a Planning Inspector, and even if the Secretary of State recovers the decision for his own consideration, then an Inspector will report to him first. Appeals are dealt with either by written representations, a hearing, or a public inquiry. If a developer is refused planning permission, and considers that the local planning authority has misinterpreted the NPPF, then this is a matter which could be raised in the appeal to the Secretary of State.

15.04 The Inspector's role on appeal (or that of the Secretary of State, if the appeal is recovered) is to determine the planning application herself. She considers the planning merits, and decides whether to grant planning permission. She will interpret the NPPF, and apply her view of the meaning to the facts of the proposal before her. The Inspector is not limited to considering the legality of the local planning authority's decision.

---

[1] For instance, *De Smith's Judicial Review of Administrative Action*, 8th edn, Woolf, Jowell, Donnelly and Hare, Sweet and Maxwell 2018. For a book considering judicial review of decisions in the context of environmental law, see *Environmental Judicial Review* - Richard Moules, Hart Publishing 2011. For an account of procedural matters which is updated, see *Garner's Environmental Law*, LexisNexis, Chapter 1B.

15.05 In the case of court proceedings, the role of the court is limited to reviewing the legality of the decision. As such, an appeal on the merits is generally much more advantageous for an unsuccessful developer than a court claim. The applicant will have a second opportunity to convince a decision-maker that granting planning permission is a good idea. As such, it will only be in extremely unusual circumstances that a developer would bring a judicial review challenge to the decision of a local planning authority to refuse planning permission.[2]

15.06 After an appeal, the developer, local planning authority or other person aggrieved by the decision can challenge the decision of the Planning Inspector or the Secretary of State in the High Court under section 288 TCPA. Unlike the appeal to the Inspector, a challenge to the Inspector's decision can be brought only on the basis that the decision was not within the powers of the TCPA, or any of the relevant requirements have not been complied with in relation to the decision. Essentially, the grounds of such a challenge are very similar if not identical to challenges by way of judicial review.[3] These grounds include that the Inspector erred in relation to interpretation of the NPPF, in a way which materially affected her decision.

Enforcement Action

15.07 If a local planning authority brings enforcement action against an alleged breach of planning control, then a person on whom an enforcement notice is served has the right of appeal to a Planning Inspector under section 174 TCPA. One of the statutory grounds of appeal (Ground (a)) is that planning permission should be granted for the proposed development. If an appellant feels that the local planning authority's decision that it is expedient to bring enforcement action proceeds on the basis of a misinterpretation of the NPPF, then the appellant can raise these arguments before the Inspector on appeal. As with appeals against the refusal of planning permission, the appeal can be determined by means of written representations, hearing or public inquiry.

15.08 Again, if the person subject to enforcement action, the local planning authority or another person aggrieved by the decision wishes to appeal against the Inspector's decision, there is a right of appeal under section 289 TCPA. If the person appealing against the Inspector's decision considers that the Inspector has erred in her interpretation of the NPPF, then this is a potential ground of legal challenge under section 289.

Development Plan Documents

15.09 If a local planning authority adopts a development plan document which a person (whether a developer or an objector, or another local planning authority) considers to be based on a flawed understanding of the NPPF, then a legal challenge can be

---

[2]   Indeed, absent extremely unusual circumstances, the court would be likely to dismiss the claim if it did, on the basis that judicial review claims are supposed to be a remedy of last resort: if a claimant has an adequate alternative remedy, then the judicial review claim should not be brought and that alternative remedy should be pursued instead.

[3]   See *Seddon Properties Ltd v Secretary of State for the Environment* (1981) 42 P&CR 26.

brought under section 113 PCPA.

The Grant of Planning Permission by Local Authorities

15.10   If planning permission is granted by the local planning authority, then an objector to the planning permission does not have the right of appeal to a planning Inspector or the Secretary of State. In these circumstances, the remedy is to apply to the High Court for judicial review of the local planning authority's decision. The court will consider only whether the decision was legally open to the local planning authority; it does not consider questions of the merits of the grant of planning permission.

The Time Limit For Bringing A Claim

15.11   The details of the time limit for bringing a claim depend on the nature of the claim which is being brought. The calculation of the exact deadlines can be complex,[4] and the detail of these matters is beyond the scope of this book. However, in very crude terms, the deadlines are as follows:

•   Claim under section 288 TCPA - 6 weeks' deadline, which cannot be extended;

•   Appeal under section 289 TCPA - 28 days' deadline, which can be extended by the court;

•   Claim under section 113 PCPA - 6 weeks' deadline, which cannot be extended;

•   Judicial review claim - 6 weeks' deadline, which can be extended by the court.

15.12   All of these deadlines are short in the context of civil law claims,[5] and in the context of public law actions more specifically.[6] A potential claimant will therefore need to act swiftly. This will involve assessing whether there are grounds for a claim, whether to instruct lawyers (and taking their lawyers' view of the strength of the claim), considering funding for the claim and the potential liability in costs, and ideally engaging in pre-action correspondence with the potential defendant.

15.13   Before bringing a court claim, the potential claimant should write to the decision-maker, explaining why he, she or it thinks that the decision was flawed, and requesting that the decision-maker accepts that the decision was wrong.[7] This is known as a "Letter Before Action". As well as seeking a concession from the other side, the proposed defendant's response to a Letter Before Action may be useful to the proposed claimant in assessing the strength of the proposed defendant's answer

---

[4]   See, for instance, *R (Blue Green London Plan) v Secretary of State for the Environment, Food and Rural Affairs* [2015] EWHC 495 (Admin), although the wording of the legislation which Ouseley J considered in that case has been changed since this decision.

[5]   For which the deadlines vary, but the general limitation period for claims in contract and tort is 6 years (Limitation Act 1980, ss 2 and 5).

[6]   A judicial review claim, other than for a decision made under the Planning Acts and a claim in relation to public procurement, must be made promptly, and in any event within 3 months of the facts for the claim arising (CPR 54.5). The time limit for bringing a claim in the context of public procurement is even shorter: 28 days.

[7]   A decision-maker in the planning context is unlikely to revoke the decision (as a right to compensation may arise as a result), but may agree to the decision being quashed by the court.

to the claim, and in requesting useful information from the proposed defendant.

Who Can Bring a Court Claim?

Challenges Under Section 288

15.14　The statutory test for who may bring a claim under section 288 is that a claim can be brought only by a "person aggrieved" by the decision. This will obviously include a disappointed developer, as well as a local planning authority which has had its decision overturned. The position regarding third parties objecting to the grant of permission is more complex. The effect of the decision in *Crawford-Brunt v SSCLG*[8] is that, in order for an objector to be a person aggrieved and therefore have the ability to bring a claim under section 288, they need to have objected in the course of the appeal procedure. It is not enough to have objected to the local planning authority against the planning application, against whose decision the appeal is brought.

Appeals Under Section 289

15.15　Under section 289(1) TCPA, the only parties who may appeal against the decision of the Inspector are the appellant who appealed against the enforcement notice, the local planning authority, and any person who has an interest in the land subject to the enforcement notice.

Judicial Review

15.16　The test for bringing a claim in judicial review is that the claimant must have a "sufficient interest" in the matter in question (Senior Courts Act 1981, section 31). This is not a high threshold: a person who has objected to the proposed application for planning permission is likely to have a sufficient interest to challenge the grant of that planning permission.

What Are the Hallmarks of a Successful Claim?

15.17　There are a large number of potential grounds for bringing a claim in judicial review. This work focuses on claims alleging that there has been an error in the interpretation of national planning policy.

15.18　The interpretation of policy is, at least in theory, a legitimate ground for challenging a planning decision, because the interpretation of policy is a matter of law for the court: *Tesco Stores Ltd v Dundee CC*.[9] However, it is necessary to demonstrate that the error is one in the interpretation of policy; if the decision-maker has interpreted a policy correctly but the challenger disagrees with the application of that interpretation to the facts, then the court will not interfere with the decision. Lord Carnwath JSC stressed the distinction between interpretation and application in

---

[8]　[2015] EWHC 3580 (Admin); [2016] JPL 573. The decision is convincingly criticised by Richard Harwood QC in commentary in the Journal of Planning and Environmental Law at [2016] JPL 573, 578: an individual who has objected to a planning application will be told that their objection to the local planning authority will be considered by the Inspector on appeal.

[9]　[2012] UKSC 13; [2012] PTSR 983.

Hopkins Homes Ltd v SSCLG.[10] At paras 25-26, he held:

> "It must be remembered that, whether in a development plan or in a non-statutory statement such as the NPPF, these are statements of policy, not statutory texts, and must be read in that light. Even where there are disputes over interpretation, they may well not be determinative of the outcomes. (As will appear, the present can be seen as such a case.) Furthermore, the courts should respect the expertise of the specialist planning inspectors, and start at least from the presumption that they will have understood the policy framework correctly. With the support and guidance of the planning inspectorate, they have primary responsibility for resolving disputes between planning authorities, developers and others, over the practical application of the policies, national or local. ...
>
> Recourse to the courts may sometimes be needed to resolve distinct issues of law, or to ensure consistency of interpretation in relation to specific policies, as in the *Tesco* case. In that exercise the specialist judges of the Planning Court have an important role. However, the judges are entitled to look to applicants, seeking to rely on matters of planning policy in applications to quash planning decisions (at local or appellate level), to distinguish clearly between issues of interpretation of policy, appropriate for judicial analysis, and issues of judgment in the application of that policy; and not to elide the two."

15.19   Unfortunately, the line between interpretation of a policy, and its application to a set of facts, is not clear in every case. In *R (Tate) v Northumberland CC*,[11] the issue related to whether proposed development constituted limited infilling in a village. The claimant sought to argue that the local planning authority had misinterpreted the phrase, arguing as a matter of law that "village" has certain characteristics; a settlement without those characteristics is not a village. Whilst the claim was successful (both in the High Court,[12] and before the Court of Appeal), the claimant's approach to the definition of village was rejected. It seems likely that whether a settlement was a village was a matter of judgment for the decision-maker. The matter would have been different if the term "village" was defined in the Glossary to the NPPF; as it was not defined, the question of whether a settlement was a village was a matter of application of policy to the facts, rather than a matter of interpretation.[13]

15.20   In *Trustees of the Barker Mill Estates v SSCLG*,[14] Holgate J held at para. 84:

> "Normally a claimant fails to raise a genuine case of *misinterpretation* of policy unless he identifies (i) the policy wording said to have been misinterpreted, (ii)

---

[10]   [2017] UKSC 37; [2017] 1 WLR 1865.

[11]   [2018] EWCA Civ 1519.

[12]   [2017] EWHC 664 (Admin).

[13]   That does not mean that the judgment is subject to no limits whatsoever. Describing the whole of Greater Manchester as a "village", for instance, would be likely to be unlawful as not being a reasonable application of the concept of village.

[14]   [2016] EWHC 3028 (Admin); [2017] PTSR 408.

the interpretation of that language adopted by the decision-maker and (iii) how that interpretation departs from the correct interpretation of the policy wording in question. A failure by the claimant to address these points, as in the present case, is likely to indicate that the complaint is really concerned with *application*, rather than *misinterpretation*, of policy."

15.21   The Court of Appeal has stressed that the Secretary of State, and an experienced Planning Inspector, is unlikely to misunderstand the NPPF. In *St Modwen Developments Ltd v SSCLG*,[15] Lindblom LJ held at para. 32:

> "In my view it would have been most surprising if the Secretary of State had gone astray in his understanding an application of these fundamental components of national planning policy for the supply of housing, contained as they are in the Government's primary policy document for the planning system in England, which had been published some three years before he came to make his decision in this case. Nor is it likely that an experienced inspector would err in that way: see the judgment of Lord Carnwath JSC in the *Hopkins Homes Ltd* case… I think the court should approach arguments like this with great hesitation. Here I am in no doubt that the argument is bad…"

15.22   There is some indication that similar reasoning may apply to decisions of the planning committees of local planning authorities, which are informed by reports written by professional planning officers. Planning committee members themselves are familiar with particular matters relating to their area: *Mansell v Tonbridge and Malling BC*[16] [see Chapter 3: The Interpretation of Policy].

15.23   A challenger should take points before the local planning authority, or before an Inspector on appeal, if it wishes to rely on such a challenge before the courts. In the context of judicial review of a decision of a local planning authority, in *R (Luton BC) v Central Bedfordshire Council*,[17] Holgate J held at para. 97 that "a failure by parties to raise an issue in their representations to the local planning authority may be highly material, if not determinative, unless that issue was one which the legislation required the authority to take into account in any event". In the context of a challenge to a decision of a Planning Inspector, Ouseley J stated in *Humphris v SSCLG*,[18] at para. 23:

> "[w]hatever may be the limited circumstances in which it can be contended that the inspector has reached a decision that is erroneous in law and beyond his powers by reference to a point not raised before him, this is not one of them. This is not a point that has not been available to be taken; it is not a point that can be described as an error of fact which becomes an error of law not known to the parties at the time. It is not a point where it can be said it has arisen without the parties being given an opportunity to deal with it…"

---

[15]   [2017] EWCA Civ 1643; [2018] PTSR 746.

[16]   [2017] EWCA Civ 1314; [2018] JPL 176.

[17]   [2014] EWHC 4325 (Admin).

[18]   [2012] EWHC 1237 (Admin).

15.24   In *St Modwen Developments Ltd*, Lindblom LJ at para. 47 agreed with Ouseley J in the High Court in that case that one must "be cautious lest a point on a [section] 288 challenge takes a very different shape and emphasis from that which it had before the inspector". This comment was made in the course of dismissing a challenge that insufficient reasons had been given for the dismissal of an appeal.

15.25   The courts should not permit litigants to "go behind the inspector's conclusions on the credibility and reliability of the parties' respective cases on housing land supply", where these are made "in the light of all the relevant evidence": this would be to trespass beyond the role of the court in reviewing decisions (*St Modwen Developments Ltd*, para. 51, Lindblom LJ).

15.26   In order to give rise to a successful claim, a claimant must demonstrate not only that there has been an error in the interpretation of the NPPF, but that this error was material to the decision-maker's decision. Take the example of a Planning Inspector who decides that a particular proposal for development of land is harmful to the openness of the Green Belt, and refuses planning permission. In making a decision on openness, the Inspector states "visual impact is entirely irrelevant to the assessment of openness, which is a spatial question only". This constitutes an error of law, following from the decision of the Court of Appeal in *Samuel Smith Old Brewery (Tadcaster) v North Yorkshire CC* [see Chapter 10: The Green Belt].[19] If the Inspector finds (i) harm to openness by virtue of the spatial impact of the development; (ii) the proposal would constitute inappropriate development; (iii) no very special circumstances, then the Inspector's error would have made no difference. Had he not made the error, that would have made his decision to refuse planning permission even stronger. A challenge by the developer on the basis of his misinterpretation of the NPPF would be pointless, and therefore doomed to fail.

15.27   In the field of judicial review claims, this position is reflected in section 31(2A)-(2C), (3C)-(3F) of the Senior Courts Act 1981: generally speaking, a court must dismiss a claim if satisfied that it is very likely that the decision-maker would have made the same decision even if it had not made the error identified by the claimant. Section 31 applies only to judicial review claims; it does not apply to statutory challenges, for instance brought under section 288 TCPA. In the case of statutory challenges, case law establishes that a decision containing an error should be quashed unless the court is clear that the decision could not have been the same were it not for the error: *Simplex GE (Holdings) Ltd v Secretary of State for the Environment*.[20] In *East Northamptonshire CC v SSCLG*,[21] Lindblom LJ appears to consider both the *Simplex* approach and the test under section 31(2A) of the Senior Courts Act 1981. The

---

[19]   [2018] EWCA Civ 489.

[20]   (1989) 57 P&CR 306. In *R (Smech Properties Ltd) v Runnymede DC* [2015] EWHC 823 (Admin), Patterson J identified a serious error in the local planning authority's identification of its housing land supply. However, Patterson J considered that, if the error had not been made, the situation regarding housing land supply would have been even worse. As such, the error was not material, and the decision to grant planning permission was not quashed. Patterson J's decision was upheld on appeal by the Court of Appeal [2016] EWCA Civ 42; [2016] JPL 677.

[21]   [2017] EWCA Civ 893; [2018] PTSR 88.

better view is that the section 31 test does not apply outside the context of judicial review, but the distinction was not relevant to Lindblom LJ's decision.

15.28   There are signs that the courts are becoming frustrated with challenges concerning the interpretation of planning policy. In *Trustees of the Barker Mill Estates v SSCLG*,[22] Holgate J noted at para. 141 "the ingenuity with which lawyers (whether acting for or against a development proposal) put forward interpretations of policy in challenges before the courts". Lindblom LJ in *Oadby and Wigston BC v SSCLG*[23] noted at para. 33 that some challenges which have been brought in relation to the interpretation of the NPPF have been successful, "[b]ut most have not... the NPPF contains many broadly expressed statements of national policy, which, when they fall to be applied in the making of a development control decision, will require of the decision-maker an exercise of planning judgment in the particular circumstances of the case in hand." Lindblom LJ in *Mansell v Tonbridge and Malling BC*[24] held at para. 41 that the court's approach to the interpretation of policy should be "straightforward, without undue or elaborate exposition", and that the court's review of a planning decision should not take "the hypercritical approach the court is often urged to adopt". In the context of a judicial review Sir Terence Etherton C at para. 62 deprecated "minute legalistic dissection" of an officer's report to a planning committee. At para. 63, he held:

> "Such reports are not, and should not be, written for lawyers, but for councillors who are well-versed in local affairs and local factors. Planning committees approach such reports utilising that local knowledge and much common-sense. They should be allowed to make their judgments freely and fairly without undue interference by courts or judges who have picked apart the planning officer's advice on which they relied."

15.29   Notwithstanding these warnings, challenges continue to be made, and some are won. The decision of the Court of Appeal in March 2018 in *Samuel Smith Old Brewery (Tadcaster) v North Yorkshire CC*[25] was one in which the Court of Appeal overturned the decision of the High Court, finding that there had been an error in the interpretation of national planning policy concerning the NPPF, and that this error had infected the officer report, such that the decision to grant planning permission had to be quashed. The officer had not considered visual impact when considering the impact of the proposed development on the openness of the Green Belt, despite visual impact having been considered elsewhere in the report. Notwithstanding the decisions warning against "excessive legalism", the court was still bound "to intervene where a planning decision has been made by a local planning authority on the basis of a misunderstanding and misapplication of national planning policy" (para. 33).

15.30   If the decision is made on a single basis, and the interpretation of a single policy is

---

[22]   [2016] EWHC 3028 (Admin); [2017] PTSR 408.

[23]   [2016] EWCA Civ 1040; [2017] JPL 358.

[24]   [2017] EWCA Civ 1314; [2018] JPL 176.

[25]   [2018] EWCA Civ 489.

of key relevance to that decision, then if there has been a misinterpretation of the policy, then it is more likely that challenge to the decision will succeed.

Outline of Procedure

Judicial Review

15.31 A claim in judicial review against a grant of planning permission is brought in the High Court. It is in two stages: the permission stage, and the substantive stage. Before a claim can even proceed to a full hearing, a claim must be granted permission to proceed. The focus of a judge in deciding whether to grant permission will normally be on whether the claim is "arguable". The threshold of the arguability test varies in practice, but it is supposed to weed out claims which are hopeless, and do not have a proper chance of succeeding at the substantive hearing.

15.32 Whilst arguability is often the most important question at the permission stage, there are other matters which will need to be considered, including whether the claim is brought in time, whether there are any alternative remedies which the claimant should have taken rather than applying for judicial review, and whether the claimant has standing to bring the claim.

15.33 Permission is first considered on the papers filed with the claim, and the formal response by the defendant and any party seeking to resist the claim. A claimant should therefore put before the court the arguments seeking to demonstrate that the decision is flawed, and the documents which support those arguments. However, in accordance with the "duty of candour", the claimant should also make clear facts which are unhelpful to the claim. The claim, once issued by the court, will need to be "served"[26] on the defendant, and any interested party. The defendant will be the local planning authority who granted planning permission. Interested parties are those who may have an interest in the outcome of the judicial review. They will include the recipient of the grant of planning permission, and may include the owners of the land over which planning permission was granted (if different). The defendant, and any interested party, can at this stage put in a brief response to the claim, arguing why permission should not be granted (unless they are willing to concede the claim). This is in a document called the Acknowledgment of Service.

15.34 If the judge grants permission, then the matter will proceed to a substantive hearing.[27] If the judge refuses permission, then generally the claimant will have the ability, if it wishes, to "renew" the application for permission at an oral hearing before a judge. This is a short hearing at which the judge decides whether the claim is arguable, and whether there are other reasons why the claim should not proceed. However, the claimant does not always have the right to an oral renewal of its application for permission. If the claim is utterly hopeless, the court may mark the claim as "Totally Without Merit". The effect of such a designation is to take away the right of oral renewal.[28] If the claimant still wants to press its claim, in the

---

[26] A technical term essentially meaning "sent to" or "given to".

[27] Although it may be that the defendant thinks seriously about conceding the claim at this stage.

[28] CPR 54.12(7).

face of a TWM designation, then its recourse is to the Court of Appeal against the High Court's order.

15.35   On a grant of permission, the defendant has the opportunity to put in detailed arguments as to why the claim should fail, and put in any evidence to resist the claim. As with the claimant, the defendant is under a duty of candour, to make clear facts which are helpful to the claim (and unhelpful to the defence).

15.36   Before the hearing of the substantive challenge, the parties should agree a bundle of authorities (i.e. legislation and previous court decisions) to put before the court. Parties participating in the hearing (if legally represented) should send to the court and to the other parties a "skeleton argument". Notwithstanding the name, skeleton arguments are often fairly detailed works of oral advocacy, setting out the respective parties' positions. However, a skeleton argument should be as short as practicable, and should not generally exceed 20 pages in the High Court.[29]

15.37   At the hearing, the judge will set the procedure, but will usually hear from the claimant first, followed by the defendant, and then any interested parties; the claimant will generally have an opportunity to reply to what has been said at the end. If the case is relatively short and uncomplicated, the judge may give an oral judgment on the day (known as an *ex tempore* judgment). However, if it is not possible to do so, then the judge will "reserve" her decision. This may be read out on a later day in court, but more usually will be written out, and handed down in court. The parties will usually be sent a copy of the judgment in draft beforehand, and will be requested to point out any typographical or obvious errors which can be corrected in the final version of the judgment. This also gives the parties the opportunity to agree, or set out their arguments in writing, in relation to matters consequential to the judgment (for instance, which party should bear the costs, and how much they should be, and whether the losing party should be granted permission to appeal to the Court of Appeal).

15.38   Although planning judicial reviews are dealt with in the High Court, they are not all heard by full-time High Court Judges. A review of the cases in this book will show that a number are considered by Deputy High Court Judges (usually legal practitioners who sit as judges of the High Court on a part-time basis), or by Circuit Judges (judges of the County Court or Crown Court, who sometimes sit in the High Court). The status of a court's decision is formally set by the level of court which decides it, not the judge who decides it, and so the decision of a Deputy High Court Judge is, formally, of the same status as a decision by a full-time High Court Judge. However, in later cases, other judges may find decisions of judges particularly experienced in the field to be more persuasive when considering their reasoning. The court may designate certain decisions not suitable to be heard by a Deputy High Court Judge.[30]

---

[29]   See Administrative Court Judicial Review Guide, July 2018, para. 17.3.3.

[30]   Although the existence of such a designation does not necessarily mean that a Deputy High Court Judge will not hear the substantive hearing: this was the case in the (non-planning) case of *R (Taste of India Ltd) v Secretary of State for the Home Department* [2018] EWHC 414 (Admin).

15.39   Within the Administrative Court,[31] the Planning Court has been designated to hear planning claims. The purpose of this designation is to promote the existence of a "list" of judges with experience of planning matters. The Planning Court is led by the Planning Liaison Judge, currently Holgate J. The Planning Court has a procedure whereby certain cases can be designated as "significant planning cases". Such cases are supposed to be subject to an expedited timetable, so that they can be resolved swiftly.

Statutory Planning Challenges

15.40   Although there used to be dramatic differences (section 288 challenges used not to have a permission filter), the differences between the procedure in judicial review, and in statutory planning challenges, are much less than they used to be.

15.41   The main difference is between section 289 appeals and other procedures. Under section 289, the time limit for bringing an appeal is much shorter, and there is no decision on permission on the papers: the matter proceeds straight to an oral hearing (for which the Secretary of State should prepare a skeleton argument). There is no general requirement for the Secretary of State to file detailed grounds of resistance in a section 289 appeal. The procedure under section 288 is different to judicial review in that in the former the court does not have the ability to extend time to bring the claim.

Who Will Bear the Costs of a Claim?

15.42   The general principle in English civil litigation is that the loser of a court case pays the winner's costs. The winning party to litigation should not be out of pocket for correctly establishing its legal rights. Put another way, if a local planning authority made a lawful decision in granting planning permission, and if a claim against that grant of planning permission fails, then the local planning authority should not be put to the expense of that unsuccessful claim. The local planning authority should, in general, be able to recover the costs of defending the judicial review challenge. By contrast, if the claim against the grant of planning permission succeeds, then the claimant should not be put to the expense of establishing the correct legal position and quashing the grant of planning permission. The local planning authority should pay the legal costs of the claimant bringing the claim.

15.43   There are some exceptions to this principle. CPR 45.41-44 set out provisions for fixed costs in certain environmental claims falling within the scope of the Aarhus Convention.[32] Where costs are fixed, even if a party is successful, they will not be able to recover from the other side a sum above the fixed cap on recovery. The details of the provisions for fixed costs are beyond the scope of this book,[33] but the scope of protection is wider in judicial review claims than for statutory challenges. Furthermore, the fixed costs regime does not affect who is liable to pay costs, but

---

[31]   Which itself falls within the Queen's Bench Division of the High Court.

[32]   More fully known as the UNECE Convention on Access to Information, Public Participation in Decision-making and Access to Justice in Environmental Matters.

[33]   For a more detailed account, see Chapter 1B of *Garner's Environmental Law*.

only the <u>amount</u> of costs which would be payable.

15.44   Generally speaking,[34] if a claim proceeds to a full substantive hearing but is ultimately unsuccessful, then the claimant should have to pay only one set of costs: it will not generally have to pay the costs of the local planning authority and the interested party: *Bolton MDC v Secretary of State for the Environment*[35]. If the claim is refused at permission stage, and permission is refused, then generally the defendant, and any interested party, will get their costs of filing their acknowledgement of service (see below). However, if the claimant renews its claim orally, which is then refused permission, the defendant and interested party will generally not obtain their costs of attending the oral renewal hearing.[36] In a claim under section 289, a defendant who succeeds in getting an appeal refused at permission stage will be more likely to obtain the costs of the hearing than would be the case in a judicial review or section 288 challenge: *Williams v SSCLG*.[37]

15.45   If the local planning authority decides not to contest a challenge to a grant of planning permission, but it is contested by the developer who was the recipient of the grant of planning permission, then the developer will usually have to pay the claimant's costs if the claim is successful. The same applies in challenges to Inspectors' decisions; if one party seeks to defend the Inspector's decision, then they will be likely to need to pay the costs of the appeal if the Secretary of State drops out.

15.46   The costs situation is different in appeals to the Planning Inspector or the Secretary of State against the refusal of planning permission by a local planning authority. Unlike in litigation, in such appeals a party has to pay another party's costs only if they have somehow acted unreasonably.[38] Costs awards are therefore rare. Costs awards in planning appeals by or against third parties (i.e. someone other than the developer bringing the appeal, or the local planning authority) are extremely rare.[39]

---

[34]   The circumstances regarding costs, particularly where there are more than two parties to a court case, are fairly complex. For more detail, see 'Costs, Permission and Interested Parties' - Alistair Mills [2014] JR 173.

[35]   [1995] 1 WLR 1176.

[36]   *R (Mount Cook Land Ltd) v Westminster CC* [2003] EWCA Civ 1346; [2017] PTSR 1166.

[37]   [2009] EWHC 475 (Admin).

[38]   PPG, Section on Appeals, para. 030.

[39]   The PPG indicates that such an award of costs will be exceptional: PPG, Section on Appeals, para. 056.

Index

V

W